Praise for The Way of Fire and Ice

"*The Way of Fire and Ice* offers a vision of an inclusive, welcoming, spiritually rich, and socially responsible Norse Paganism. Written in a friendly, direct voice, this book presents a guided pathway for developing practice and community in this tradition, with much-needed and clear-headed education to help ensure a foundation in justice and positive core values."

—Morpheus Ravenna, author of *The Book of the Great Queen*

"Engaging, thoughtful, and most importantly inclusive, *The Way of Fire and Ice* is an excellent introduction to Norse Paganism. Author Ryan Smith includes everything a newcomer needs to get started, but there's plenty here for the experienced practitioner as well. Whether you want a deeper understanding of practice, lore, or the magick of the Norse, you'll find it all in *The Way of Fire and Ice*. Destined to become the 'go to' book for a new generation of Norse Pagans."

—Jason Mankey, author of *Transformative Witchcraft* and *The Witch's Wheel of the Year*

"*The Way of Fire and Ice* is Ryan Smith's magnum opus; a declaration of how we connect with the gods while using that fire to transform our world."

—Shane Burley, author of *Fascism Today: What It Is and How to End It*

"With *The Way of Fire and Ice* Ryan Smith has crafted a highly skilled and inspiring book for the modern heathen ... He also forges a path into Norse heathenism that lets you engage with our mythology regardless of your heritage, and provides a guide for navigating away from the ethnocentric uses of our tradition. In that way, Smith has demonstrated that Norse heathenism is truly a part of a global culture that can find its expression anywhere in the world, through anyone who so chooses."

—Mathias Nordvig, Scandinavian Studies, University of Colorado at Boulder, USA

"An incredible read for the faithful and the curious alike, *The Way of Fire and Ice* brings to life ideals and traditions of ancient times and makes them tangible today. Empowering and dedicated."

—Richard "Lord Gaylord" Weeks of Blackened Death Records

THE WAY *of* FIRE AND ICE

THE WAY *of* FIRE AND ICE

THE LIVING TRADITION OF NORSE PAGANISM

RYAN SMITH

LLEWELLYN PUBLICATIONS
WOODBURY, MINNESOTA

First Edition
Seventh Printing, 2024

Book design by Samantha Penn
Cover design by Shira Atakpu
Interior art by Llewellyn Art Department

Library of Congress Cataloging-in-Publication Data
The Library of Congress has already cataloged an earlier printing under LCCN: 2019285812

Llewellyn Publications
A Division of Llewellyn Worldwide Ltd.
2143 Wooddale Drive
Woodbury, MN 55125-2989
www.llewellyn.com

Printed in the United States of America

DEDICATION

This book was the work of many people who must be recognized.

This would not have been possible without Patricia's love and support. Her patience, guidance, and confidence were invaluable for making this possible. I could never have done it without her. Her knowledge of reclaiming Witchcraft ritual practices, organization, and theater are major influences on this book.

The ideas and practices Sophia Fate-Changer and other members of the little community we made in the Bay Area were the seed that grew into this book. Her ideas, uncompromising stands for the right thing, brainstorming, and partnership in crime made this unique form of practice possible.

Maia's combination of patience and blunt advice were critical for refining community practices, working through some serious mistakes on the journey here, and reaching a point where this book could happen. Thank you for your example and honing of this rough blade.

Kevin is an unparalleled lore master. Whenever I had questions on any Old Norse subject, no matter how obscure, he always had an excellent, thorough answer along with recommendations of many brilliant academic works.

Dave's experiences in many parts of the Norse Pagan and Heathen communities were key for understanding both the broader movement and what this book represents. He gave essential insights for explaining clearly why the neo-Volkisch are a danger for all people, including to members of that sect and our broader community.

My fellow workers Steve and Morgen have been major inspirations for me through their knowledge and their example. May their work continue and see rich fruit.

When I first got started as a Pagan, my experiences in San Diego were some of the most critical in my life. The guidance I received helped set me on the right path before I knew I was on it.

I would not be who I am or have written this without my family or their love and support.

This book is dedicated to all who feel the pull of the Norse gods and see their example as a way forward in these troubled times. Regardless of where you come from or how you live, I hope this work inspires, guides, and gives you everything you need for building a meaningful, fulfilling practice.

CONTENTS

EXERCISES

chapter one

WHAT IS THE WAY OF FIRE & ICE?

How fare the gods? How fare the elves?
All Jötunheimr groans, the gods are at council;
Loud roar the dwarfs by the doors of stone,
The masters of the rocks; would you know yet more?
VOLUSPO 48[1]

Amidst the bustling urban night, a heaving mosh pit pulses to a howling song of mighty gods doing battle at the world's end. Mystics speak a heartfelt prayer in their native tongue, raising a horn for ancient Powers beneath the boughs of a tropical rainforest. A world away, black-clad volunteers give their hammer pendants a quick kiss before locking arms with others across a freeway, demanding justice for the wrongly slain. Alone in their home a devotee opens a cupboard, lighting candles for a deity of mystery while whispering words in thanks. On the side of a snowy mountain, a group of wanderers rest a moment, feeling the presence of nature's majesty. A wounded warrior, with runes and dragons inked into their flesh, feels the comfort provided by their

1. All saga verses quoted in this book are from the Henry Adams Bellows translation of the Poetic Edda. Gender pronouns have been changed, where possible, to they / them.

path as they do the difficult work with their fellows of healing unseen injuries. All feel the tread of mighty beings.

Ever since the end of the Second World War, a remarkable new spiritual movement has come into the world. After over a thousand years where two of Abraham's three children, Christianity and Islam, have dominated religion and spirituality, the ideas that were pushed off the map have returned. Witches, druids, seers, magicians, spirit workers and storytellers carrying ancient wisdom are surfacing across the globe. Many of these practitioners call themselves Pagans, drawing inspiration from the tales, gods, and ways of the peoples of Europe, the Mediterranean, and the Middle East who lived before the rise of Christianity and Islam.

Countless people wander down these old paths seeking answers to life's many questions. For many, the source answering the call are the Norse gods. The ways people reach them are as numerous as there are seekers. Many first encounter them through popular culture, whether through Marvel's Thor, television shows like *The Vikings* or *The Last Kingdom,* comic books or bestselling novels like Neil Gaiman's *Norse Mythology* and *American Gods*. Others find them when researching personal heritage. Some feel your way through the frenzy of mosh pits and hear them in music inspired by the ancients, such as metal bands like Tyr and Amon Amarth. Many arrive through direct experiences they can't explain any other way than spiritual.

This may seem strange at first blush. In these times, it is no surprise people are seeking and finding answers on paths most have forgotten. Much in this world has been thrown greatly out of balance. For anyone seeking guidance and strength in the face of challenges, the ways of the ancient Norse and their gods offers a clear, heroic example.

Those who are drawn to these gods and the ways of ancient Norse societies are found all over the world. Norse Pagans are found everywhere in Scandinavia, where these ways first returned, and across Europe. Adherents hold rituals all over the United States and Canada, celebrating in parks and homes alike. In Mexico, Brazil, and Latin America, practitioners honor the ways of Norse practice in their daily lives and communities. From New Zealand and Australia to West Africa, people are finding Norse-inspired practice speaks to them and their concerns like nothing else.

Many may wonder why there are people turning to these ways in the modern day. It may seem strange, at first blush, for anyone in the present to be seeking guidance and inspiration from a time as far removed from the present as we are from the surface of the Moon. To the uninformed observer, what Pagans do is little more than escapism, fantasy disguised as religion to avoid the problems in our daily lives. Nothing could be further from the truth.

Even so, most Norse Pagans go to the same schools, work very normal jobs, shop in the same stores, and deal with the same news and worries everyone else does. There are many ideas and values in Norse Paganism that provide a compelling answer for the problems that come with modern life. The Norse ways offer guidance for addressing these challenges that is meaningful and satisfying. Norse Pagans turn to ancient gods and ancient ways because their example is as valid today as it was a thousand years ago.

The Source

All forms of modern Norse Paganism draw inspiration from the pre-Christian societies of Scandinavia. Some also include sources from Anglo-Saxon England and the pre-Christian Germanic tribes of continental Europe. The most commonly used sources are the sagas of Scandinavia. The most important of these are the Poetic Eddas, a collection of sagas that deal with the Norse gods, and the Prose Edda, a single work written by Icelandic monk and antiquarian Snorri Sturluson in the early thirteenth century to preserve the necessary knowledge of Icelandic lore and ideas for ensuring the art of Icelandic poetry would survive. Some other commonly used written sources are the Icelandic sagas, the Old English epic *Beowulf*, the Saga of the Jomsvikings, and other surviving historical sagas. Norse Pagans also turn to surviving relics, runestones, folklore, and Scandinavian oral traditions.

These materials were produced by a group of peoples who lived in a very different time and life from the present day. The Norse peoples of Scandinavia were a collection of many different societies, ranging from small clans to vast kingdoms, who lived over a thousand years ago in very harsh lands whose survival depended on working effectively with their environment. Most settled disputes, made laws and governed their affairs through democratic assemblies, known as Things (pronounced *ting*), that also had the power to crown and depose kings. Unlike other societies in nearby Christian Europe, women enjoyed nearly equal status to men, with the right to inherit property and divorce their husbands. Some fought on the battlefield as shieldmaidens. The Norse were master mariners, skilled traders, gifted artists, and fierce warriors.

The Norse are most well-known for a time known as the Viking Age. Beginning in 793 CE with the raid on the Lindisfarne Monastery in northern England, and ending in 1066 CE with the Battle of Stamford Bridge, this era was an age of war. Pressed from the south by expanding Christian powers and led by emperors like Charlemagne, the Norse peoples struck back against encroaching empires by raiding most of Christendom and conquering large swaths of modern England and northern France. Some chased the horizon as far as Baghdad in the Middle East and North America, trading with the people they met along the way. Despite their celebrated ferocity, the Norse were eventually converted to Christianity by force through armed invasions, opportunistic Vikings who used the new faith as a tool to dominate other Norse peoples, and power-hungry kings who used the cross to cement their rule.[2]

During this upheaval, these ancient Scandinavians produced the sagas, relics, and runestones that guide modern Norse Pagans. At the heart of their knowledge were three core ideas: the World Tree, Fate, and the Powers. The World Tree is a great cosmic tree that holds up all the realms of reality, including physical reality, which is known as Midgard. Fate is a great force that influences everything in existence, even the mightiest of the Powers, shaping everything while also being shaped by all things. The Powers are the Norse gods—including famous beings like Odin and Thor—the living spirits they honored, elves, dwarves, trolls, spirits of the natural world and the dead. More information on the World Tree, Fate and the spirits, both living and dead, and working with them is in chapter two. Information on the gods, working with them, and what they represent is in chapter three.

There is no question that the present day is totally different from when these gods were widely worshiped. The values that came with them were accepted as the norm, but conditions have changed dramatically in the centuries since Christianity became the dominant religion of Europe and much of the world. Yet for those who see wisdom in Norse Pagan practice, these changes

---

2. If you want to learn more about the Norse peoples and the Viking Age, check out the books listed in the Further Reading section

are what make the ideas, values, and worldview of these peoples a powerful source of inspiration in the present day.

Each tradition of Norse Paganism uses and interprets these sources in different ways. What is in this book—Radical Norse Paganism, or the Way of Fire and Ice—is one way of living with the Powers and applying the example of the Norse peoples in the present day. It came into existence through the experiments, trial and error, mistakes, and ideas of a group of Norse Pagans from California looking for a better way to live Norse spirituality.

The Way of Fire and Ice

What is in this book—the Way of Fire and Ice which is also known as Radical Norse Paganism, Fire and Ice Paganism, and the radical tradition that set it apart from all other forms of Norse Paganism: first, this is this is a living tradition. Meaningful spirituality grows, develops, and changes as necessary to fulfill the needs of practitioners. Second, the past is a source for inspired adaptation. Such adaptions must provide concrete guidance for tackling the challenges of daily life in a meaningful, just, and effective fashion. Third, these practices must serve the needs of people in their daily lives and not be a tool for wielding power over others. Fourth, radical Norse Paganism is open to all who feel it speaks to them and treat all people with dignity and respect. Fifth and finally, this way calls on all to actively participate in modern life through our spiritual, physical, and social communities. Just as radical Norse Paganism is a living tradition, it is also always a part of your life, in and out of sacred space.

A Living Tradition

Living tradition is this way's beating heart. It is a spiritual practice that grows and changes as times and needs require it to. We are always developing and are never chained to the dictates of holy books or anointed leaders. The ancient lore that inspires us leaves no doubt reality is not fixed and unmoving. The world as we know it has not always been and will not always exist as it currently does. In the sagas the only guarantees are life, death, and change.

If you accept these are the only things certain in this existence, it makes no sense to freeze practice in a place of unmoving perfection. This is why the way you live spirituality must be engaging, just, and fulfilling for all who share it.

Values are a compass steering you toward the right path, not a map dictating what that path is and must always be.

Inspired Adaptation

The source for ideas is the surviving information on pre-Christian Norse practices. Fire and Ice Paganism revives their ideas, spirituality, and practices in ways that are meaningful for modern life. The past is the spark for igniting effective practice. It is more important to adapt the past into practices that meet people's needs than to put theory or academic perfection first.

This is different from many other forms of Norse Paganism in the world today. Most other traditions place heavy emphasis on what is commonly referred to as reconstructionism. Reconstructionism seeks to rebuild what once existed as completely as possible for the practice's framework. In reconstructionism, it is necessary to fully understand the mentality of these peoples as they once were before their ideas can be applied to the present. This sometimes means the details of the past are focused on, at the expense of what matters today or how people practice in the present.

Though reconstructionism can be useful as a starting point, it cannot be the end-all, be-all of spirituality. One thing Fire and Ice Paganism shares with reconstructionism is the idea that revived practice should be informed and understand our source of inspiration in its historic context. You cannot pluck one element out of another time or culture with no regard for its broader significance or meaning and expect to put it to good use. That said, the place the Way of Fire and Ice diverges from reconstructionists is what you do next. This tradition uses the past as inspiration for developing practices that meet the needs of the present. It is not the final word; possessing in-depth historical knowledge is not required or necessary for meaningful practice.

Modern Relevance

Inspired adaptation fuels modern relevance. The values, philosophy, and broader worldview of the ancients offers guidance for dilemmas people face in the present, providing understanding of how you should act today. If inspired adaptation answers what to do with the source material, then modern relevance challenges you with the question, "How would the Powers expect me to handle this now?"

In the radical tradition, you act in a right fashion because the values the Powers represent are worthy and build better lives. The gods, spirits, and dead give us examples of right and wrong through the stories of their actions. No one lives constantly seeking their approval or in fear of their condemnation. If you are truly living a worthy life, they will be pleased whether or not your actions are different from how people in a very different time would have handled a similar problem. What matters is how you live and the consequences of your actions, not adherence to precise steps or rigid lists.

Modern relevance argues that spiritual practice must always serve the genuine needs of people. This also urges us to challenge anyone using Norse-inspired spirituality as a tool for wielding power over others. Whether you look to history or the news, there is no question needless suffering and hardship has been caused by powerful people invoking holiness or established institutions to justify horrible actions. Everyone must learn from these examples and not do what is clearly harmful to life. Anyone with knowledge of the Powers must guide others and never rule or dictate righteousness.

Inclusive Practice

Anyone can live the Way of Fire and Ice, regardless of heritage, race, ethnicity, physical or mental ability, sexuality or gender. The Norse gods speak to people across the globe. Some of the most famous of the gods, such as Odin and Thor, have parents who were from very different divine clans. Just as the gods themselves are of many backgrounds, all spirits of nature are worthy of reverence and every ancestor of every person, be they of blood culture or shared purpose, is worthy of honor. Fire and Ice Paganism welcomes all.

The foundation for this belief, discussed further in chapter five, holds that the measure of a person is in their deeds. This means the inherent traits of race, gender, sexuality, national origin, physical or mental ability, are not and never should be used for assessing anyone's worth. Anyone who respects others and treats people with the dignity all deserve is welcome. Those who reject this core truth by calling for or actively excluding, denying, or directly harming anyone based on inherent facts of their existence are opposed to everything that is the Way of Fire and Ice.

Active Involvement

Based on these core concepts, you should always be as active in the world as you can. Radical Norse Paganism doesn't start and stop with ritual or at the edge of sacred spaces. It is lived every day in the values you live, uphold, and honor with deeds. This means engaging in worthy deeds that make your life, communities, and the world a better place. You should always be pushing to do better, make better, and build better for all while never resting on the laurels of past successes.

Engaging with the world may mean doing volunteer work or community service. It may also mean participating in direct action for just causes. It could also mean getting involved in civic affairs locally, regionally, or globally. You might also choose to focus on talking about ideas inspired by your practice, like human dignity and fairness, on the job, in the classroom, on YouTube, or with your family and friends. Regardless of how you put the ethics of Norse Paganism into practice, there is no question this way calls all of us to be involved in the world we are all a part of. This form of spirituality is not for escaping or hiding from the troubles of the world; honoring these Powers means actively living in the here and now.

The Other Norse Traditions

There are many other forms of Norse Paganism in the world today. Fire and Ice Paganism is one of the many different takes on Norse Paganism. These traditions are not all there is to Norse Paganism. There are many more people who follow Norse Paganism who weave Norse practices into other forms of Paganism or a more uniquely personal approach to spirituality.

One thing you need to understand about Norse Paganism is the word "Heathenry." Heathenry is the most commonly used term of identification by Norse Pagans, with many (though not all) using "Heathen" and "Norse Pagan" interchangeably. However, in Scandinavia and Germany, the term "Heathen" is used the same way as "Pagan" is in the rest of the world. There are also those who identify as either Norse Pagan or Heathen while arguing these words are not interchangeable but are distinctly different things. Always make sure to ask which term is preferred before making assumptions.[3]

Asatru, Vanatru, and Rokkatru

The most well-known group of Norse traditions is made up of the three subgroups known as Asatru, Vanatru, and Rokkatru. These siblings share a common origin in the 1960s and 1970s. Each is based on worshiping one of the three tribes of Norse gods. Asatru, the oldest of the three, mostly worship the Aesir. The Aesir are gods associated with human society and include some of the most well-known Norse gods, such as Odin, Thor, and Loki. The term was first used in Iceland and was adopted across the world, becoming more Aesir-centric as time passed. One of the most influential authors for English-speaking Asatru is Diana Paxson.[4]

Vanatru and Rokkatru are newer traditions that branched off from Asatru. They share common practices with Asatru but have a different emphasis. Vanatru focuses on the Vanir, the gods associated with the interactions between humanity and nature. Vanatru developed in response to the Aesir-centric practices of Asatru by people who felt the Vanir were not honored enough and were more called to that tribe. The gods of the Vanir include Freyr and Freyja. Rokkatru, also called Thursatru, is the newest of the three and is founded on reverence for the Jötnar, the gods who are also called giants that are associated with the powers of nature in its fullest. Some Rokkatru practitioners are influenced by Left Hand Path spirituality and borrow ideas from them.[5]

---

3. "Religions—Paganism: Heathenry." BBC. October 30, 2003. Accessed November 06, 2017. http://www.bbc.co.uk/religion/religions/paganism/subdivisions/heathenry_1.shtml.

4. "Asatru: Norse Heathenism." ASATRU (Norse Heathenism). Accessed November 06, 2017. http://www.religioustolerance.org/asatru.htm., Diana Paxson, *Essential Asatru: walking the path of Norse paganism*. New York: Citadel, 2007, XIV-XV.

5. Ember Cooke, "What is Vanatru? Who are the Vanir?" EmberVoices: Listening for the Vanir. October 28, 2015. Accessed November 06, 2017. https://embervoices.wordpress.com/2013/10/02/what-is-vanatru-who-are-the-vanir/ and "What is Rökkatru?" Northern Tradition Paganism. Accessed November 06, 2017. http://www.northernpaganism.org/rokkatru/what-is-rokkatru.html.

Reconstructionist Heathenry and Theodism

Some see Heathenry as a different thing from Norse Paganism. According to these Heathens, the essence of the difference is they, unlike Norse Pagans, are reconstructionist polytheists. Their goal is building Heathen spirituality by reconstructing it as best as possible in the modern world through studying the folklore, written sources, archeology, and other research on pre-Christian Germanic peoples. Reconstructionist Heathens often define their spirituality as Germanic in origin instead of just being exclusively Norse. For reconstructionist Heathens there is a major emphasis on scholarship and direct reconstruction over revived adaptation.[6]

Theodism is a unique form of Heathenry that takes reconstructionism to greater lengths. Theodism was founded by Garman Lord and argues for total reconstruction, as much as possible, of the spirituality of pre-Christian Anglo-Saxons and their social systems. They say the best way to practice their form of spirituality is in something as close as possible to the historical social environment. Theodism is very hierarchical and believes the leaders of their groups, known as theods, are the intermediaries between members and the divine. Theodists require aspiring members to join the community as thralls, who are effectively initiates or apprentices. In Theodism, being part of an active community is essential to practice; it is not possible to be Theodish without being a part of a Theod.[7]

Folklore-Inspired Practices

Another common form of Norse Paganism is Forn Sed, also known as Forn Sidr. Forn Sed means "the Old Way" and is mostly found in Scandinavia and Northern Europe. For Forn Sed practitioners the main source is folklore and oral traditions. Preserving these customs, practices, and beliefs is more important than reconstructing the past. However, much like Reconstructionist Heathenry, there is a strong emphasis on tradition over adaptation. There is also a

6. Xander. "The Reconstructionist Method." Huginn's Heathen Hof. October 27, 2016. Accessed August 21, 2018. http://www.heathenhof.com/the-reconstructionist-method/.

7. "Theodish Belief: Oft-Askings (Frequently Asked Questions)." The Ealdríce Théodish Fellowship. May 04, 2017. Accessed November 06, 2017. https://ealdrice.org/theodish-belief-oft-askings-frequently-asked-questions/.

much stronger focus on reverence for the spirits of nature and place instead of the gods.[8]

Urglaawe, first organized by Robert Schreiwer, is another tradition that comes from North America. It draws some inspiration from the rest of Norse Paganism, but its primary focus is the folk practices of the Pennsylvania Deutsch (commonly called the Pennsylvania Dutch). The Pennsylvania Deutsch are a group of people who first emigrated to Pennsylvania, located in the northeastern United States, from western Germany and Switzerland, beginning in the seventeenth century. They brought their folklore and customs with them, developing a unique language and culture in their new home. Many of their traditional practices were pushed to the fringes of society during the early twentieth century. Urglaawe focuses on reviving what was until recently suppressed. This makes Urglaawe very similar in some ways to Forn Sed, but it draws on a very different source of inspiration.[9]

The Neo-Volkisch Movement

There is a final group that uses Norse language, symbols, mythology, and folklore who claim to be the most "true" form of Norse Paganism. They are best known, through an in-depth report by the Southern Poverty Law Center, as the neo-Volkisch movement. When you get past the Norse trappings, what they are really doing is disguising fascism as religion; they worship that they were born with white skin and live in total fear of everything in the world that isn't just like them. This sect is known by many names. The most common are: Folkish Asatru or Folkish Heathenry, created by Stephen McNallen and the Asatru Folk Assembly; Odinism, founded by Else Christensen and the Odinic Rite, Varg Vikernes' Odalism; and David Lane and Ron McVan's Wotanism. For all their talk of glory, pride, and honor, these groups run on fear and panic. Anyone in these groups who is not part of the ruling cliques must constantly

8. Räv Skogsberg, Markus. "What is Forn Sed?" Huginn's Heathen Hof. July 07, 2016. Accessed November 06, 2017. http://www.heathenhof.com/what-is-forn-sed/.

9. Miller, Stevie. "Urglaawe: One of History's Best-Kept Secrets." Huginn's Heathen Hof. September 16, 2016. Accessed November 06, 2017. http://www.heathenhof.com/urglaawe-one-of-historys-best-kept-secrets/.

prove their purity, and any who come up short for any possible reason are cast out with next to no warning.[10]

The neo-Volkisch claim the Norse gods are genetically transmitted cultural archetypes that are unique to the so-called Nordic race. This belief has no roots in the ancient lore but actually comes from a 1936 essay written by Carl Jung, called "Wotan." In this essay, Jung claimed Adolf Hitler's success was due to his being an avatar of these blood-borne ideas. Based on this theory, the neo-Volkisch say a person can only honor the Norse gods if they are of the appropriate heritage and strongly imply the gods aren't really gods. On paper, this means a direct blood tie is necessary to worship the Norse gods. In practice, this always means being sufficiently white. Anyone who doesn't pass the paint swatch test is, at best, told to "drink from their own well."[11]

The only real connections between the neo-Volkisch and the rest of Norse Paganism are superficial; the neo-Volkisch actively recruit anyone they believe to be "white enough" without showing any interest in the ancients. They reduce the gods to mere blood-borne traits that primarily exist to exclude, denigrate, and discriminate against anyone judged insufficiently pure. Even though they claim to "love their own race and don't hate others," many of their leaders, like Stephen McNallen, call for race war one minute while claiming the gods will die if the so-called Peoples of the North disappear in the next. Left unsaid is who qualifies as a Person of the North, leaving it entirely in the hands of neo-Volkisch leaders. McNallen himself has dispelled some of this ambiguity in a more recent video where he called for putting unity with the white

---

10. "Neo-Volkisch." Southern Poverty Law Center. Accessed March 23, 2018. https://www.splcenter.org/fighting-hate/extremist-files/ideology/neo-volkisch.

11. Eoghan. "Declaration of Purpose." Asatru Folk Assembly. Accessed November 06, 2017. http://runestone.org/oldsite/index.php?option=com_content&view=article&id=69&Itemid=475., Gambanreiði Statement describes the Characteristics of a Folk Religion. Accessed November 06, 2017. http://www.gambanreidistatement.com/AFolkreligionIS.html; Tan, Edwardson. "Jung's Shadow: Two Troubling Essays by Jung." Jung's Shadow: Two Troubling Essays by Jung. October 27, 2013. Accessed November 06, 2017. http://www.cgjungpage.org/learn/articles/analytical-psychology/47-jungs-shadow-two-troubling-essays-by-jung; "Stephen McNallen and Racialist Asatru Part 2: The Roots of Racialized Religion." Circle Ansuz. September 10, 2013. Accessed November 06, 2017. https://circleansuz.wordpress.com/2013/08/26/stephen-mcnallen-part-two/.

power movement ahead of spiritual beliefs, making it clear that race matters more to him than religion. Unfortunately, their dishonesty, deliberate misrepresentation of their beliefs, active recruitment, and failure by some in the Norse Pagan community to confront them have allowed them to hog the proverbial microphone, effectively appearing to be the norm when they are in fact a very loud fringe.[12]

Radical Norse Paganism is totally opposed to neo-Volkisch sects, as the former twist the lore into a club for brutalizing others. They insult the history they claim to honor with their salad bar approach to the facts, reinforcing their false sense of superiority by watering down truth into empty lies. They are cowards dressing up their vile agenda in odds and ends stolen from ancient lore. The actions of the neo-Volkisch are harmful to people, and dismantling their movement is absolutely necessary for all Norse Pagans regardless of tradition who want to see these beliefs survive and thrive.

Living the Way

This book is a toolkit for developing personal and communal Norse spirituality, whether you practice on your own, are with a community, or are trying to start your own community. It is a starting point, a source of inspiration, and a guide for your journey. The way forward is different for everyone. This book will help you make sense of the path and find fellow travelers to keep you company on the road ahead.

Each chapter in this book covers a different aspect of how to do this. Chapters two through five have all the information you need to start building your personal practice. They cover the world of Radical Norse Paganism, the gods, developing your personal practice, and the ethics of the Way of Fire and Ice. Chapters six and seven will help you start exploring the deeper mysteries of runelore and the arts of seiðr (pronounced *say-th*). Chapters three and six have a lot of information in them on gods and runes. You can go through those sections at your own pace and use them later for reference. Chapters eight and

12. "David Lane" Southern Poverty Law Center. Accessed November 06, 2017. https://www.splcenter.org/fighting-hate/extremist-files/individual/david-lane.; "Stephen McNallen and Racialist Asatru Part 3: In His Own Words." Circle Ansuz. September 10, 2013. Accessed November 06, 2017. https://circleansuz.wordpress.com/2013/09/02/stephen-mcnallen-part-3/.; https://youtu.be/MxcOLFMTzMI?t=197

nine have information on finding community, organizing your own, and resisting fascists, both neo-Volkisch and any others who try to hide behind Norse trappings. There are also two appendices with further reading recommendations and a brief history of modern Norse Paganism.

Every chapter finishes with an exercise that will help you learn and grow on your own. The first exercise in this book is a simple breathing exercise. Breath is life and the first of the three gifts from the gods to humanity. Control over the breath is the foundation of all the other exercises and can help in your daily life.

exercise
UNDERSTANDING THE BREATH

Begin by finding a quiet space where you can sit comfortably.

Close your eyes and breathe normally at a relaxed pace.

Take a slow, deep breath in through your nose. As you draw in your breath slowly count to nine. Your breath should begin at number one and finish at number nine.

Hold your breath for a slow count from one to nine.

When you have reached nine while holding your breath, begin to slowly exhale through your mouth, counting down from nine to one. Breathe out on nine; by the time you reach one, you should have completely emptied your lungs of air.

This process of breathing in to the count of nine, holding for the count of nine, and breathing out to the count of nine is one breath cycle.

Begin a second breath cycle. On this cycle, focus on how your lungs feel as they fill with air, hold breath, and release it.

Now begin a third breath cycle. On this cycle, focus on how your heartbeat feels during each stage of the cycle. Pay attention to what causes it to speed up and slow down.

If you need to repeat the second or third cycles to better observe how these parts of your body feel, go right ahead. You should not rush ahead to the next step until you have a firm sense of what is taking place during each cycle. What matters is feeling and understanding the interactions between your breath, your heart, and your lungs.

Once you are comfortable with what you are feeling during the second and third cycles, begin a fourth breath cycle. In this cycle, focus on how the rest of your body feels during each stage. Do you feel tense during some moments and relaxed in others? How does it feel when your heart speeds up and slows down? Pay attention to what you sense during these moments.

You may repeat the fourth cycle as necessary.

The breath cycles of this exercise will be used in further exercises in this book to help you achieve a state of relaxation.

You can also use breath cycles in daily life to help relax your body when stressed or upset. The more you practice this exercise, the easier it becomes to control your breath, and through it, your state of being and reactions to what is happening in your life.

chapter two

THE NORSE PAGAN WORLD

They alone are aware who have wandered wide,
And far abroad have fared,
How great a mind is guided by they
That wealth of wisdom have
HAVAMAL 18

The world is alive, and everything in it moves to an eternal song. Reality for Norse Pagans is far greater than what can be seen and touched. From crude matter and the smallest living things to the mightiest of the Powers, all existence is shaped by greater rhythms. The first step in understanding Norse Paganism is learning these cycles and how they influence your life, and how they bind together.

The core of the world according to Norse Paganism is shaped by four great truths: the World Tree, the cyclical processes that shape reality, the spirits in the world around us, and the all-encompassing web of fate. These truths are at the heart of the universe, shaping all that is. They are as central to reality as the laws of science. Whether you see them as literal fact or powerful metaphors for explaining existence, the three truths carry deep wisdom. Heeding their lessons offers powerful insights for leading worthy, meaningful lives.

The World Tree

The center of the Norse Pagan universe is the World Tree, which is also known as the Yggdrasil (pronounced *IGG-druh-sil*). It is the backbone of Norse Paganism's cosmic ecosystem. Its branches reach in every direction, cradling all the worlds of Norse Paganism. The World Tree's roots plunge into unfathomable depths and are watered by the three great wells. Everything is connected to and through the Yggdrasil.

On the Yggdrasil are nine worlds. They are different realms, like parallel universes, governed by their own laws and norms. The highest reaches of the Yggdrasil hold the realms of Asgard and Vanaheim, the homes of the Aesir and Vanir. The gods travel from Asgard to the other realms using the Bifrost, a rainbow bridge guarded by the god Heimdall. Nearby is Alfheim, the home of the Alfar, a powerful group of spirits who have great beauty and mystical prowess.

Halfway down the Tree is Midgard, the Middle Realm. Midgard is all of physical reality as we know it. Earth, the sun, the stars, and the rest of the universe are in Midgard. Encircling the outer limits of Midgard is Jormungandr (pronounced *YOR-mun-gan-dir*), a serpent so massive it circles all of reality and holds its tail in its jaws. Nearest to Midgard are Jötunheim, the realm of the third group of gods known as the Jötnar, and Nidavellir (also called Svartalfheim) on the other side, the home of the dwarves.

In the great depths watering Yggdrasil are the three great wells of Urd, Mimir, and Hvergelmir (pronounced *VER-gel-meer*). On either side of the base are the realms of fire and ice named Muspelheim and Niflheim. When these primal realms collided, in a time separated from ours by an unfathomable abyss, the explosion unleashed by their meeting created the building blocks of Midgard and the ancestors of the gods. The last realm at the World Tree's base is Helheim, the land of the dead. The dead dwell here in their eternal rest, watching over the living in the comforts of the goddess Hel's Hall. Gnawing at Yggdrasil's roots is the dragon Niddhogr (pronounced *NEED-hog*), a great dragon whose hunger for the World Tree will never be satisfied and who can never stop chewing at the backbone of reality.[13]

The World Tree's place as the supporter and sustainer of all worlds makes it essential in Norse Paganism. Everything depends on it. All need the World

13. Ibid

Tree to exist just as all life on Earth needs healthy, sustainable, and thriving ecosystems to survive. If you could cut any of the Nine Worlds off Yggdrasil, it would probably suffer the same fate as a healthy branch torn from a tree. Even so, the World Tree does not stand above all things like a transcendent deity. It is connected to all and is fed by the waters of the three great wells at its roots. The soil beneath it supports it, giving it life and foundation.

Life is very similar to the World Tree. As has been proven by modern biology, all living beings are made up of countless tiny cells, all too small for the eye to see. Each cell has its own needs that must be met so it can live, thrive and reproduce. These cells do not operate solely on their own, nor in their own narrow interests. When cells come together, they form tissues, organs, and the stuff that makes up all life, from the simplest molds and lichen to complex beings like plants, animals, and humans. Connection and cooperation at the smallest level is the backbone of life as we know it.[14]

Following the same pattern is the way in which the broader forces that define our existence work. Living cells are made up of atoms and molecules which are held together by electromagnetic forces. These tiny particles are the building blocks of nonliving matter and the proteins, DNA, and other chemicals that make living beings. Everything is held together by forces we cannot see or touch, yet their influence is as intimate as your heartbeat and as far-reaching as the horizon. This unseen yet indispensable web of connections is the essence of what the World Tree is, means, and how it upholds reality on every level.[15]

The Cycles of Reality

In the Eddas, the ancient sagas of the Norse, it is said that in the beginning there was no Earth. In its place was the Ginnungagap, a great empty void flanked by the fires of Muspelheim and the ice of Niflheim. None know how long this primordial age of opposing forces, separated by the Yawning Gap,

---

14. "KS3 Bitesize Science—Cells to Systems: Revision, Page 5." BBC. Accessed August 22, 2018. http://www.bbc.co.uk/bitesize/ks3/science/organisms_behaviour_health/cells_systems/revision/5/.

15. "How Do Molecules Interact?" OpenLearn. August 08, 2006. Accessed August 22, 2018. http://www.open.edu/openlearn/science-maths-technology/science/chemistry/how-do-molecules-interact.

endured. On one fateful day in the primeval past, for reasons unknown, this tense equilibrium was shattered by a mighty clash of cosmic power. Muspelheim's flames roared into the gap just as Nifelheim's ice surged forward with furious intensity. These twin primal forces collided in the empty abyss, unleashing a cataclysmic explosion. In that moment everything changed.[16]

The first to emerge from the cooling steam released by the clash of mighty forces were the mighty giant Ymir (pronounced *EE-meer*) and the great cow Audumla (pronounced *OW-doom-lah*). Ymir gave birth to the first of the Jötnar, spawning them from their thighs, arms, legs and sides. Audumla and the giants lived by licking moss off the rocks, while Ymir alone dined on Audumla's everlasting meat and milk. After an unfathomable eternity, the smallest of things would unwittingly cause reality's next great upheaval. One day when Audumla was eating, her licking on a patch of frozen lichen freed a bright, shining being from the tundra. This being's name was Buri, the first of the Aesir. Buri had children with a frost giant, including a son named Bor. Bor, in turn, sired three sons—Odin, Vili, and Ve—with a frost giant. The brothers would end the age of the Great Giant and bring forth the world as we know it.[17]

Odin, Vili, and Ve lived under the same poverty as their forebears and the other Jötnar. Throughout these long ages, Ymir had kept Audumla's bounty for themselves, leaving everyone else to scrape a meager living out of the frosty ground. No matter how hard Buri, Bor, their spouse, or the Jötnar worked, nothing changed. None know how long the brothers endured such toil before deciding they'd had enough. One day they rose up, struck against Ymir, and slew them.[18]

This time, all the gods were given a say in making the new reality, and they used Ymir's bones, flesh, and blood as material for crafting existence. As it says in the Voluspo:

Then sought the gods their assembly seats,
The holy ones, and council held;
Names gave they to noon and twilight,

---

16. Voluspo 3, Poetic Edda; Gylfaginning 4, Prose Edda, Jesse L. Byock Translation

17. Voluspo 3, Vafthruthnismol 21, Poetic Edda; Gylfaginning 5, Prose Edda

18. Voluspo 4-6, Poetic Edda; Gylfaginning 8, Prose Edda

Morning they named, and the waning moon,
Night and evening, the years to number.[19]

Together they made Midgard, deciding all matters through councils and deliberation. After setting the shape of reality, Odin, Lodur, and Hoenir went into Midgard.[20] As it says in the Voluspo:

Then from the throng did three come forth,
From the home of the gods, the mighty and gracious;
Two without fate on the land they found,
Ask and Embla, empty of might.
Soul they had not, sense they had not,
Heat nor motion, nor goodly hue;
Soul gave Odin, sense gave Hoenir,
Heat gave Lodur and goodly hue.[21]

The first humans then opened their eyes, wandering out into Midgard. With no commands, limits, or decrees handed down by their makers, they took their first steps freely, aided by the gifts the gods gave them.

These great acts created the world as we know it, crafting the rules that govern this universe and setting it in motion. Yet even the gods, though they demonstrated great power and wisdom in these transformative deeds of destruction and re-creation, are not immune to even greater laws that govern all things on the World Tree. Just as Midgard was created through revolution against Ymir's power, so too will a new age ultimately come in the distant future. Its onset will be immensely terrible, and many of the gods work tirelessly to delay its arrival. This time is known as Ragnarok, the Doom of the Powers.

Ragnarok was foretold by the Nameless Seeress, a dead mystic who is uniquely gifted in the arts of prophecy. The Seeress was forced to reveal this terrible future by Odin, who pulled her up from beyond the grave using terrible magics. In the Song of the Seeress, also known as the Voluspo, she revealed

19. Voluspo 6, Poetic Edda

20. Some say Lodur and Loki are the same being, not much is known about Hoenir due to a lack of surviving material

21. Voluspo 17-18, Poetic Edda

horrifying truths to the One-Eyed God: in a time to come, all the works of the gods will be undone. Yet despite these visions of fear and loss, a spark of hope burns brightly.

It will begin in Midgard. As it says in the Voluspo:

Brother shall kill brother and sisters' sons will slay
Hard it is on Midgard with all in reckless abandon
Axe-time, sword-time shields are sundered
Wind-time, wolf-time ere the world falls
No one will each other spare[22]

Three roosters will crow, alerting all the final battle is coming. The god Heimdall will sound his great horn for the first and last time, summoning the gods and their allies to battle. They hold council and prepare for the war to end all worlds. The Einherjar, mighty warriors plucked from battlefields across Midgard by the Valkyries throught the centuries to serve in Odin's great host, muster in Valhalla for the last time.[23]

Up and down the World Tree, destruction reigns. Slaughter unceasing in Midgard is made worse with the coming of the Fimbulwinter, a time of bitter cold so fierce it unleashes a new ice age. Fenrir, the Great Wolf, shatters the bonds imposed by the gods and runs free, seeking bloody vengeance. Jormungandr, the Midgard serpent, will rise from beneath the waves, flooding the land as it surges forward to slay the gods. In the depths of Muspelheim, Surtr gathers an army of fire giants so vast that Asgard's Rainbow Bridge will shatter beneath their weight. As disaster grows, the multitudes of newly dead flee for Helheim, hoping for refuge with a great inferno licking at their heels.[24]

The armies of Muspelheim march on Asgard. They break the great wall surrounding the realm of the Aesir, charging onto the great fields behind it. There they clash with the host of the gods and the warriors of Valhalla.[25]

---

22. Voluspo 45, Poetic Edda
23. Voluspo 42-48, Poetic Edda
24. Voluspo 46-52, Poetic Edda
25. Voluspo 53-56, Poetic Edda; HR Ellis Davidson, *The Road to Hel: A Study of the Conception of the Dead in Old Norse Literature*, Greenwood Press (Westport, Connecticut: 1968), 66-82

Surtr duels Freyr, slaying the King of Plenty with a blade forged from white-hot flames. Thor wrestles the Midgard Serpent in a mighty clash for the ages. The two champions rend the ground beneath them in their struggle. Thor just barely breaks his foe, yet will only take nine steps before Jormungandr's last poisonous breath brings the Thunderer down. Odin charges fiercely into the field but is devoured by Fenrir in a single bite. The great hound Garm, who sat at the roots of Yggdrasil for an endless age, slays Tyr, the god of Justice. Amidst the chaos, Loki arrives with a ship crewed by the dead and unleashes them into the bloodbath, causing further confusion.[26]

In the swirling carnage, Surtr charges the base of Yggdrasil. He strikes the trunk with his fiery sword, setting all alight. Everything on the World Tree will burn as flames consume all worlds, victor and vanquished alike, and nothing will escape the blaze. All the works of gods and humanity will end. Yet even as this is a cataclysmic ending, Ragnarok is not the end of everything.[27]

Odin's son Vidar tears the Great Wolf in two, avenging his father. Thor's children pull his hammer from the wreckage, standing beside the gods who survive. Two humans, Lif and Lifrasir, ride out the storm hidden in the leaves of the World Tree and will bring a new birth of humanity. The slain god Baldr rises from Helheim to join the new gods in a new world raised from the ruins of the old. Even in the face of Ragnarok's destruction, another reality will rise, just as this one was born from the great upheaval unleashed by Ymir's downfall.

The story of the Nine Worlds is driven by a consistent cycle. At the beginning of each age of creation is an existing status quo; order itself is maintained by the deeds of those who benefit the most from it. Due to the actions and decisions of those on top, opposing forces develop and seek a new ordering of existence. They eventually rise up and overthrow the old order, creating a new one using the components of what came before.

This cycle mirrors processes found in the natural world. The vast pine forests of Scandinavia and central Europe follow a similar pattern of new life emerging from destruction. In these regions, pine trees spread their seeds by growing and dropping pine cones. They can only scatter their seeds when wildfires ignite the sap holding the cones together, flinging seeds in every direction.

---

26. Voluspo 53-56, Poetic Edda

27. Voluspo 57, Poetic Edda

The soil they land in is invigorated by the ashes of the flames, which provide critical nutrients that are essential for new life. This dynamic is not unique to Scandinavia and is seen in many ecosystems worldwide where destruction begets new creation.[28]

The march of the seasons moves to the same rhythm. In spring and summer, living beings flourish as plants grow, herbivores eat the plants, carnivores hunt the herbivores and life multiplies. The gifts given by water, wind, and sun nurture everything, nourishing what is and could be. As the days grow shorter and conditions become less hospitable, everything prepares for leaner times. When winter comes, life retreats but does not end. Plants go dormant, and some animals hibernate while others conserve their energy to survive until spring returns.[29]

Philosophically speaking, this process is very similar to what is known as dialectical logic. In dialectics, all ideas, social systems, and communities are shaped by a continuous process as they grow and change. The components of this process are thesis, antithesis, and synthesis. The thesis is existing status quo, whether that is a widely accepted idea or a community's current state. The antithesis is a challenge to the thesis, often arising because of flaws or shortcomings in the thesis. Their struggle leads to the synthesis, a new situation made up of elements of thesis and antithesis combined with new ideas and solutions that arose from the earlier struggle.[30]

The creation of humanity by the gods follows this same dynamic. The gods did not simply will the first humans into existence any more than they com-

---

28. "Scandinavian Mountains over 2000 metres - James Baxter." Scandinavian Mountains - Flora and Fauna. Accessed November 12, 2017. http://www.scandinavianmountains.com/flora-fauna/trees-shrubs/index.htm.; "How Do Pine Trees Reproduce?" Sciencing. Accessed November 12, 2017. https://sciencing.com/do-pine-trees-reproduce-5173107.html.; "How Trees Survive and Thrive After A Fire." National Forest Foundation. Accessed November 12, 2017. https://www.nationalforests.org/our-forests/your-national-forests-magazine/how-trees-survive-and-thrive-after-a-fire.

29. "The Seasonal Cycle of Atmospheric Heating and Temperature." American Meteorological Society. Accessed November 30, 2015. http://journals.ametsoc.org/doi/abs/10.1175/JCLI-D-12-00713.1

30. Maybee, Julie E. "Hegel's Dialectics." Stanford Encyclopedia of Philosophy. June 03, 2016. Accessed November 12, 2017. https://plato.stanford.edu/entries/hegel-dialectics/

manded Midgard to rise from nothingness. They took up two pieces of dead wood, reshaped them, and gave these new creations the gifts of breath, mind, and heat. Much like the creation of Midgard from Ymir's body or the seeding of new trees in the ashen ground, the gods made humanity by taking existing material they changed and shaped into new forms.

The decisions made in the great cycle are just as critical as the cycle itself. The contrast between the rule of Ymir and the time of Midgardr is critical. Under Ymir, only the great giant feasted on the only source of wealth in all existence. The hoarding and poverty of their lives moved Odin, Vili, and Ve to rebellion. In cooperation with the rest of the gods, they then used Ymir's body to fashion a new world where all would have space to thrive. Even the surviving Jötnar children of Ymir have a home in Jötunheim and are not ruthlessly hunted into extinction. Humanity and all other beings in the Nine Worlds have the freedom to live as all choose in a world with space for everyone. They replaced an order of domination and inequity with one of freedom and shared prosperity.

There was nothing compelling the rebels against Ymir to share as they did. In fact, Ymir's own rise shows that the gods could have ruled this world just as absolutely as the great giant did. Instead, they built Midgard and Asgard, giving space for all to find their own paths. Their main actions, as shown in the lore, are driven by keeping this order intact instead of imposing their power on those who live in it.

In Radical Norse Paganism, reality moves in cycles. When anything dies, breaks down, or falls apart, its elements and components go back into the world to facilitate new life and new creations. Even if a person or animal dies without siring offspring, they contribute to new life—directly in the form of their decomposing body, and indirectly through the wisdom they shared while living, the fruits of their labor, and the effect their deeds had on the world around them. These broad strokes are consistent even as the details vary.

The only constants in these cycles are life, death, and change. Life endures, adapts, and persists, while always seeking new ways to thrive. Though certain, death does not dictate the moments between beginnings and endings. Change is also certain—sometimes it is the product of time's ceaseless march and other times it is caused by deliberate action. All things age and eventually pass on, but they are only replaced by newer forms through deeds, not by waiting for life to happen on its own.

If you accept a reality that's driven by cycles of great upheaval and transformation, then you need to consider some very tough questions. As existence on all levels and its organization was shaped through action, it is reasonable to conclude the same must be true for your life, the society you live in, and the world around you. The ultimate challenge is to ask yourself what is worth keeping, what must be destroyed, what can be repurposed for something better, and how to do it in the most equitable way possible.

Spirits All Around Us

In Radical Norse Paganism, everything is alive. From the breeze at our backs to the ground beneath our feet, we live in a world filled with spirits. Oceans roar, forests stretch, and electricity hums all around us. Nothing is ever at rest, whether it is a chunk of concrete underfoot or the mightiest of mountains. In Radical Norse Paganism you live in a world that is constantly in motion. There are entities, beings and intelligences all around you, with their own goals, desires, and drives. This idea is what is commonly known as animism.[31]

Animism is the belief that everything, no matter how big or small, has some sort of spirit within it. In Norse Paganism many things, no matter what they are or how unremarkable or insignificant they may seem, have a sacred essence known as a spirit called a vættr, collectively known as the vættir (pronounced *vite* and *vie-tear*.) This is just as true of living beings, such as plant and animal life, as it is of inanimate objects and places. In the lore were often specific things, such as rivers or homes, with their own spirits, though it is difficult to know today what does and does not have its own spirit. Regardless, all things should be treated as if they have a spirit which deserves dignity, respect, and honor. Each has its own critical role to play in the grand design of existence.[32]

---

31. Park, George Kerlin. "Animism." Encyclopædia Britannica. December 19, 2016. Accessed August 22, 2018. https://www.britannica.com/topic/animism.

32. Reimund Kvideland and Henning K. Sehmsdorf, *Scandinavian Folk Belief and Legend*, University of Minnesota Press (Minneapolis: 1988), 8-10; Alda Sigmunsdottir, *The Little Book of the Hidden People*, Little Books Publishing (Reykjavik: 2015), 11-13; "1179 (Svensk Etymologisk Ordbok)." Project Runeberg. Accessed August 22, 2018. http://runeberg.org/svetym/1267.html.

The idea that everything has a spirit that deserves our consideration has enormous implications for how life should be lived on a day-to-day basis. If you accept that any number of things around you have a sacred essence worthy of respect, this changes how you live. Objects become more than things and living beings must be given greater respect than what is often shown by modern society. The effect of your actions, decisions, and their consequences take on far greater significance when you act as if uncountable things in the world must be treated with dignity and honor. Everything becomes more than just the chemical reactions and matter that make them possible.

One good way for explaining how this works is to consider what this perspective means when you think of trees. For most people living today, a tree, while unquestionably alive, is mostly seen in terms of what it provides. Whether they are fruit-bearing, a source of shade, good for climbing, or measured by the potential volume of lumber that can be harvested, trees are viewed based on how people can use them. That a tree is a living being with its own needs is usually secondary for many people to what it can do for them.

For animists, this materialistic approach is the exact opposite of how the living world should be considered and experienced. A tree is a living being that must be respected, revered, and honored, simply for being alive. By existing, it contributes to everything around it in many ways. If it becomes necessary for us to harvest from the tree, it isn't a simple matter of dispassionately collecting the desired materials; the tree should be honored, thanked, and respected for the gifts it gives every step of the way, especially if those gifts come at the cost of the tree's existence. You should also only harvest from the tree when it is necessary and not to satisfy a passing urge or out of immediate convenience.

All known evidence from pre-Christian times suggests that on a day-to-day level, the bulk of the spiritual focus for Norse peoples was on their relationships with such nature spirits. Of course the gods were still important, but people tended to interact most often with the spirits, the forces they were associated with, and the places they were tied to. Earning the favor of the gods was as important as keeping the spirits in their communities and homes happy for living day-to-day.[33]

---

33. Kvideland and Sehmsdorf 9

The Spirits of Norse Paganism

In the ancient world, many things and places were believed to have their own spirit. The most common spirits were associated with specific places like groves of trees, open fields, and bodies of water. As mentioned earlier, the spirits of natural places are commonly called vættir, and one group in particular is known as husvættir (pronounced *HUS-vie-tear*), who are tied to specific homes and other dwellings. The island nation of Iceland, according to folklore, is protected by four especially powerful spirits—a vulture, a dragon, a giant, and a bull—that are included in the official Icelandic coat of arms.[34] It is certainly possible in the present day for individual vættr to be tied to specific streets, neighborhoods, and urban communities.

In addition to the vættr of Norse lore are the well-known alfar, also known as elves. Unfortunately, there is little consistent information on them in the lore; it is known the elves are ruled by Freyr, one of the Vanic gods, have their own realm called Alfheim, are strongly associated with magic, and are described as beautiful and unpredictable. You may have already seen something like them in popular culture. The Norse Alfar directly inspired the elves of J.R.R. Tolkien's *Lord of the Rings* and many other works of fantasy that followed in Tolkien's footsteps.[35]

Another famous group of spirits are the dwarves, who are also known as the Svartalfar or Dark Alfar. They are better understood than the alfar and are said to live in the realm of Nidavellir, also known as Svartalfheim.[36] They are masters of craftwork, industry, and construction. They made many of the greatest treasures of the Aesir and Vanir, including Thor's hammer. Whenever the gods need something especially potent, beautiful, or specialized, they

---

34. Davidson, Hilda Roderick Ellis. *Myths and Symbols in Pagan Europe: Early Scandinavian and Celtic Religions*. Syracuse: Syracuse Univ. Press, 2006. 102-104; Davidson, Hilda Roderick Ellis. *The Lost Beliefs of Northern Europe*. London: Routledge, 1994, 119-121; Kvideland and Sehmsdorf 8-10; "History | Icelandic Coat of Arms." Prime Minister's Office. Accessed November 12, 2017. https://eng.forsaetisraduneyti.is/state-symbols/icelandic-coat-of-arms/history/#Guardian_spirits

35. Davidson, *Myths and Symbols in Pagan Europe: Early Scandinavian and Celtic Religions*, 109,172-173; Sigmundsdottir 11-12

36. Crossley-Holland xxxi-xxxii; Ross, Margaret Clunies. *Prolonged Echoes: Old Norse Myths in Medieval Northern Society*. Odense: Odense University Press, 1994, 73-74

nearly always ask the dwarves to make what they need. Given these associations, you could say that they are very close to all forms of present-day crafting, technology, and production.

Another famous type of spirits are trolls. Unlike the other spirits, who can be friendly, hostile, or indifferent depending on the spirit, trolls are usually a source of mischief and challenges. Their actions range from annoying pranks to far more dangerous deeds. There is no concrete proof the Norse folklore on trolls is the source of the modern term for certain people on the internet, even though the actions of these digital trolls are rather like their counterparts in folklore. In contrast to trolls are the guardian spirits known as disir. Usually depicted as women, disir watch over specific people and families.[37]

The last group of spirits are the dead. In Norse Paganism, death is only an end for physical life. A part of your self—and every person's self—passes on after death to one of many different fates. There is no single destination awaiting those who have passed through this veil, although most people go to Helheim to live in a great community of the dead enjoying a well-deserved rest from the labors of life. The other most well-known places are Freyja's Hall of Folkvangr and Odin's Hall of Valhalla, which play host to those who died heroically on the battlefield. Anyone who dies at sea live in the Hall of Aegir and Ran, deep beneath the waves. Some dwell at their grave sites and there are many stories of people who wrestle with the dead to claim their treasures or secrets.[38]

With the sole exception of those who commit the most unspeakable crimes (whose ultimate end is to be devoured by the great dragon Niddhogr), there are no eternal punishments—or rewards—doled out to the dead. This idea goes hand-in-hand with the veneration of the dead for their deeds while alive and the effect they had on the world. In Norse Paganism, death is only a change of how you exist. Either through the effect of your deeds while alive or in a more spiritual sense, it is not the end of your presence in the world.[39]

---

37. John Lindow, *Trolls: An Unnatural History*, Reaktion Books (London: 2014), 14-25; Davidson, *The Lost Beliefs of Northern Europe*, 113

38. Ross 251-256; Davidson, *The Road to Hel* 2-6, 83-95, 99-104

39. Voluspo 39, Poetic Edda

Working with the Spirits

There are many ways to connect with the spirits in the world around you and build enduring relationships with them. The most common way is leaving regular offerings of food, drink, or small gifts of valued, biodegradable materials like hops, grain, or flowers. The practice of offerings dates back to pre-Christian times, where families left out offerings of milk, honey, or grain for the spirits of their homes and the lands they lived on. Showing appreciation for the world around you shows respect for the spirits living there, and it also makes them more aware of you. You can build ties through exploring these places and meditating in them using the methods described in chapter four. Spending time in places that may be homes for vættir will help you gain a greater understanding of those spaces, what they are connected to, and how they influence your life.[40]

An even deeper, more powerful way of connecting with the spirits and their environments is by caring for the spaces where they make their homes. You could do this by regularly watering a particular tree, cleaning up trash, and other acts of care. Such deeds show respect and reverence for the place and what lives there. If leaving gifts for the vættir shows respect for the spirits, then acts of service demonstrate an even deeper level of reverence. This work also helps by restoring the space, making it whole, and ensuring it is hospitable for all who need it.

On a broader level, animism challenges the manner in which we should live in the modern world. Society today operates as if everything on Earth should be treated as disposable commodities. Trees are assessed in tons of lumber, hills and mountains by the size of their mineral deposits, oceans for oil drilling and fish stocks, and even the sky is carved into lanes for air traffic. If you see a cow as so many cuts of beef instead of a living thing whose death will sustain many, or an open field as space to be developed for maximum profit instead of as a home for many living things, it becomes dangerously easy to abuse anything.

In this world of disposable, replaceable things is little room for dignity or respect. When the most important kind of value measures only how many expensive things you own and the size of your paycheck, everything suffers.

---

40. Davidson, *The Lost Beliefs of Northern Europe*, 103-104,137; Kvideland and Sehmsdorf, 8–10.

Such crude reduction of the beautiful, interconnected reality everything needs to survive into mere commodities denies the essence inside of all things. There is no question that this alienation stands in clear opposition to living an animistically guided life. However, when your understanding of the natural world and society is based on a complex web of dynamic relationships, nothing can be treated as a lone object operating in isolation. All things depend on and influence each other. When you cut down a tree, every living thing in it faces destruction. Tearing up a cherished city park to make way for a high-rise block of luxury condos destroys the heart of a community along with the greenery and playing fields.

Modern society's practice of reducing places, beings, communities, and people to numbers on balance sheets has unleashed unprecedented environmental destruction on the world and has justified awful acts of total dehumanization. At its worst, this materialistic mentality has enabled the horrors of the slave trade and wholesale genocide, including the destruction of the First Nations of the Americas and the Nazi death camps. According to the latest scientific research on the health of the environment, life on Earth will soon be an impossibility if modern society does not change.

Practitioners of Radical Norse Paganism believe that everything is alive in one way or another, and its animistic perspective urges us to live with respect for all things around us. The consequences of your actions are felt in many ways, some of which may not be obvious. You should always move in life fully aware of the consequences of your decisions and their impact on the world. Living in this way brings you closer to the world around you and helps you lead a more complete life.

Fate

The final truth guiding Radical Norse Paganism is Fate, the influencer of all things. Its tug, touch and tensions shape life. No thing, not even the gods, are free from Fate. Yet the Norse concept of Fate is not that of an immutable, unchanging thing dictating how all events will always unfold. Instead, it is an active, dynamic force shaped by the deeds of all things in every world. Though you may not be able to dictate what card Fate deals you, you can decide how to play your hand and, through sustained work, change the game for the better. There are two forces shaping how Fate's influence shapes everything in the

Nine Worlds—Ørlog and hamingja (pronounced *OAR-log* and *ha-ming-ya)*—who represent the sum of all actions and every individual's capacity to change Fate.

The skeletal framework of Fate is Ørlog. Ørlog is made up of all the things in life that have already been determined by past deeds beyond our control, existing elements of society that come about through the accumulation of many actions over time, or the consequences of all actions. This includes the time and place of your birth, your parents, the consequences of others' actions, and the other elements of your life that cannot be changed. The beings with the most influence over Ørlog are the Norns, three goddesses who dictate when you and all other living things are born and when all will ultimately die. They also feed the World Tree with waters drawn from the wells that hold the pure potential of Fate. Beneath the Norns Ørlog is shaped by the accumulated weight of the deeds of all who have ever lived. Every life can change the shape of the Ørlog surrounding their lives in ways both obvious and hidden.

To break it down to a personal level, the fact that you were born in the present time, place, and circumstances is because of the decisions made by others. For example, that you were born in a particular place was the result of how your parents met and what they chose to do after you were conceived. The decisions made by your parents created what are, for you, inalterable facts. In turn, their choices were likely shaped by other circumstances beyond their control, such as what kind of work they found to support themselves, the circumstances of the place where they live, the conditions they work in, how they were born into world, and how it affected them.

Your past and present actions, choices, and effect on the world are then shaped both by circumstances you can't control (such as the conditions of the community where you were born, what sort of opportunities for supporting yourself or others were available, traits that are an inherent part of who you are,) as well as the effect any existing prejudices or biases in society had on those circumstances. Some of these circumstances result from actions of specific individuals, the accumulated weight of the actions of many unfolding across history and collective action by groups of people working to change their circumstances. This is all before even going into the way any of the Powers —from the humblest spirit to the mightiest god—affect the state of the world and everything in it. All of this is Ørlog, and all of these decisions are shaped by Ørlog.[41]

This all probably sounds very intimidating, and you may be wondering how it's possible to change Fate in any meaningful way when there is so much inertia behind all that is. The answer is your hamingja, also known as luck. For most people living today, luck is little more than random chance or unexpected encounters. In Radical Norse Paganism, nothing could be further from the truth. Your hamingja is inherently part of you, made of all your skills, means, immediate conditions, and anything else in your life capable of changing yourself and your circumstances. Hamingja comes from what is passed on to you from the circumstances of your birth by those who came before. Anything in the Ørlog affecting your life affects your capacity to cause change. Actions you take grow or shrink your ability to cause change. By making decisions and doing deeds that use what is part of your hamingja, you can change Ørlog.[42]

The place where these forces meet is where Fate is shaped. When people use their hamingja to change their lives, their circumstances, or conditions facing others, they change existing Ørlog. In changing the Ørlog, they also create a new and different Ørlog that will affect lives in different ways. Some things that are Ørlog, particularly when the circumstance in question is a product of social institutions, are more resistant to being changed by your hamingja than others. Sometimes it is only possible for you to change a small portion of Ørlog, while in other cases it may be possible to have a much greater influence. This also means your actions and the actions of others are intimately connected, with all playing a role in shaping the world.

There might be times when you are facing Ørlog that it looks bigger than what you on your own can change with your hamingja. Sometimes the solution is to think of different ways of applying your capabilities. There might be an indirect way to solve a problem when a direct solution doesn't work. You might also be facing Ørlog that will take time and sustained effort to alter. In other cases, especially if you are dealing with Ørlog impacting communities or society, you may need to work with others to achieve your goal. When people work collectively to change Ørlog, the manner in which they interact with Fate

41. Ross, 242–243; Davidson, *Gods and Myths of Northern Europe* 217–219

42. Davidson, *Myths and Symbols in Pagan Europe*, 134, 166

changes. People working together pool their hamingja into a greater force than any of their individual means, creating a far greater capacity for causing change.

It is important to remember every person's hamingja is different, just as every individual is different. This means some things that are Ørlog impact people in different ways. The possession or lack of specific components of hamingja does not make any one person inherently greater or lesser than anyone else. It is simply a matter of means, conditions, and how Ørlog affects them. Sometimes there are also Ørlog that are too great to be changed easily (e.g., powerful institutions), or even at all, as is the case in universal laws. This does not mean you should simply accept what is. If there is Ørlog that is harmful to yourself, others, or whole communities, you should still do everything in your power to change it. In Radical Norse Paganism, it is always better for you to try your best to improve your circumstances than to meekly accept them without complaint. As the example of the gods and Ragnarok shows, even if something is inevitable or more powerful than you can handle, you should still do everything you can to change your circumstances, community, and society for the better.

Pulse of Reality

At the heart of Radical Norse Paganism are four central truths: the World Tree sustaining all of reality, the cycles that define everything, the living world of the spirits around us, and Fate's dynamic and inescapable influence. When put together, they show the world is deeply interconnected and our actions can change it. By understanding these greater patterns and dynamics, you can better understand the Powers, develop an understanding of spirituality, and find the best way to lead a worthy, fulfilling life.

As massive (and at times overwhelming) as this all may look, there is a kind of comfort you can take from it. When you accept the world as one where even the greatest gods live under the same laws as the smallest living things, it opens up incredible possibilities. The struggles and challenges you face are shared by many others, including the mightiest Powers. This means you can learn from the examples, successes, and mistakes of others and find ways to use this wisdom to improve your life. It also means you can genuinely make such changes in your life, your community, and the world.

The following exercise will help you better understand how you and everything around you is connected. You may find this exercise gives you even greater insights when you do it in different places, times, or circumstances. With time and practice, it will also improve your day-to-day awareness of the world around you.

exercise
SPATIAL AWARENESS

Begin by finding a place outdoors where you can sit in place without fear of being disturbed or made unsafe. Follow the steps of the breathing exercise outlined in chapter one. Continue the breathing exercise until your heartbeat is calm and you feel at ease. Keep your eyes closed throughout the exercise.

Once your body is in this resting state, focus on your hearing. Let your attention drift and take in everything around you. Let the sounds of the immediate environment fill your mind. Listen deeply, savoring every sound you can.

You can also do the same with your sight. If you choose this approach, keep your eyes open and take in all the sights around you. Do not focus on any specific detail, item, or thing present; instead, let your eyes take in everything around you. Let your vision drift without focusing on any specific thing. Regardless of the method you use, once you have taken in your surroundings, you are ready for the next step in this exercise.

You should now focus on seeking out four specific things with your senses. If you are using your ears, search for the quietest sound you can hear, the loudest sound you can hear, the farthest sound from you that you can hear, and the closest sound to you that you can hear. If you are using your eyes, look for the smallest thing you can see without moving your head or eyes. Look again for the largest thing, the closest thing, and the farthest thing.

Once you have found what you are seeking, listen or watch for whatever is in their vicinity. Everything in the world moves in relationship with everything else, just as we all live in relationships with the spirits around us. Once you have determined the closest things to each of the four things you have observed, you may return your focus to normal.

Take time to reflect on what you have observed.

chapter three

THE NORSE GODS

At Idavoll met the mighty gods,
Shrines and temples they timbered high;
Forges they set, and they smithied ore,
Tongs they wrought, and tools they fashioned.
Voluspo 7

There are moments in everyone's lives where you may have felt the movements of things that cannot be explained. Perhaps you've had a flash of insight that solved an intractable puzzle in the space of a breath. There might have been a tingle running up your spine in the wake of a storm's fury. Maybe you saw *something* out of the corner of your eye that seemed impossibly ancient and indescribable. There could've been an instant when you suddenly felt as if a mighty presence was in the room with you even though you'd swear you were all alone. Even more unsettling are those times when you weren't the only one who felt the company of the enigmatic.

If any of this sounds familiar, you may have already been touched by gods. For Radical Norse Paganism they are guides, mentors, protectors, mighty allies and examples of worthy and unworthy conduct in facing life's struggles. Though they have their own goals that may push you in unexpected ways, they are not rulers. In the Radical tradition, they have shown they trust everyone to govern ourselves even as they offer help.

Understanding Divinity

In Norse Paganism there are many gods, an understanding of divinity that is also known as polytheism. Each god is an independent, autonomous being with their own name, titles, personality, abilities, purviews and desires. Even this is but a fragment of what the gods truly are. Though the Norse gods, like all polytheistic gods, are not limitless or all-powerful, they are still **gods**. Even though they are subject to the same greater laws as everything else in the Nine Worlds, they are the Powers who lit the stars, raised the mountains, filled the seas, and set the cosmos in motion. Knowing what each is called, tied to, and the driving behind them will help you better understand beings whose true forms are far beyond the limits of human comprehension.

Even as mighty as the Norse gods are, they are far from perfect. Some bear scars, others are missing limbs. Like all people, the gods have made mistakes and sometimes done terrible things—just because a god does something doesn't make that action justified. The gods offer powerful examples, at their best and worst, for everyone.

Their imperfection may seem strange in the face of modern society, which believes divinity means infallibility. But it is the flaws of the Norse gods that make their conduct even more relevant to our lives. They show the gods struggle with many of the same challenges you may face every day. They are encouraging, experienced mentors who want you to do the best you can and are not waiting to punish you for mistakes or setbacks. They've been there and know that the right or best action isn't always easy.

The gods are also a means for understanding the human experience. The stories of their actions are one way of giving you worthy examples for life. Another is through what they are associated with. Many people these days dismiss nature-based, polytheistic gods as primitive superstitions used to explain the natural world before the rise of modern science, but nothing could be further from the truth. Whether talking about a god of the ocean depths, a harvest deity, or one of words and wisdom, a specific god's associations helps understand that deity and explain why things are. Associations provide you with a frame of reference for understanding the aspect of life that deity is associated with, and the ties also mean that the deity can provide people guidance if their lives are shaped by an area or field associated with that deity. The influence of the gods is a different view of reality; it doesn't contradict, negate, or nullify scientific explanations. If anything, science and spirituality enhance each other when applied with an open mind.

Just like animism, the heart of working with the Norse gods is building enduring relationships. There are many ways you can do this. The information that follows will give you a better idea of what each of the gods are like, what they are associated with, and the guidance they offer. There is also an exercise at the end of this chapter that can get you started on your spiritual journey. More specifics on building these relationships can be found in chapter four. There are no specific gods that are better to start off with than others; just as everyone is different, the gods you connect with most easily are the ones who are most suited to meeting your needs. One good place to go for some ideas is author Niki Ruggerio's work on relational polytheism.[43]

In Norse Paganism, most of the gods of the Nine Worlds belong to one of three clans, known as the Aesir, the Vanir, and the Jötnar. Each of these clans is associated with an element of how people understand reality. There are also gods with similar potency, importance, and influence who aren't part of any of the three, known as the Others. They do not make up a specific clan, as each is tied to the most primordial powers in existence, putting them beyond the rest of the gods in many key ways, making each a highly unique Power.

The Aesir are the gods associated with humanity and society, with connections to words, law, labor, and conflict. They also show up the most in pop culture. The Vanir are the gods related to how humanity interacts with the natural world, with connections to fertility, magic, and working with nature. The Jötnar are the gods of the wilderness, with ties to raw natural forces like wildfires, the ocean depths, and Earth itself.[44]

The three clans and the Others have some very complicated relationships. Sometimes they fight, most spectacularly when the Aesir and Vanir fought a drawn-out war in the days following Midgard's creation, or as seen in the many scuffles between the Aesir and some of the Jötnar. They also have friendly

43. https://www.patheos.com/blogs/awitchsashram/2015/08/11/relational-polytheism/

44. Crossley-Holland, xx; Crossley-Holland, xxxi-xxxii

relationships; some have even intermarried. There are no clear, bright lines defining good versus evil or light against dark between any of the three clans and the Others—they are all simply different Powers with different drives and associations, with many facets of existence.[45]

Even though the relationships between the three clans and the Others are sometimes tense or complicated, all honor the shared customs that were part of everyday life for the ancient Norse peoples. For example, all recognize the sanctity of hospitality, offering and receiving the protections of guest-right. Compensation for injury and death, known as weregild, is often requested and granted even between members of different groups. Oaths are taken and recognized even if they aren't always kept. They all, generally, resolve their affairs through open councils, debates and popular assemblies instead of decree. The relationships between different groups of gods and individual deities are shaped by specific circumstances. There is no overarching, cosmic struggle that pits specific groups against each other; many of the conflicts between them are thanks to quite human, easily understood causes.

The Aesir: The Gods of Society

You may have already heard of some of the more famous Aesir, like Odin, Thor, and Loki. Their popularity is in part because so much information on them has survived, as well as due to their very direct associations with humanity. As gods of all aspects of social life, culture, and the human experience, the Aesir are closely tied to concepts like writing, justice, and warfare. There are many Aesir recorded in the sagas and countless more whose names survive to the present day, like Baldr, Forseti, Ullr, Bragi, Idunna, and many others. The information covered in this chapter provide enough information for you to get a sense of who the Aesir are and get started on your practice. The unmentioned Aesir are still important in their own ways and you may find yourself drawn to them as your practice develops.

One aspect shared by most of the Aesir that needs its own discussion is their well-known connection to war and conflict. Most of the Aesir have a martial aspect, something that caused many to believe they are warrior gods who *only* accept warrior peoples and see battle as more important than anything

45. Davidson, *gods and Myths of Northern Europe*, 45.

else. This assumption is based on an incomplete understanding of the ancient world. For many of the Norse peoples, war was civic duty. When their communities were threatened, everyone was expected to help defend their homes however they could. It would be more accurate to say that the Aesir's warlike nature reflects these conditions. We may extrapolate that all members of every community have a part to play in facing shared struggles, no matter what form those dangers take. So, contrary to popular assumption, the Aesir won't turn you away for not being "macho"—their examples show they have very different priorities.

Odin: The Many-Named God

Odin is one of the most complicated deities in the Nine Worlds. In the lore is a name for Odin for every place he's ever been. He's also picked up many other names, kennings, and titles thanks to his deeds while wandering the pathways of reality. As complex as he is, many reduce him to a ruling warrior patriarch with some brief mention of his wisdom. However, these superficial understandings of the One-Eyed God just barely scratch the surface of this multi-faceted deity.

The best way to think of Odin is as an experienced elder, world-weary traveler, and cunning sage who has seen it all, done it all, wrote the book, and then rewrote it after realizing his first attempt wasn't good enough. Odin's story begins when he and his brothers, Vili and Ve, overthrew Ymir and crafted a new world from the bones of the old, winning the names *Ygg*, meaning the terrible, and *Allfather*. Following this revolution, Odin kept pushing the envelope, sacrificing one of his eyes for knowledge of the future, stealing the mead of poetry, and learning seiðr from Freyja. His greatest feat was winning the runes by hanging from the World Tree for nine days and nights. When finished, he shared the fruits of his sacrifice with all the Worlds. This deed earned him the name of the "Hanged God."[46]

Ever since these first adventures, Odin has restlessly wandered all the Worlds, seeking knowledge no matter where it was or who held it, earning him the name Wanderer. Many celebrate him as the Father of Victory, yet Odin usually wins through deception and trickery instead of battle, often aided

46. Gylfaginning 3, translated by Jesse L. Byock.

by his great knowledge of magic. As the God of Ecstasy, he is the patron of the skalds (the storytellers and poets of the ancients and modern Norse Paganism), mystics, and the ferocious berserker warriors.[47]

Odin usually appears wearing a broad-brimmed hat pulled down to one side to cover his missing eye when he doesn't have an eyepatch, and a well-worn traveling cloak. He carries a great spear, Gugnir, which has the power to grant victory; all the Aesir swear their oaths on it. He is accompanied by two wolves, Geri and Freki, who devour all that is put before them. The twin ravens Huginn and Muninn (meaning Thought and Memory) fly through all the Nine Worlds telling Odin everything they see. He rides an eight-legged horse named Sleipnir, a child of Loki, so that he may travel effortlessly between the Worlds. When not traveling, his home in Asgard is the hall of Hlidskjalf. In this hall is a great seat that grants whoever is in it the power to see anything anywhere in the Nine Worlds. Two symbols most often associated with Odin are the Valknut, representing sacrifice in his name, and the Triple Horn, representing his wisdom and cunning.[48]

The Valknut and the Triple Horn

Odin can offer you great wisdom, though always with the expectation of work and sacrifice. As Odin gave up his eye and hanged from the World Tree

47. Crossley-Holland, xxv–xxvi.

48. Crossley-Holland, xxv–xxvi; Gylfaginning 9, Byock translation.

for wisdom, his example is one that expects you to endure challenge and hardship to achieve your goals. Odin's endless journeys for knowledge mean he offers great insights for anyone whose work involves digging up information, understanding difficult theories, and finding secrets. He offers inspiration of the sort that challenges your core assumptions, ideas, and beliefs. He provides guidance for resolving challenges, trials, and struggles through seeking out unconventional or unexpected solutions. If you seek Odin's wisdom, always remember nothing of the Many-Named God is ever what it seems to be.

Frigga: the Key-Holder

Frigga, Odin's spouse and partner, is as potent as the Old Man. Many assume, due to her ties to hearth and home, that she is simply a mother goddess figure defined by domesticity. Such assumptions ignore far greater depths. Frigga is one of the wisest of the Aesir thanks to her associations with hidden knowledge and knowing how to acquire it.[49]

In her role as goddess of the home, Frigga is often underappreciated thanks to how society undervalues domestic labor. Considering how Odin is often absent from Asgard on his journeys and getting into trouble, Frigga is frequently keeping a lot of wheels spinning. This type of patient work is essential for keeping a community functioning and is often the most critical. After all, there is little point in fighting for a place, seeking out wisdom, or creating great works if there is no community served by any of those deeds. Someone must keep the lights on, and Frigga excels at this.

Hearth and home only scratch the surface of Frigga. Equally critical to Frigga is her well-proven wisdom, as shown in the sagas. Frigga is the only one of the Aesir who knows all fates, yet says nothing, possessing even greater knowledge of events and their causes than Odin. Frigga does not passively seek knowledge for its own sake—Frigga has used information to change Fates, bring favor to any she believes are worthy, trick Odin, bring down a tyrant, and attempt to protect her son Baldr from all harm. She has consistently shown masterful skill in the magical arts of seiðr. Frigga is said to dwell in her own

49. Crossley-Holland, xxxi.

hall of Fensalir ("Fen Hall"), which has associations with wetlands and everything found within them.[50]

What best sums up Frigga's complex nature is understanding the meaning of keys in ancient Norse society. As they granted control over access to restricted spaces, keys were an unmatched symbol of a person's—usually a woman's—power. Keys can open more than just homes, as treasure, tools, records and secrets were kept behind strong locks. Frigga, as both the domestic goddess and the keeper of great secrets, holds the ultimate key. Her actions show she is not afraid to use it, releasing critical nuggets of information in the right moment to achieve her ends. If Odin's plans are like those of a scheming high-stakes gambler then Frigga's designs are those of a patient chess player.[51]

Frigga offers her own unique wisdom. Frigga's way is patient observation, steady work, and methodical planning. Frigga's example provides guidance for any engaging in work that requires these qualities, whether it's study and research, keeping a home, or holding a community together. Thanks to her domestic associations, she is also strongly tied to hospitality and provides wisdom in this area of conduct. Her most well-known symbols are a weaver's distaff and a key.

Thor: Defender of Midgard

Thor is the most well-known and popular of the Aesir. The son of Odin and Jötun Jord, the Thunder God, his hammer and great red beard are known all over the world. As shown by the popularity of Thorian place and personal names and the sheer number of Thor's hammers found by archeologists, he was also one of the most popular Aesir in pre-Christian times. Mightiest of the gods, with the strength to topple mountains, his appetites are equally large, as shown in his famous journey into Utgard, when his thirst lowers all the oceans of Midgard.[52]

Yet for all the emphasis on his physical power, Thor is so much more than a musclebound sky god. He is Midgard's defender against dangerous entities.

---

50. Lokasenna 29, Poetic Edda; Davidson, *Gods and Myths of Northern Europe*, 111–112, 114; Gylfaginning 35.

51. Jesch, Judith. "History: Viking Women." BBC. March 29, 2011. http://www.bbc.co.uk/history/ancient/vikings/women_01.shtml.

52. Davidson, *Gods and Myths of Northern Europe*, 84–85; Crossley-Holland, xxvi-xxvii

Lightning strikes and thunder claps when his hammer, Mjolnir (pronounced *MYOL-neer*), falls on a foe. Though often assumed to be dense and thick-witted, there are many times where Thor demonstrates great cunning and patience in pursuit of victory.[53]

Of all the gods, only Thor was known by the kenning "Friend of Man" in ancient times. In the Harbardsljoth, Thor proudly proclaims how he takes common workers into his hall in Asgard, scoffing at the more elite dead. His great hammer echoes the first tool ever made by human hands, as a hammer is a weapon and tool that anyone, rich or poor, could own and use. The Son of Earth is a defender without prejudice, standing for all in danger, no matter who they are or where they hail from.[54]

For the modern Norse Pagan, Thor has many roles and associations. First and foremost is his role as Defender. Thor takes up Mjolnir in defense of others and not to show domination or power, guaranteeing safety and security for all. His associations with workers show his protection is for securing people's needs and not maintaining the status quo for its own sake. Just as lightning strikes with precise, overwhelming force, the Thunderer moves decisively against threats to Midgard and all its people.

Mjolnir, the Hammer of Thor

53. Davidson, *Gods and Myths of Northern Europe*, 73–75.

54. Harbardsljoth 24-25, Poetic Edda.

Along with Mjolnir, Thor has many other symbols and names. He is sometimes called the Red God, a color associated in ancient times with blood, boldness, and fury. He is also associated with goats, thanks to the two goats Tanngrisnir and Tanngnjóstr, who pull his chariot across the sky.

Sif: The Harvester

The goddess of grain and harvest, Sif is Thor's wife. Her most well-known story is where she is the butt of one of Loki's pranks. For reasons unknown (most likely because Loki thought it would be funny), the God of Mischief snuck into Thor and Sif's hall and shaved her head. Thinking quickly, Loki escaped Thor's wrath by convincing dwarves to spin her new hair from gold. The shearing of hair is generally interpreted as a parallel to the act of harvesting grain, tying her very directly to grain and the harvest. Sif is also said to be one of the few of the Aesir who has no quarrels with any of the other gods, as is mentioned in the saga of the Lokasenna.[55]

It's possible to describe her simply as a fertility goddess, but the work of the harvest is much more than having rich soil. Raising and harvesting crops is essential for life as we know it. In the ancient days, when the best tools available were ox- or horse-pulled plows, hand tools, and often rocky soil with a short growing season, it was very difficult work. Harvest in particular was incredibly dangerous labor where injury, maiming, and death were very common. It took strength, determination, and intimate knowledge of the land to bring in a big enough harvest to feed a community of any size. The strength and danger involved in harvesting gives greater meaning to Sif's marriage with Thor. Just as she is closely associated with workers, Sif stands closest to farmers and field workers. Her rains feed the fields made fertile by her labor.

Sif, as the goddess of both crop and its collection, embodies many qualities. Her work and wisdom have great meaning for any form of labor where patient, steady work produces necessary results. Sif's example matters whether you are teaching, an artist, studying, or involved in any other project where long-term dedication and planning is necessary. She stands with all who work the long, hard hours that make life possible. She offers the wisdom of patience, determination, and the knowledge necessary to get the job done. The most

55. Davidson, *Gods and Myths of Northern Europe*, 30, 84.

well-known symbols of Sif are her golden hair and shorn scalp, the grain sheaf, the sickle and the scythe.

Tyr: The One-Handed

Tyr, son of the Jötun Hymir and God of Justice, is harsh yet fair. He is the embodiment of the letter and the spirit of all that law is meant to be. He is renowned for his might, yet sacrificed some of his strength for the sake of all. Many believe this means Tyr stands for strict adherence to the law, but there is much in Tyr's conduct and associations arguing strongly to the contrary. Tyr's example calls for upholding higher principles even when that means making hard choices.[56]

Tyr's most well-known story is when he sacrificed his sword-hand to bind the Great Wolf, Fenrir. Even when Fenrir was a pup, all the other gods feared him. Only Tyr was courageous and sympathetic enough to care for him. As Fenrir grew, his appetite swelled, causing many to fear he would devour everything, so the gods plotted to chain the Wolf. To ensure their success, Tyr swore an oath to Fenrir, his de facto foster son, that if the gods successfully bound the wolf, he could take Tyr's sword hand. When the ribbon Gleipnir succeeded where all other bonds failed, Tyr upheld his end of the bargain, letting Fenrir take his hand in a single bite, making him the one-handed god. Despite the personal loss, his sacrifice staved off a potential threat in more ways than one.[57]

The tale of Tyr and Fenrir is only the beginning of Tyr's complex relationship with justice. In ancient times, Tyr was associated with the democratic popular assemblies known as Things (pronounced *tings*), the bedrock of ancient Norse societies. These assemblies set laws, resolved disputes, empowered and deposed leaders. In the Things all free people could speak, propose legislation, and demand justice. These spaces were presided over by Lawspeakers, community members who held office based on their knowledge of the customs, beliefs, and norms of their communities. In his role as protector of Things, Tyr is not just an enforcer of law—he also upholds the means for creating truly equitable justice.

---

56. Davidson, *Gods and Myths of Northern Europe,* 57–60; Hymiskvida 5, Poetic Edda.

57. Gylfaginning 34, Byock translation.

In the present, Tyr offers powerful lessons. His associations show the importance of consent and dialog in creating equitable social relations. He shows the letter of what is set down must reflect higher principles and how sometimes you must make great sacrifices to uphold them. Tyr is also known as the Leavings of the Wolf and Oathkeeper. His most common symbol is an open hand, representing what he lost to Fenrir's jaws, and the rune Tiwaz.

Tiwaz, the Rune of Tyr

Loki: The Maker of Change

Loki is, without question, the most notorious of all the Norse gods. Often maligned as an untrustworthy bringer of chaos, some even consider this god to be more of a devil figure. When digging further, however, you find they are a far more complex deity than being just some discount Viking Satan. Loki is originally of the Jötnar, yet they are Odin's sworn blood-brother and are accepted as one of the Aesir. Loki is a critical figure in bringing about many necessary changes, creating valuable artifacts, and toppling old structures. Loki's role as a transformer is shown in their malleable form and their actions.[58]

Loki's role as a bringer of change is consistent in all their stories. Such tales all tend to follow a consistent pattern. Loki does something, sometimes for their own amusement or to fulfill an immediate need, which causes a problem. They fix the problems caused by their actions by also winning, creating, or taking something that makes the Aesir stronger and wiser. There are exceptions, however. One good example is when Loki ensured a new defensive wall for Asgard would be completed by turning into a horse, seducing a giant's stallion, getting impregnated, and, as a bonus to go with the wall's completion, gave birth to Odin's mount Sleipnir. Two of Loki's most consistent attributes are their skills as a shapeshifter and their ambiguous gender. Loki has taken on masculine and feminine shapes, along with many other forms at will, and doesn't seem terribly attached to any gender, making them a very genderfluid deity.

58. Davidson, *Gods and Myths of Northern Europe*, 176-182.

Two of Loki's more infamous moments show why some view them as a Norse Satan. The first is in the saga of the Lokasenna where Loki enters a feast and calls out all the gods for their shortcomings. The gods responded by slaughtering their children, tying them up with the entrails of Loki's offspring, and imprisoning them in a cave until Ragnarok. When Ragnarok comes, Loki will lead an army of the dead into battle while their other children, Fenrir and Jormungandr, wreak havoc. You could assume these actions make them a clear enemy of the gods, yet both show the same consistent theme as Loki's beneficial deeds. In each case, Loki is challenging longstanding problems and upsetting stagnant systems to clear the way for necessary change. This is especially true of Ragnarok, an event that is inevitable and unavoidable. You don't have to like Loki or their methods to agree that their actions are nearly always necessary.

The Urnes Snakes

Loki offers a compelling example in the present day. Their malleable form shows people can change many things about themselves, even what may appear to be fixed or unalterable. They urge you to challenge everything in your life and test what is before you to see if it has the strength to stand on its own merits. Loki's wisdom lies in never resting on past successes, accepting something simply for the sake of comfort or convention, and to always question authority. They cause change in the world, inspire new developments, and prevent stagnation. One symbol commonly associated with Loki is the interlocked serpents known as the Urnes Snakes. Anything representing change or transformation is also fitting for Loki.[59]

The Vanir: The Gods of Nature

If the Aesir are the gods of society, then the Vanir could be considered as the gods of nature, but would be better to say the Vanir are closely associated with how humanity works with nature. The Vanir exist on both sides of the boundaries between the human experience and the world beyond. Their associations with mystical practices and the outsider status of seiðr practitioners in ancient society reinforces their ties to boundaries and transcending them. Even though the Vanir are famous for their magical prowess and the Aesir get all the press when it comes to strife, the gods of nature as just as ferocious as the wilds they hold dear.[60]

Though only three of the Vanir—Freyr, Freya, and Njord—are discussed in this book, there are probably many more, including some mentioned in Snorri Sturluson's Prose Edda. The Vanir covered here are the most well-known and commonly honored by Norse Pagans today. As gods associated with the space between society and the natural world, it is not surprising that some of the Vanir passed out of written record, compared to the well-documented Aesir.

As gods of liminal space, human interactions with the natural world, and the more mystical side of things, the Vanir offer a very different perspective from the Aesir. They urge you to consider the deeper connections between you and your environment. Where the Aesir challenge you to consider society, the Vanir push you to examine the broader ecosystems that shape you.

Freyr: The Bringer of Plenty

Freyr (pronounced *FREY-er*) is a god of fertility, understanding the land and natural cycles. In ancient and modern practice Freyr is associated with masculine fertility, desirability and potency. This is shown in the many statues from ancient times depicting him with a large erect penis. He is Freyja's twin

---

59. Lokeanwelcomingcommittee. "30 Days of Deity Devotion: Loki Day Three." Lokean Welcoming Committee. June 27, 2015. Accessed August 28, 2018. http://lokeanwelcomingcommittee.tumblr.com/post/122544282338/30-days-of-deity-devotion-loki-day-three.

60. Davidson, *Gods and Myths of Northern Europe*, 92-93; Ross 204–211.

brother, the son of Njord and one of the Vanir who was sent to the Aesir as a hostage following the end of the war between the two tribes. He is also the King of the Alfar, a group of spirits closely tied to the natural world, in and is hailed as Bringer of Peace.[61] In many ways, Freyr represents a more nurturing and empathetic form of masculinity.

Two of the most widely known stories of Freyr are the courtship of his wife, the Jötun Gerd, and his last stand at Ragnarok. As written in the saga of the Skirnismol, Freyr sought out Gerd's hand in marriage after he saw her while sitting in Odin's magic seat in Hlidskjalf, leaving him totally smitten and determined to win her love. As part of the arrangements to win her over Freyr gave up his magic sword, a blade that could fight on its own with no need for a hand to guide it or arm to swing it. Freyr willingly sacrificed an item of great power in pursuit of something he saw as greater than any magic sword even though this decision may have sealed his doom at Ragnarok.[62]

In the final battle, Freyr, along with many of the other gods, will ride out first into the fray. On the Idavoll plain he will face the mighty Surtr in a ferocious duel. The two will clash, but Freyr, facing a living inferno only armed only with an antler spear, will fall. Even in defeat, what Freyr represents does not die with him. A new green world springs up from the ashes of Surtr's blaze just as new life follows ferocious wildfires. You could say the fertility Freyr embodies is served through this sacrifice.[63]

Freyr is associated with peace and abundance. His wisdom is useful when starting a new project, working with plants and animals, or cultivating new possibilities. Freyr is also very strongly tied to masculine energy, male fertility, and masculine-identified people. That said, one should be very clear about their desires when working with this aspect of Freyr. Freyr is often honored in seasonal rites, particularly at the time of the Spring and Fall Equinoxes. Some of his other names are the Bringer of Plenty and Peace, the Peace-Giver, and his name means Lord. Freyr's most common symbols are antlers, boars (thanks to his golden boar, Gullinbursti), and the plant life of spring and autumn.

61. Gylfaginning 24, Byock translation

62. Gylfaginning 37, Byock translation

63. Voluspo 52-53, Poetic Edda; Gylfaginning 37, Byock translation

Freyja: The Free Heart

Freyja (pronounced *FREY-yah*), Freyr's twin sister, is one of the most famous of the Norse gods. Usually cast as a Scandinavian Aphrodite due to being described as the most beautiful of all deities, Freyja is far more than that. Fiercely independent, with ties to war and sorcery, Freyja embodies all passions. She is the embodiment of feminine power, understands her own desires, and always stands up for her autonomy. One of the many symbols of her power is her chariot, which is drawn by a team of cats that work together and obey her commands.[64]

As a goddess of all passions, Freyja is as much this as the embodiment of the independent woman. In fact, her name is the word for "lady." Freyja is said to have had many lovers, all of her own choosing, yet she lives alone on her own terms. Her famous Brisingamen necklace was said to have been made for her by dwarven lovers and is one of her most well-known possessions. Amber is also associated with her, as it is believed to come from her tears falling to Midgard, making it a popular gift between lovers. Even though she is known for love, beauty, and sensuality, Freyja is also closely tied to warfare. As the Queen of the Valkyries, a group of spirits who stalk every battlefield, Freyja gets the first choice of any of the slain brought before the gods by these fierce battle spirits. Odin then takes the rest for Valhalla. Freyja is a powerful force in war or when using her formidable command of the mystic arts.[65]

One of the most important aspects of Freyja is her mastery of the arts of seiðr, a form of Norse magic. She first taught Odin these arts, and there are many instances of her skills surpassing his, such as one case where she punished him for stealing the Brisingamen by trapping two armies he wanted for Valhalla with her magic in an endless battle. This display of power was so awe-inspiring that Odin has never attempted such a stunt since. In the lore, the Vanir's mystical might was potent enough to evenly match the more martial Aesir's power. Freyja also wears a feathered cloak that she uses to shapeshift into the form of hawks and falcons.[66]

---

64. Gylfaginning 24, Byock translation

65. Gylfaginning 24, 36, Byock translation

66. Ross, 206.

Freyja's wisdom lies in the power you hold by standing strong on your own terms. Her conduct gives stellar examples of personal autonomy and consent. She offers guidance in these matters, especially for women and feminine-identified people. Her close ties to mystical practice also mean she is often invoked for such work and can help you understand the secrets of these mystic arts. Her most common names are the Lady of the Slain, the Giver, and Sea Brightener. Her most common symbols are cats, birds of prey, the seiðworker's staff, amber, and gold.

Njord: The Wave-Rider

Njord (pronounced *NYORD*) was one of the Vanir who was traded as a hostage with the Aesir to end their war with the Vanir. He has lived with the Aesir ever since. He is associated with the sea, ocean waves, and sailing. He lives in his hall of Noatun, by the water. Even with these strong maritime ties, Njord is not associated directly with the oceans themselves. This makes Njord is a perfect example of how the Vanir embody human interactions with nature in contrast to the Jötnar's direct embodiment of nature itself.[67]

What is critical for understanding Njord is knowing the importance of sea travel in ancient Scandinavia. For the Norse, the fastest and most reliable way to travel was by ship. Mariners also brought in food from the sea through fishing, whaling, and seal hunting. Sailors navigated using tools like sunstones, astronomy, and the art of dead reckoning, a form of navigation that depended on a sailor's intimate knowledge of local currents, tides and even the taste of different bodies of water. Every voyage was a risk with no guarantee of survival. This dangerous trade was a matter of survival for whole communities.[68]

Along with his associations with sailing and sea travel is his most well-known story. When the Jötun Skadi came to Asgard demanding justice for the Aesir's role in killing her father Thiazi, Njord was one of the many offered as a possible husband as compensation. He was picked in a blind contest where the only feature Skadi could see was the candidates' feet—and thanks to his living

67. Gylfaginning 23, Byock translation

68. Konung Skuggsja 5, translated by Laurence M. Larson; "Wayfinders: Wayfinding." PBS. Accessed November 13, 2017. http://www.pbs.org/wayfinders/wayfinding2.html

by the water, Njord's were the cleanest. Sadly, Njord and Skadi's relationship was not a harmonious one. Njord was kept awake at night in Skadi's hall by the howling of wolves and the wind in the trees and missed the sounds of the sea. Due to these problems and other irreconcilable differences, they amicably separated, yet there is no hint of ill will between them.[69]

For modern Norse Pagans, Njord offers especially keen guidance for any who live on or by water, work in maritime trades, or whose lives depend on their ship coming in. He offers the wisdom of charting a course through difficult conditions, pressing on in the face of great uncertainty and finding ways to bring in critical wealth for those in need of it. Njord is sometimes also called the Giver and is associated with navigational and maritime tools, fish hooks, items used in sailing, and seashells.

The Jötnar: The Gods of the Wilderness

If the Vanir are the gods of humanity's interactions with nature, the Jötnar are nature itself in all its unbridled fury and mystery. Closely tied with elemental forces like the ocean depths, the Earth itself, and the fury of flame, the Jötnar are all that lies beyond humanity in every sense of the word. Even in the modern world, with all the discoveries made by science and society, there are mysteries and aspects of the natural world that lie well beyond human control or understanding.[70]

The interactions between the Aesir and Jötnar mirror humanity's relationship with nature. Though humanity as a species is often in conflict with nature, humans have found ways to work with the many ecosystems of the world. Even where modern technology gives a sense of power and dominance, it is still stumbling as a result of the many unanticipated consequences of pressing against nature's power. As Powers who dwell in the unknown, the Jötnar are gods of the deeper wisdom that lies beyond the limits of knowledge and comfort.

There are many writings on the Jötnar; surviving texts and folklore often speak of many tribes of hill Jötnar, ice Jötnar, fire Jötnar, and countless others. The Jötnar discussed here are the most well-known and documented in the sa-

69. Gylfaginning 23, Byock translation

70. Crossley-Holland xxxi-xxxii

gas. There are likely many more Jötnar who are unknown, unnamed, or have yet to be met or worked with.

Ymir: The Progenitor

Ymir is one of the most important gods in Norse Paganism. As one of the first beings that emerged following the collision of fire and ice, Ymir was there at the beginning of all things. All around was a vast, frosty tundra where nothing else existed. Ymir lived off the meat and milk of Audumla, while the cow lived by licking moss and lichen off the ice and rocks. It was from Ymir that the first of the frost giants came into existence, spawning from the primordial giant's arms, legs, and torso.[71]

One day, as Audumla was foraging for lichen, the great cow came upon a bright being trapped in the ice named Buri. Its licking freed this being of light, setting in motion the greatest change since fire and ice collided. Buri wed an unknown frost giant, and they had a son named Bor. Bor, in turn, married the giant Bestla and they begat three sons named Odin, Vili, and Ve. Even in these days when the world was inhabited by many frost giants and the children of Buri, only Ymir could partake of Audumla's milk and meat.[72]

There was no question this order was one that mostly benefited Ymir at the expense of all others. Under these conditions and after living for three generations of unknown length under Ymir's domination, the three brothers would upend everything. After seeing all of what was around them and how reality operated, Odin, Vili, and Ve rose up against Ymir. They slew the great giant, unleashing a torrent of its blood to wash over existence. As the flood subsided, the brothers, along with many other gods, came together to forge a new reality. They used Ymir's bones, flesh, and organs to build Midgard and all of physical reality as we know it.[73]

The story of Ymir's downfall is critical for two reasons. The first is everything comes from something else; nothing comes from nothing. All things are made from the materials, ideas, and influences of something else. Things can

---

71. Gylfaginning 6, Byock translation
72. Ibid
73. Gylfaginning 7-8, Byock translation; Voluspo 3-4, Poetic Edda; Vafthruthnismol 20-21, Poetic Edda

be taken and reshaped into new, more beneficial forms for the present and future. The second is that Ymir, as is shown in many other sagas, is a clear example of the evils of greed, hoarding, and dominating others. Many other hostile figures, like the dragon Fafnir, were in the wrong because they hoarded of wealth for themselves instead of sharing their bounty freely.[74]

Ymir's story shows presently existing conditions can be adapted into new forms and people do not have to accept what is if the current order is harmful for them. Reality is not a fixed, unalterable creation. It can be changed, refashioned, and rebuilt into new forms by deliberate, decisive action. For those who meditate on the vast primordial being, Ymir itself carries the mystery of the primordial times before Midgard. As the first being to come from fire and ice, its wisdom is unique and potent for those who would seek it. Be wary for if you would plumb the depths of reality to commune with a dead giant. You may find answers you did not expect or were prepared for.

Surtr: The Walking Inferno

Surtr dwells in Muspelheim, the land of eternal fire and heat, and rules over the fire giants living there. He is a massive, furious entity of great power embodying raging flame. Surtr carries a flaming sword that will ignite the World Tree at the climax of Ragnarok, burning all the Nine Worlds.[75] In the lore, Surtr is a bringer of great destruction, catastrophe, and crisis.

It is easy to see Surtr as the ultimate enemy and opponent of the gods. There is some truth to this—however, Surtr's role is much more complex than being a simple adversary. Surtr is as much an agent of destruction as Odin and his brothers were when they slew Ymir, yet their rising paved the way for Midgard as we know it. Even though Surtr will not rule over the realm created by his acts of destruction, he is as much an agent of change as Odin, Vili, and Ve.

Surtr's fire has many parallels in the natural world. The great pine forests of Scandinavia are dependent on flame to bring new life, just as the World Tree is to bring forth new realities. Their seed-bearing cones drop regularly throughout the seasons, but this alone is insufficient to make new pine trees. It takes a wildfire, whether caused by natural or human sources, to make this possible. During

74. Gripisspo 11-13, Poetic Edda

75. Gylfaginning 51, Byock translation; Voluspo 52, 57, Poetic Edda

the blaze the sticky, combustible sap holding the pine cones together heats up and explodes, flinging the seeds in every direction. The ash from the blazes fertilizes the ground and clears the way for new life to grow and flourish.[76]

Even though Surtr fulfills this broader cosmic role, it doesn't make him harmless or lacking in agency. His war against the Aesir at Ragnarok, as is shown in the lore, has its roots in deeper feuds between these clans. Many actions, such as Ymir's death and the deception in the building of Asgard's wall, motivate Surtr and his followers to move against the Aesir and their allies. The role of Surtr is both cosmically necessary and driven by his own desires in response to the actions of other Powers on the World Tree.

Jord: The Living Earth

Jord is the Earth itself. She is the ground beneath our feet and everything it sustains. Jord is the closest there is in Norse Paganism to an Earth goddess figure. Also known as Fjorgyn, Jord is best known as Thor's mother, making the thunder god half Jötnar. This also shows any claim of constant, unceasing hostility between Jötnar and Aesir has no basis in the lore. If this were the case, then Thor would never have come into existence in the first place.[77]

Jord is a goddess to be reckoned with—she is everything that makes up the air we breathe, the soil that grows our food, the waters that sustain us, and all else that makes life possible. She is the rage of volcanos, the tremble of the rumbling earth, and ferocious landslides. Where other deities like Freyr are associated with the ways humanity interacts with nature, Jord is the cradle, home, and support needed for nature to be possible.

In modern practice, Jord's potency, breadth, and depth reflect nature's diversity, majesty, and fury. She invites contemplating the great paradoxes of life, both its nurturing and destructive sides. She is the beauty and danger of all the things that lie beyond human control. Jord's wisdom shows how to confront these limitations, humanity's place in the natural world, and how utterly dependent humans are on forces that are, at best, indifferent to human needs.

---

76. "Gymnosperma (Pine)." Afzender. Accessed November 13, 2017. http://www.vcbio.science.ru.nl/en/virtuallessons/gymnosperma/.

77. Ross 54-56; Voluspo 56, Poetic Edda

Jord calls for respect and humility before nature's might. Anything representing Earth and the natural world are her symbols, showing her diversity and power.

Aegir and Ran: The Ocean Depths

Aegir and Ran are directly associated with the ocean in a more direct way than Njord. They live in a hall deep beneath the ocean depths that is also home to all who die at sea. Even with this fearsome reputation, Aegir and Ran are not simply cold, ferocious gods ruling what lies beneath the waves. They have hosted the Aesir and Vanir at feasts in their great hall. Aegir himself, who is also called the Brewer, possesses the only kettle large enough to make enough ale for all the gods. Like the great oceans of the world, Aegir and Ran can be cruel or kind, giving and taking as they will.[78]

Aegir and Ran offer many things. They show how hospitality is widely honored across the Nine Worlds by hosting the Aesir and Vanir in their hall. This relationship shows the dynamic between Aesir, Vanir, and Jötnar is not a clear-cut order-versus-chaos dichotomy, but is far more complex. The cooperation between the Aesir, Vanir, and these two gods shows the necessity of working with great forces of the wilds. The best symbols for them are creatures of the deep like sharks, whales and octopi, ocean waves, and other representations of the sea. Another common symbol for Aegir and Ran is a fishing net, as it was said in the ancient days anyone who died of drowning had been caught in Ran's net.

Skadi: The Frosty Mountains

Skadi is one of the most well-known of the Jötnar, in part due to the amount of information about her that survives to the modern day, as well as her close ties to the Aesir. Skadi first comes into the lore following the death of her father, Thiazi. After his demise at the hands of the Aesir, Skadi took up her weapons and armor, setting out for Asgard to demand the Aesir give her justice for his death. Due to the nature of her request and her clear display of martial prowess, the gods agreed.[79]

---

78. Davidson, *Gods and Myths of Northern Europe*, 128-129; Hymistvithka 1, Poetic Edda.

79. Gylfaginning 23, Byock translation; Davidson, *Gods and Myths of Northern Europe*, 106–107.

They offered her a husband as compensation and to make her laugh. They further said Skadi had to choose her husband by only looking at the feet of her potential betrothed. All the eligible bachelors were lined up behind a screen and she picked the cleanest feet she saw, which belonged to Njord. Unfortunately this marriage was an unhappy one. Skadi loved woods and snow of her mountains and Njord loved the sea. Skadi was no more comfortable at his hall of Noatun, where the cry of seagulls and crash of the waves disturbed her slumber. The two felt their differences were irreconcilable and so they agreed to part ways, amicably divorcing. Even so, Skadi regularly associated with the Aesir afterward.[80]

Skadi is tied to skis, snowshoes, hunting, mountains, wolves, and winter. In modern practice she is also associated with sports, the great outdoors and the cold. Her role as one of the punishers of Loki for their perceived breaches of hospitality during the Lokasenna also sees her invoked as a goddess of Vengeance. Her great wisdom is in the example of her strong, independent personality and willingness to take direct action to achieve justice. If you seek Skadi's guidance, she will urge you to act while helping you find the strength and best way to achieve justice. Her separation from Njord is regularly cited as an example of how people in romantic relationships can amicably resolve great differences and part ways while remaining friendly. Snowflakes, icicles, mountains, skis, snowshoes, and wolves are her most common symbols, as are implements of the hunt such as knives, spears, and bows.

The Others: Gods of the Primal

Outside of the three tribes are other entities who live in the Nine Worlds. They don't belong to any tribe of their own. Each is a unique entity with its own history, personality, traits, and role to play. They embody primordial forces even more potent, unknown, and vast than the three tribes. They offer their own wisdom, though it is often more terrible than any other's. Three of these beings are children of Loki and the troll Angrboda; the others are potent entities whose origins are a mystery. To study these beings is to explore some of the deepest and most terrifying yet enlightening mysteries in existence.

80. Gylfaginning 23, Byock translation; Davidson, *Gods and Myths of Northern Europe*, 106–107; Lokasenna 49-51, Poetic Edda.

The Norns: Fate-Shapers

The Norns are three goddesses who live at the base of the World Tree. Their names are Urd, meaning what is, Verdandi, meaning what is becoming, and Skuld, meaning what shall be. The roots of their names are a reflection of the Norse understanding of time where the past determined what currently is, the present as the here and now that is constantly in a state of becoming, and the future as what shall be as a direct consequence of past events and present developments. They are the shapers of Ørlog and the tenders of the World Tree. Over the course of countless ages, they sat at the base of the Tree, drawing water from the Well of Urdr to nourish the Yggdrasil with pure possibility. They set the Ørlog of the living into the World Tree, which then moves with Yggdrasil as it grows, changing with time.[81]

Some compare them to the Moirai of Greek mythology, the three spinners who dictate the lives of all. There is some superficial truth to this comparison; after all, they dictate the lengths of the lives of all beings and how much time is allotted to them. A key difference is how much power they hold over the time between. Though they set the lengths of lives and their Ørlog, they hold no sway over what happens during that time. As the drawers of the Well of Urdr's water, they interact with possibility like everything else, using it as best they can.[82]

None are sure when the Norns first came to be. Their first known appearance in the lore is shortly after Ymir's demise and the shaping of Midgard. They are not mentioned often, and the rest of the gods seem to give them a wide berth, never interfering in their timeless task. Even Odin and Loki, two deities known for showing little regard for boundaries when it suits them, are never known to have sought out the three. It is possible they even have influence over the fates of gods.

The Norns represent the primordial power of time. They are its inevitability and inescapable nature. They also show all are shaped by life's circumstances and how those can change. Their endless work to feed the World Tree shows a steady, patient dedication for keeping reality intact and dynamic. The wisdom they offer is accepting the inevitability of time's march and how to

81. Gylfaginning 15-16

82. Voluspo 20, Poetic Edda; Ross 202-203

cope with it. By keeping everything moving, growing, and changing, the Norns keep possibility flowing instead of freezing all in place.

Fenrir: The Great Wolf

Fenrir is the wolf child of Loki and Angrboda, queen of the trolls. He was born and raised in Asgard by the gods. Due to his fearsome appearance, Tyr was the only god brave enough to care for the pup. As he grew, his cravings kept up with his size, and he needed more and more to be satisfied. This swelling appetite alarmed the gods who feared the Wolf, whose growth showed no signs of slowing down or stopping, would eventually swallow up everything in existence. He became so vast that when he opened his jaws they stretched from the ground to the furthest reaches of the sky.[83]

Driven by fear, the gods plotted to bind the wolf and spare reality from his vast hunger. The dwarves made three great chains, one after the other, to hold Fenrir and the gods presented them to Fenrir as a test of his might. Fenrir, however, was suspicious of their intentions and demanded a guarantee for his safety. Tyr, in exchange, placed his sword-hand in Fenrir's maw, swearing an oath that if anything happened to impede Fenrir's freedom, the Wolf could take Tyr's hand. The first two chains, one forged from heavy iron and the other made of stone, were easily broken. The third, the ribbon Gleipnir, was forged from seven things that were removed from reality the moment the dwarves took them for Gleipnir. This bond held fast, keeping Fenrir locked in place. In a rage, Fenrir tore off Tyr's hand, swearing revenge on the gods and declaring he would devour Odin at Ragnarok.[84]

Like so many other examples of dangerous forces in the lore, like the dragon Fafnir of the Volsungsaga and Grendel of Beowulf, greed is the driving force that makes Fenrir so threatening. Fenrir's all-consuming greed convinced the gods to bind him at the depths of the World Tree. Yet Fenrir is not simply a villain. His rage and vengeance exist because of betrayal by the gods, guaranteeing he will be an agent of destruction at Ragnarok. Fear was just as critical as hunger in shaping the Wolf. Fenrir's imprisonment shows the dangers of letting

---

83. Gylfaginning 34, Byock translation

84. Ibid

fear overpower your better judgment, urging you to always question the roots of your distress and ask if what you feel is justified.

Jormungandr: The Migdard Serpent

Jormungandr is the great serpent child of Loki and Angrboda, so long that it circles all of Midgard and holds its own tail in its mouth. When Jormungandr was born, Odin hurled it into the seas surrounding Midgard, where it sank, wrapping around the borders of the physical realm. There it dwells, hidden and undisturbed.[85]

It comes back into the lore when Thor, Tyr, and the giant Hymir go on a fishing trip. In an attempt to catch the largest fish imaginable, Thor uses the head off Hymir's ox for bait. Before long, Jormungandr bites down on the hook. Thor holds on, attempting to reel in his massive catch only to see the enormous serpent surge from beneath the waves. The two grapple back and forth before Hymir, in a panic, cuts the line to stop Thor and the Midgard Serpent from tearing the boat in two.[86]

The serpent will emerge again at Ragnarok. Its rising from beneath will unleash waves that drown Midgard. It will surge forward with the other enemies of the gods to settle its long-standing score with Thor. The two will wrestle in a match that shakes the world before Thor finally triumphs over the great serpent. In spite of this great victory, Midgard's champion will only take nine steps before Jormungandr's venom overpowers him, laying Thor low.[87]

Jormungandr is the edge of known reality. It represents the limits of existence. When it turns against the reality it once defined, everything we know will come crashing down, unleashing untold havoc. Some fans of pulp horror literature may note there is some similarity between Jormungandr's resurgence at Ragnarok and the fictional deity Cthulhu, another indescribable being said to slumber beneath the ocean, whose awakening will usher in the end of civilization. That said, any resemblance between the two is probably a total coincidence.

---

85. Ibid

86. Hymisvithka, 23–25.

87. Voluspo 55–56, Poetic Edda.

Hel: Guardian of the Dead

Hel is the daughter of Loki by Angrboda. Born half-living and half-corpse, Odin hurled this crossroads Goddess as far from Asgard as he could, launching her into the depths of what became Helheim. Since that moment, no other god or goddess is as closely associated with Helheim and the dead as Hel. In this place of rest, she keeps watch over the deceased as they retire from the toil of their living days.[88]

As keeper of the dead, Hel is connected to the spirits of the departed, the grave, and decay. She is the certainty of death and the memories that remain in spite of it. If you work closely with the dead, you may find her to be a key guide for understanding the deceased. She also provides a way of grappling with the inevitability of mortality, offering some degree of comfort that some part of you will endure long after your passing.

Nidhoggr: The Devourer

At the base of the World Tree, by the shores of a lake called Nastrond, is the great dragon Nidhoggr. It dwells there forever feasting on the dishonored dead who committed deeds too horrible to enter Helheim, like murdering the defenseless and kinslaying. When the Corpse-Gnawer is not consuming the few who fall into its maw, it chews endlessly on the roots and trunk of the World Tree. The dragon will never stop eating, gaining no final success in devouring its greatest target, and it is one of the few that will survive Ragnarok. None know when it first came into existence.[89]

Nidhoggr is the embodiment of entropy and decay. It is ceaseless in its labor, as eternal as the tree it devours. Just as Nidhoggr's hunger will never be satisfied, entropy will never cease. Yet in spite of the serpent's determination, Yggdrasil endures thanks to the care of those who maintain it. Nidhoggr's unceasing dedication to this task, along with the endless efforts to keep its harm at bay, neatly summarize the challenge presented by the inevitable march of time. Nowhere is there any consideration of surrender to the dragon. Even the fate said to await the worst of the living in Nidhoggr's belly links back to

---

88. Gylfaginning 34, Byock translation; Davidson, *Gods and Myths of Northern Europe*, 29–32.

89. Voluspo 39, 66, Poetic Edda.

its embodiment of decay. Those who commit terrible deeds in life have all save the most terrible actions worn away by time until the only things remaining of them are their most shameful actions.

The Nameless Seeress: The Terrible Truth

The Nameless Seeress is an obscure figure who often escapes notice in modern practice. In Radical Norse Paganism, however, she is far more important. She is different from all the others in this chapter because in both of her appearances she is clearly dead, raised up from under a mound. Both times she appears in the lore she plays a highly critical role, revealing visions of Ragnarok and Baldr's death to Odin. She gives access to some of the greatest secrets in the lore and what she reveals is truly awful to behold.[90]

Beyond these two specific moments there is little known about the Nameless Seeress. Even her name or any titles she holds are a mystery. Even so, these episodes provide considerable insight into her nature. In each case, Odin actively seeks her out for information, claiming she has answers he cannot get anywhere else. She only divulges this information after being pulled from her mound unwillingly by Odin's magic. Though this could imply Odin has control over each encounter, he is powerless to silence her once she begins reciting these dire prophecies. That Odin seeks the Seeress suggests she possessed great oracular skills in life and death gives her special insights into Fate's design beyond all other the other Powers.

For modern practitioners, the Nameless Seeress represents the most terrible of all knowledge. What she offers is true and inescapable. Her status as dead, yet active and insightful, further suggests this wisdom comes from a permanent, irreversible change. The Seeress' wisdom is of confronting the most primordial truths, greatest fears, and the biggest assumptions of life in search of deeper knowledge. This comes with the warning that her answers may not be ones you want to hear.

Many Gods, No Masters

The gods of Norse Paganism offer many pathways to wisdom, understanding, and answers. Though this tradition honors all gods, regardless of clan, you may

90. Voluspo 1, 66, Poetic Edda; Baldrs Draumar 4-5, Poetic Edda 1.

only end up regularly working with one or a few. Which gods you work with may also change over time as your life changes, you face new challenges, and seek different solutions to the problems ahead. What matters is always seeking out the best way for you and trying out different perspectives. Working with the gods won't always be easy or simple but the ways they push you will ultimately make you stronger.

The next exercise will help you work with the gods by learning how to reach out to them. Do not be discouraged if nothing dramatic seems to happen the first few times you try this exercise. The gods work in many different ways and interact with lived existence in means beyond human comprehension. What you learn during this exercise may manifest itself in many different ways, ranging from flashes of insight to intense visions and visitations.

exercise
REACHING THE DIVINE

Before you start this exercise, skim through chapter three until you find a deity that calls to you. The best ones for your first attempt are the Aesir or Vanir, as they are the most human in their associations, activities, and desires. As you get comfortable with some of these deities, you can then try working with some of the Jötnar.

Begin with the breath exercise at the end of chapter one. Continue until you have reached a state of relaxed calm with steady heartbeat and breathing.

Start whispering the names and titles of the deity you are working with. Start with their name before continuing with their other titles. Once you have gotten through all the ones included, go back to their name and repeat them all again. Go through this process at least three times.

As you whisper the names of the specific deity, visualize their symbols in your mind. Start with the first that comes most easily, and as you whisper more names, visualize additional symbols.

As the symbols become clearer, begin thinking about what that deity is associated with. Focus on what that means for you, how those associations make you feel, and what ideas or images come to the surface as you do.

Let your mind drift. Sit in this unfocused space silently for as long as you feel comfortable doing so. When you feel the time is right, open your eyes.

Write down everything you felt during this meditation. Pay particular attention to anything you didn't expect or can't easily explain. These moments of insight are the beginnings of when the gods came directly to you.

As you practice this exercise more with the same deity, your impressions and experiences will become clearer. This will make it more possible for you to build a reciprocal relationship with the Norse gods.

chapter four

DEVELOPING SPIRITUAL PRACTICE

Hail to the Aesir! Hail to the Asynjur!
Hail to the bounteous Earth!
Words and wisdom, gives to us noble twain
And healing hands while we live.
SIGRDRIFUMAL 4

Knowing the lore is just the beginning. In the Way of Fire and Ice, this information is a starting point for building your life. The next step, then, is realizing ideas in the lore through your actions and experiences. You can do this through learning how to open yourself up to greater wisdom, push beyond what you have accepted as normal or ordinary, and challenge what is to reach for something even better.

The tools for doing this are very simple, yet profound. Becoming a spiritually active person is not restricted to a few select mystics, gurus, or devoted handful who must wall themselves off from the mundane. In Radical Norse Paganism, developing an engaging, personal, and meaningful spiritual practice is open to everyone. By building your skills, refining your understanding of the tools presented in this chapter, and continued practice, you can cultivate your spirituality into something you feel in every waking moment. In this tradition, the wisdom of the Powers strengthens every moment of your life.

Building Your Spirituality

The foundation of all practice is your personal spirituality. Whether you are practicing as a solitary individual, working with a local group, or are part of an active fellowship or a larger organization, much of your day-to-day work, practice, and development is primarily personal. Developing your personal practice will lead you to deeper insights, self-awareness, and understanding, and it will help build your confidence for working with other Pagans.

Your personal development will be shaped by your needs, life experiences, and what works best for you. Just as every person is a unique individual, the same is true of personal practices. Even so, there are common themes, methods, and techniques that are effective starting points for building your skills and inspiring further growth. These jumping-off points for your journey will help you find your way forward.

The Ecstatic State

The ecstatic state is the foundation of all spiritual work in Radical Norse Paganism. You may have already entered an ecstatic state without even knowing it. Have you ever been completely swept away by music or been out for a night of dancing that took you out of your body? Have you ever been in the thrum of a mosh pit, feeling the press of the crowd like an extension of yourself? Have you ever sat in quiet thought so deep you got lost in your own mind? Have you felt total serenity, peace, and calm while carrying out some sort of daily ritual like preparing your morning coffee?

All these experiences are moments when you slipped into an ecstatic state. In this state your consciousness shifts outside of how you usually experience life. During an ecstatic state, your consciousness becomes open to new experiences and insights. There are many methods used for reaching an ecstatic state. They do this by engaging different parts of your brain in unconventional ways while helping the more logical parts of your mind justify them.

There are many examples from the pre-Christian world showing ecstatic states were a part of ancient Norse spiritual practice. There are countless tales of seers, known as vǫlur, delivering messages from beyond in halls and on grave mounds while deep in mystic trances. Skalds sought wisdom found under trees and entranced their communities with mighty spell-songs. The famous berserker and ulfhendar warriors clothed themselves in the hides of bears or wolves, taking on the attributes of their chosen animals before charging into battle in ferocious, ecstatic states.[91]

There is also a growing body of research showing the ecstatic state is a very real, verifiable shift in consciousness. Numerous studies conducted by doctors working in the field of neurotheology, a medical field where scientists study what happens to the brain during spiritual experiences, show this. This research has consistently found people engaging in specific spiritual practices associated with ecstatic state were activating their brains in totally different, unexpected ways.

In one example, test subjects engaging in mantra or prayer-based work saw increased activity in regions of the brain associated with regulating behavior, directing attention, and expression. Participants in other studies on possessory work, psychic mediumship, and speaking in tongues had decreased activity in the regions of the brain governing sensory information, located in the frontal lobes, along with increased activity in the thalamus, the area of the brain responsible for regulating the flow of information to the rest of the brain. Researchers concluded that it was possible that participants were getting information from different sources than what is regulated by the frontal lobes.[92]

When researchers studied Buddhist monks and Catholic nuns, both of whom reported feelings of timelessness and oneness with existence during meditation, brain scans showed decreased activity in the parietal lobes. The parietal lobes govern perceiving objects in three-dimensional space, and the decreased activity closely matched subjects' sense of oneness with the world. Tests also showed the same areas of the brain that light up during sexual arousal are actively engaged when subjects experience feelings of religious ecstasy during rituals and other forms of practice. Even though there is a lot of

---

91. Davidson, *The Road to Hel*, 105–110; Davidson, *Gods and Myths of Northern Europe*, 66–68, 70; Neil Price, *The Viking Way: Religion and War in Late Iron-Age Scandinavia*, Department of Archeology and Ancient History (Uppsala: 2002), 208–210, 366–373.

92. Neurotheology: This Is Your Brain On Religion. NPR. NPR, December 15, 2010. https://www.npr.org/2010/12/15/132078267/neurotheology-where-religion-and-science-collide.

debate about the meaning of these results, there is no doubt something very unique happens in the brain during ecstatic religious states.[93]

Cultivating Ecstatic Practice

There are many techniques you can use to reach an ecstatic state. These include, but are not limited to, meditation, singing, chanting, playing music and dance. What all these methods share is they provide your conscious mind with a specific action to focus on while engaging your body and creative self. This brings on a controlled ecstatic state where you can go beyond the ordinary and touch the extraordinary.

For the new practitioner, meditation is the best tool for consistently reaching an ecstatic state. This is because meditation is ideal for cultivating discipline and focus, builds a foundation for other techniques like chanting, dancing or playing music and, as shown by recent medical studies, has proven mental health benefits like reducing stress. The exercises in this book will help you build your skills in meditation.[94]

The best way to start is finding a comfortable place to sit that is free of distractions and beginning the breathing exercise at the end of chapter one. After reaching a state of physical calm, begin the Sea and Sky exercise from chapter five. This will prepare you for the World Tree Within exercise at the end of this chapter. When you have finished, you can then do the exercises in chapters six and seven, focus on a specific Power, or let your mind wander and see what happens.

The best way to improve your proficiency with meditation is scheduling a regular time to practice in private, ideally once a day. You may find it helpful to set an alarm signaling the end of your session before you begin. This will help you focus on meditation by removing the need for you to keep track of time. As you get more comfortable, stretch out the length of your sessions. If you have started with ten-minute sessions, try lengthening them to fifteen or even

---

93. Ibid

94. Walton, Alice G. "7 Ways Meditation Can Actually Change The Brain." Forbes. January 17, 2018. Accessed May 29, 2018. https://www.forbes.com/sites/alicegwalton/2015/02/09/7-ways-meditation-can-actually-change-the-brain/#4b37c4791465.

twenty minutes. When you're first starting, it does not matter how long you can meditate—as long as you regularly practice, your skills will improve.

One recommendation for starting out from Patricia, an experienced Reclaiming Witch and theater professional, is to use props. Props help train your conscious mind to relax by signaling there is about to be a shift in consciousness. Some commonly used props are incense, candles, recorded music, or covering yourself in a cloak. As she became more comfortable in meditation, Patricia needed her props less, reaching the point where she could perform her daily practice even on a busy, noisy subway.

Once you get comfortable with regular meditation, you can add other techniques like playing an instrument, chanting, singing, or dancing to your practice sessions. Before experimenting with these other techniques, you should study them outside of ecstatic work to help you better understand how to incorporate them. This includes going out dancing regularly, taking drumming classes, joining a local choir, going to poetry slams, and attending concerts and music festivals. No matter what you choose, know that any option is just as good whether you are using meditation, music, chanting, or dance.

These methods are a starting point for reaching the ecstatic state. There are many other techniques and approaches for shifting consciousness. The techniques covered in this chapter give you a set of tools for building a reliable ecstatic practice. From here, the sky is the limit.

Sacred Space

Creating a dedicated sacred space is a very potent tool for enhancing your personal practice, deepening your relationships with the powers and honing your ecstatic skills. Sacred space creates an area where, through regular practice and association, you train your conscious self that any work done in sacred space is associated with sacred ecstasy and the Powers. Using sacred space for ecstatic work reinforces the connection between the space and ecstasy in your conscious mind, making sacred space a useful boost for shifting your consciousness.

Creating sacred space is very simple. What makes the space sacred is your use of it for sacred purposes. The more you use a specific space and set of tools for such work, the more it reinforces their sacred purpose. Tools and items representing the Powers can help reinforce this status, but ultimately it is your actions that are far more important for sanctifying space than any trappings could ever be.

The center of most sacred spaces is a shrine, a space devoted to the Powers. Shrines can be as simple as a candle and shoebox for holding sacred items to highly elaborate setups with displays of artwork, items, and tools dedicated to sacred work. They can be indoors or outdoors, fixed or portable, and dedicated to a single Power, several Powers, or even all them. Shrines can also include other items that are very important to you. What matters is your shrine resonates with you and your practice.

The center of a shrine is an altar. Altars are the focal point of a shrine where offerings are made and tools are kept. In contrast to shrines (which can be pretty elaborate), altars are very simple because they are working spaces. A good starting altar is an offering vessel, like a cup, plate, or bowl, to hold offerings for the Powers and some space for setting other items next to it.

There is also one specific kind of sacred space sometimes used in Radical Norse Paganism called a horgr (pronounced *HORG*), or a harrow. They are a pile of stones dedicated to the Powers and are always located outside under the open sky. In ancient days, people using harrows for honoring the Powers by pouring offerings onto the stones, letting their offering be absorbed by the ground beneath them. The same is done in the present, making harrows a shrine and an altar at the same time.[95]

Working with the Powers

The bedrock of working with the holy Powers is building reciprocal and healthy relationships with them. All the Powers, from the humblest of the dead to the mightiest of the gods, have their own goals, desires, and personalities. They are more than tools, perspectives, or manifestations of ancient culture and should be treated with the respect all autonomous entities deserve.

One of the most useful techniques for starting work with any of the Powers is entering an ecstatic state. By shifting your consciousness, you open yourself to direct experiences with the Powers. How they interact with us differs from person to person and Power to Power. Practitioners have experienced them in

---

95. Eldar Heide, "Hǫrgr in Norwegian names of mountains and other natural features," *Namn og nemne* 31 (2014), 7-10

many ways, including intense visions, hearing their voices, indescribable feelings of a strong presence, intuitive flashes of insight, and strange coincidences interpreted as omens. No matter what happens, pay attention to everything you experience. Be clear in telling them what you are okay with doing and are looking for. Listen to what they say. No matter what, just because a being is a Power does not mean they get to ignore your needs or demand you do anything you do not want to do. If you make any agreements, be sure the terms are clear and acceptable to you and the Power you are working with.

After first contact, you should set aside regular time for building your relationships with them. A good way to do this is working with that Power during your daily practice. You can also do other things to create a connection like taking a hike in the woods, writing poetry or songs, creating works of art dedicated to that Power, leaving regular offerings of food or drink on your altar, participating in community action, or going to performances that seem pleasing to them. What is important is keeping up such work and maintaining it in a way that does not violate your boundaries or any agreements you have with that Power.

As you build your relationship with any of the Powers, you must always be clear when setting terms and stating your boundaries. It is important in any relationship to be clear about what is expected, your comfort zone, and what is not acceptable, whether it involves a person or a Power. These negotiations will unfold over the course of your relationship with any of the Powers, and they will develop based on mutual understanding and shared experiences. It is important to be absolutely clear and up-front to avoid any possible confusion or misunderstanding.

It is perfectly alright to break off a relationship with a Power if they violate their agreements with you, just as would be the case in any other relationship. It is also important to listen to what the Powers say, what they claim they can and cannot do, and their expectations. As is the case in any relationship, failing to listen or respect the Powers can lead to confusion and serious problems. The Powers are not pets or apps you can order around or ignore whenever it is convenient for you. Entering a relationship with any Power means opening yourself to unexpected and sometimes challenging experiences. Even so, as uncomfortable as it may get, they are unique openings for expanding understanding of yourself and the world around you.

Old Norse Poetry

A very useful addition to personal practice, unique to Norse Paganism, is Old Norse poetry. In ancient times, these poems were sung in and out of rituals, delivering their wisdom in an easy-to-remember and highly engaging format. These poems were believed to carry great power, and anything set to verse could change fate. For modern practitioners, the Old Norse poetic forms can do the same while also providing a useful framework for writing chants, songs, and invocations.

According to literary scholar Preben Meulengracht Sørenson, two of the central elements of Old Norse poetry were alliteration and kennings. Alliteration is a poetic device where words with the same beginning sound are repeated in the same verse. A kenning is a way of describing something in poetic terms that includes references to Norse lore, some of which were particularly indirect and obscure. Understanding these kennings is essential for understanding the meaning of the Norse sagas.[96]

Kennings usually describe their subject in terms of the subject being a possession of another thing. For one example the kenning "the gull's land" refers to the sea by describing the sea in terms of its relationship to a gull. A kenning for battle, "the sword's play," uses a similar logic. A more mythic example is the kenning for the sky, "the dwarves' burden," which refers to the dwarves who hold up the dome of the sky. An even more lore-dependent kenning would be "the wave's fire," a reference to gold. This kenning refers to the lost Rhinegold treasure of the Volsungsaga which was hidden by tossing it into a river. The same patterns can be used for making your own in ritual or artistic work.[97]

The three types of verse described in this chapter are some of the more common forms encountered in the sagas, according to Sørenson. They work very well for writing meditative mantras, ritual chants, and songs. They are listed from least to most complex. In the ancient days these verses would have been spoken or sung with rhyme and rhythm worked out by how a verse sounded instead of how it appeared on a page. To help you understand how this would work, all the example verses below will have dots showing the syllables, line

96. Preben Meulengracht Sørenson translated by John Tucker, *Saga and Society: An Introduction to Old Norse Literature*, Odense University Press: 1993, 162-163.

97. Ibid

pairs will be marked, any syllables that need to be stressed will be underlined, and alliterations will be in bold.[98]

Ljóðaháttr

Ljóðaháttr (pronounced *LEYO-tha-hatt-ar*), the incantation meter, was often used for religious or mystical purposes such as invocations, prayer, and magical incantations. In Ljóðaháttr, each stanza has six lines with five syllables per line. Where and how alliteration happens in Ljóðaháttr depends on the specific line of the stanza. The first line will contain a word that alliterates with a word in the second line. The fourth line does the same with the fifth line. The third line and the sixth line each have words that alliterate within the same line. Here is an example verse showing how this works:

Thor-the-Son-of-Earth
Thun-der-god-smash-ing
Claw-ing-**cl**ang-ing-chains
Re-lease-from-so-rrow
Re-dress-for-many
Li-ber-ates-all-**li**ves

Fornyrdislag[99]

Fornyrdislag (pronounced *for-NEAR-dis-lag*), the old story-telling meter, usually appears in the sagas of the Poetic Edda for telling tales of the lore. In Fornyrdislag, each stanza has eight lines, which are divided into two four-line halves. There are four syllables per line and two of those syllables are emphasized. Alliteration in Fornyrdislag happens in the sets of paired lines. The first line of a pair has one or two words that alliterate within the line. The second line in each pair has one word that alliterates with the alliterated, accented first syllable of that line. Here is an example verse that shows how this works:

Come-on,-**climb**-on
Cour-age-ri-ses

98. All verses in this chapter were written by the author

99. Sørenson 161

Life-beck-ons-all
Lur-ing-**for**-ward
Prom-ised-**pri**-zes
Pe-al-ing-out
Hard-is-the-way
Hea-vy-the-load

Drottkvaett

Drottkvaett (pronounced *DROT-kv-ah-ett*), the courtly meter, is one of the most complex forms of Old Norse poetry. It was written about specific subjects by known skalds and is the most common surviving form. In Drottkvaett each stanza has eight lines. Every line has six syllables each where three of those syllables are long and stressed. Lines in this form alliterate in pairs with the first line in each pair, having two words alliterating on either the first and third or first and fifth syllable while the second line alliterates on the first syllable using the same sound as the alliteration in the first line. Drottkvaett is also the only form of Old Norse poetry with rhymes, though these are internal to each specific line. The first line of each pair has a half rhyme, while the second line of each pair has a whole rhyme. The rhymes will be shown in italic text. Here is an example verse that shows how this works:

Ri-*sing*-fall-*ing*-**roar**-ing
Rumb-ling-reach-*ing*-soar-*ing*
Crash-*ing*-sweep-*ing*-**call**-ing
Ca-ress-*ing*-ca-vort-*ing*
Play-*ing*-**pro**-*bing*-ri-sing
Press-*ing*-fall-*ing*-brush-ing
Bound-*less*-end-*less*-**burb**-ling
Beck-on-*ing*-se-duc-*ing*

Sacred Rites

There are two sacred rites in Radical Norse Pagan practice: the blot (performed to honor the Powers) and oaths. There are some terms that need to be clarified when discussing the rites. The term *rite* will be used to refer to specific spiritual actions with intentional sacred purpose. *Ritual* is a longer spiritual ceremony that includes at least one rite. Rituals are usually longer than individual rites and include other actions such as offerings, performances, chanting, meditation, and whatever else best serves the participants and the ritual's objective.

As part of Radical practice, any rite, ritual, or mystical working, such as an act of runework or seiðr, begins with invoking the powers of fire and ice. This brings the energy at the heart of creation into the space of the act. It also opens up the space for new possibilities, changing the Fate of anyone involved and signals to the Powers what is happening. The next page has a step-by-step guide for how to do this on your own. As you become more comfortable and experienced in your practice, you can add additional elements to the invocation like music, poetic verses, or movements like dance. Regardless of what you add, the core of this practice is summoning the opposing cosmic forces of fire and ice, forcing them into collision, and re-creating the moment when the Ginunngagap was filled with the building blocks of reality.

rite
INVOKING FIRE AND ICE

Stand or sit in front of your altar facing toward it

Perform the Breath exercise from chapter one

Open both of your hands with your palms facing upwards

Slowly chant the word "Isa," the name of the Elder Futhark rune of ice. As you chant, visualize the rune (shown below) being drawn on the palm of your dominant hand

ᛁ

Feel the power of ice fill that hand while you slowly chant the word "Kenaz," the name of the Elder Futhark rune of the torch and fire. As you chant, visualize the rune Kenaz (shown below) being drawn on the palm of your non-dominant hand

Feel the power of fire fill that hand and sit with the opposing forces for a moment

Clap your hands together while breathing in and pull them apart slowly as you breathe out, both palms facing each other for a moment.

Feel the energy of the moment of creation, a reflection of the time when the fire of Muspelheim and the ice of Niflheim met in the Ginnungagap.

Turn both hands away from each other, palms open, and face them toward the altar

Keep your palms open and facing out as you slowly sweep your arms extended until they are pointing in opposite directions, one on each side of your body held up at shoulder height

Stay in place, holding your arms out, while turning one full circle.

As you sweep your arms, feel the energy of the moment spread around you and push outward in every direction, opening the space for new possibilities

Blot

Blot (pronounced like the word "bloat") is the main devotional rite in Radical Norse Paganism. In Old Norse, blot means "sacrifice," which is the essence of what this rite is about. One of the best descriptions of how this was done in the ancient world comes from the Heimskringla:

> To this festival all men brought ale with them; and all kinds of cattle, as well as horses, were slaughtered, and all the blood that came from them was called "hlaut", and the vessels in which it was collected were called hlaut-vessels. Hlaut-staves were made, like sprinkling brushes, with which

> the whole of the altars and the temple walls, both inside and outside, were sprinkled over, and also the people were sprinkled with the blood; but the flesh was boiled into savory meat for those present. The fire was in the middle of the floor of the temple, and over it hung the kettles, and the full goblets were handed across the fire; and he who made the feast, and was a chief, blessed the full goblets, and all the meat of the sacrifice. And first Odin's goblet was emptied for victory and power to his king; thereafter Njord's and Freyja's goblets for peace and a good season.[100]

From this excerpt we see two key components to ancient blots: the blood of the sacrificed animals that were the property of the participants, and the meat and drink the host shared with all the people at the rite. The blood, representing the life of the animals sacrificed, was used to sanctify the ritual space and the participants. The food and drink were also blessed, with some of it offered to specific gods, before sharing it with all the participants.

A modern blot is very different from an ancient one. That said, how blot works in this tradition is based on the original practices. The core of the ancient blot was the sacrifice of precious or valuable possessions such as livestock, blessing all those present with the essence of what was sacrificed to the Powers, in thanks for their aid and as a petition for future blessings.

In Radical Norse Paganism, the main change from ancient practice is the offering, as most practitioners don't own horses or cattle. The most commonly given offerings are food and drink, purchased or prepared by the practitioner, as both are necessary for life. The first portion of this offering is given as a sacrifice to the Power being honored in the blot. This portion is sacrificed by pouring it into a special offering bowl or cup, whose contents are then poured into water or earth after the rite is completed to be buried, burned, or given to a body of water. The rest is then consumed, much like the ancient blots, to share in the bounty that has been given to the Powers. Following is an outline for performing a simple blot.

---

100. Snorri Sturluson translated by Samuel Laing, *Heimskringla*, Saga of Hakon the Good 16

rite
THE BLOT

Set sacred space by invoking fire and ice as described earlier in the chapter.

Invoke the Power being honored by this blot with a chant, a poem written in the style of Norse poetry, or by saying the name or multiple names of the Power being invoked.

Raise the plate or glass holding the offering to the altar and say, "Hail X" (where X is the Power honored by the blot).

Now give the first portion by pouring out the first sip of a beverage or placing a piece of food in the offering bowl on your altar. If you are offering something that isn't food or drink, place that offering in the bowl.

If you have offered food or drink, consume the rest of what you have. If the offering is anything else, then dispose of it by burning, burying, putting in water, or otherwise destroying it and disposing of the remnants in a safe, environmentally friendly way.

When blot is used as the center of a ritual, it is common to do multiple blot rites, also known as rounds, in the same ceremony. When doing a Radical blot ritual, one blot rite is done for the gods, one for the spirits, and one for the dead. This approach is implied in the description from the Heimskringla where after offerings are given to the gods, the dead were honored:

> Then it was the custom of many to empty the brage-goblet; and then the guests emptied a goblet to the memory of departed friends, called the remembrance goblet.[101]

In Radical Norse Paganism, there is a specific way to do three round blot rituals. The first thing you always do is ask the local spirits and dead for permission to hold the blot and invite them to join you.

---

101. Ibid

You then begin with the first round in honor of the spirits. The second round is for the gods and may honor a specific god, a group of gods (like the Aesir), multiple specific gods, or all the gods. The third round honors the dead. For this round you may recognize specific dead people, groups of the dead (e.g., those who died in a similar way or were associated with a specific place), or all of the dead. After completing these three rounds, you can add additional rounds in honor of specific Powers or individuals, boasting of deeds, or formally bestowing nicknames and kennings on any who are present for the blot ritual. These actions are not a required part of the blot rite but can improve the rite by further engaging participants.

Oath-Making

Oaths are a critical, sacred practice in Norse Paganism. An oath is a very solemn vow binding all parties to fulfill its terms. Oaths bind the Luck of all parties together, creating Fate-forged ties. In modern practice, an oath is more than a sacred promise; an oath is a deep moral and spiritual obligation. In your spiritual practice, you may feel the best way to cement a relationship with one of the Powers is by swearing an oath to them. This is a perfectly acceptable practice; in this case, the approach for oath-swearing is the same.

There are two main parties to any oath: the person making the oath is the oath-maker, and those who are present for and hearing or receiving the oath are the oath-takers. If you are swearing an oath to a specific Power, that Power is an oath-taker. If they feel it is appropriate, you may name additional Powers as witnesses to the oath. Regardless of who is making and taking the oath, all involved are obligated to help uphold it, or if it is broken, help set things right.

Outside of affirming relationships with the Powers, there are many circumstances when an oath should always be sworn. A mutual oath should be sworn by student and teacher when beginning an apprenticeship for a sacred role, swearing both will uphold the duties and ethics of the position. Ceremonies like weddings can include an oath affirming commitment to the relationship and what it means.

Oaths can also be used for binding a community together. It is quite common for people joining a fellowship, *thing*, or other Norse Pagan organization to swear an oath stating they will uphold the principles and bylaws of the group in question. Anyone holding a position of trust, responsibility, or leadership in a community should swear an oath. It should be witnessed by the community they will serve, affirming their commitment to the duties, obligations and responsibilities of their position before taking office. If testimony needs to be given during dispute resolution, the person giving such testimony should swear an oath affirming they will tell the whole truth to those questioning them.

You can also swear oaths in specific situations where you believe it is necessary or appropriate. People embarking on major life-changing journeys or setting specific goals may bind themselves to that goal with an oath. If there are people engaging in shared, risky work of any kind they may choose to swear a mutual oath to each other and their success. In any of these situations, such oaths are just as binding and potent as oaths taken for any other reason. An oath is not a thing to be taken lightly and should be treated as a highly esteemed, sacred act.

There are three situations where breaking an oath is justifiable; all are highly exceptional situations. The first is if an oath is made to achieve some sort of task and there is a serious risk of failure. In these situations, it is highly recommended for the oath-takers to require the oath-makers to include a pre-determined weregild to be provided if the oath is broken by falling short. This balances the scales and provides an additional incentive to do your best in fulfilling the oath. The second case is for mutual oaths where either party breaks the terms of the oath. In these instances, the oath becomes null and void and the party who broke it first is the oathbreaker.

The final case is where fulfilling the conditions of an oath requires the oath-maker to perform deeply dishonorable or unethical actions. These situations are very difficult, as oathbreaking is also an unethical action. In an ideal world, no one would never swear an oath that would put them in such a position, but assuming this will always be the case is highly unrealistic. The next best choice, if this option is possible, is asking to be released from your oath and if it is an oath for holding a position of trust, immediately resign. If you cannot be released from the oath it is better to break it than to commit the unethical act. There is no honor in upholding a shameful oath.

The best solution to these problems, as recommended by Kevin who is an informed lore scholar and experienced Heathen, is including an opt-out condition in any oaths sworn, particularly for oaths related to membership in groups or for holding a position of authority. An opt-out clause lets you withdraw from the oath if fulfilling it would force you to engage in actions you cannot support or believe are contrary to the oath. Consider it a major warning sign if other parties refuse to include an opt-out clause in an oath. Anyone who treats obedience as more important than right action will probably at some point use a sworn oath to force you into performing shameful acts. Such abusive, exploitative environments must be avoided at all costs. Any benefits a group, position, or cause might offer will always be outweighed by the harm and dishonor that will be inflicted on you.

rite

OATH-MAKING

Write out the terms of the oath in advance and make sure all parties and witnesses agree to them.

Invoke fire and ice as described earlier in the chapter.

State your name followed by, "I solemnly swear to ___" (recite the terms of the oath).

State any agreed weregild to be provided if the oath is broken and any opt-out conditions.

Say the names of the oath-taker and any Powers you wish to name as a witness.

Finish by saying, "I will, as I have sworn, uphold the terms of this oath to the best of my ability and ask all those who bear witness to support me in fulfilling it, aid me in making amends if I break it, and support me if I am released from it."

Holidays

There are many holidays in Norse Paganism. The four high holidays in this practice are Yule, the Spring Equinox, Midsummer, and the Fall Equinox. All celebrate the passage of time, the movement of the seasons, and the cycles of the world. There are other holidays honored in this practice and there might be additional holidays you decide to incorporate into your personal practice.

What Powers you honor on these holidays is up to you, although suggestions have been included here that are based on what is usually done in this practice. It is totally alright to honor other Norse Powers on these days or add more.

Yule (December 21–22)

Yule is the most important of the holidays; the winter solstice is the darkest night of the year, something that has always been quite literally true in the far northern parts of the world. In some places, the sun disappears for days and even weeks at a time, making it also one of the coldest times of the year. Yet every day after the solstice, the days grow longer and night slowly retreats. Accordingly, the ancients considered Yule the end of the old year and the beginning of the new.[102]

In the pre-Christian world, this holiday was celebrated by bringing the community together in a great hall while a small party prepared a fire. The fire was kept burning all night until dawn returned. People told tales, listened to storytellers reciting the sagas, feasted, held blots in honor of Odin, Thor, and Freyr, and collectively defied darkness as they waited for the coming light. Many modern Christmas traditions, like tree decorating and setting out stockings, have origins in Yule practices.[103]

For modern practitioners, there are many things that can be done on Yule. If you are so inclined, you could hold a vigil for the sun, staying up from when it sets until it rises again. Blots to Odin, Thor, and Freyr as the gods of Yule are very popular, though they are far from the only Powers worthy of honor on Yule. Another god worthy of recognition is Mani, the Moon God, as Yule is the night of his longest ride. As for the telling of stories, one excellent Yuletide tale is the creation of Midgard, a reminder that even in the darkest of times, life always finds a way to triumph. People also tell tales of their deeds from the past year during Yule feasts, sharing their experiences and celebrating accomplishments.

---

102. Local, TT/The. "Today Is the Shortest Day of the Year. Just Thought You'd Like to Know." The Local. December 21, 2016. Accessed August 26, 2018. https://www.thelocal.se/20161221/sweden-shortest-day-of-the-year-winter-solstice.

103. "Frozen Factors: Nordic Influences on the Festive Season - BBC News." BBC. December 20, 2014. Accessed August 26, 2018. https://www.bbc.co.uk/news/uk-scotland-highlands-islands-30411490.

Spring Equinox (March 20–21)

The Spring Equinox follows Yule in the calendar. Where Yule represents the end of the old year and beginning of the next one, the Spring Equinox is the time of renewal. Day and night are equally long, and each day after the Equinox grows longer as night retreats. This holiday is called by many names; two of the most popular are the Charming of the Plow, honoring the Equinox as a time of fertility, and Sigrblot, meaning Victory Blot which is when celebrants hold rituals calling for success over adversity in the coming year.[104]

Spring Equinox is a time for celebrating the potential of the new year. The darkness of Yule has passed with the promise of spring and summer lying ahead. Spring Equinox celebrations are a good time for honoring the Powers of fertility, like Freyr, Jord, and local land spirits, along with seeking aid in coming ventures. Stories about renewal, triumph over great odds, or events that took place in your part of the world during that time of the year all work well with Spring Equinox.

Midsummer (June 20–21)

Midsummer represents the year at its height. Where the Spring Equinox is the time of renewed life and growth, Midsummer is the time when the world's bounty is at its greatest. Warmth, light, and growth are everywhere, yet stand at the crossroads. Though Midsummer is the longest day of the year, with places in the farthest north experiencing no night at all, it also is a turning point. Every day after Midsummer grows shorter as each night grows longer.[105]

Midsummer is the time to celebrate life at its fullest. It is also a good time for seeking guidance for completing any work started earlier in the year. Midsummer is the last big hurrah for the year before night grows and light retreats. Stories for Midsummer that are especially relevant are ones dealing with triumph over obstacles, great victories, and inspiring moments. The Power must

---

104. Wyrddesigns. "Wyrd Designs - The Holy Tides - Ostara, Sigrblot & Summer Nights." Faith on the Couch. March 18, 2011. Accessed August 26, 2018. http://www.patheos.com/blogs/pantheon/2011/03/wyrd-designs-the-holy-tides-ostara-sigrblot-summer-nights/.

105. "Celebrating the Solstice: Midsummer in the Nordics." A Little Something about Easter in the Nordics. Accessed August 26, 2018. https://www.nordicvisitor.com/blog/celebrating-the-solstice-midsummer-in-the-nordics/.

associated with Mudsummer is Sunna, goddess of the sun, as Midsummer is the day of her longest ride.

Fall Equinox (September 22-23)

The Fall Equinox is harvest time. Like the Spring Equinox, the Fall Equinox is the time when day and night are equal in length. Unlike the Spring Equinox, the length of the day will continue to shrink, leading to the darkness of Yule. In ancient societies, this is the time of year for the last harvest. Supplies were stored for the coming winter, and anyone on voyages abroad returned home or found shelter. Where Spring Equinox is a time of opportunity and fertility, Fall Equinox is the time to take stock of your labor, make ready to ride out the coming adversity, and have one last moment before the work of winter begins.[106]

Fall Equinox celebrations are times of reflection. People seek blessings and guidance for completing work begun earlier in the year, hoping for the most beneficial resolution possible. Some honor the dead who passed in the previous year, holding blots to the recently deceased and all the other dead. The best stories for this time of year are of sacrifice, loss, and learning from hardship. The Powers most associated with the Fall Equinox are the goddesses Frigga and Freyja for their roles as keepers of wisdom.

Other Holidays

The solstices and equinoxes are not the only holidays honored in this practice, though they are the most important. Three additional holidays included in this practice (all inspired by modern holidays and traditions) are April Fool's Day, May Day, and Halloween. If you feel there is a day worth honoring as a holiday feel free to do so.

April Fool's Day, the first day of April, is Loki's Day. As a day honored in the present with pranks, jokes, and tricks, it makes perfect sense to recognize Loki in their role as the Catalyst on this day. Along with giving blot to Loki, you can also indulge in the merriment and humor associated with this holiday. Above all

---

106. "Religions - Paganism: Autumn Equinox." BBC. June 07, 2006. Accessed August 26, 2018. http://www.bbc.co.uk/religion/religions/paganism/holydays/autumnequinox.shtml.

else, this day is for challenging assumptions and the status quo, and upending people's expectations while questioning what is often taken for granted.

May Day, the first day of May, is the day of Thor as the Red God of Workers. This day was long celebrated as a springtime festival across Europe. In 1886, it picked up new meaning following the wrongful execution of a group of Chicago labor organizers who were advocating for the eight-hour workday. In honor of both, May Day honors Thor, the common people, labor, and the struggle for human dignity. This is a day for celebration and acting for human rights.[107]

Celebrated on October 31, Halloween is Hel's Day and the Festival of the Dead. Halloween has become a part of this practice thanks to its association in society with death and things that go bump in the night. This is the time for Hel and all the dead. Magical workings are common on Halloween thanks to the belief that the veil between worlds grows thin on this night. You could also celebrate the night with scary stories, all-night revelry, or enjoying the experiences of life in communion with the deceased.

Making Your Way

Developing spiritual practice is a life-long process, and there are many different tools, techniques, and sources of wisdom that all contribute to it. Regardless of how you proceed, what matters most is that the practice you develop is meaningful for you, addresses your concerns, and reflects your needs and desires.

The next exercise is for reaching and exploring the ecstatic state. The World Tree Within is a meditation meant to help you enter this state in a controlled fashion. It is meant to be a starting point for ecstatic work, which is why what you do after completing it is up to you. The World Tree Within can be incorporated into other workings, rituals, and parts of your personal practice.

107. "May Day 2018: Ancient Origins, Strange Customs and Modern Interpretations." The Week UK. Accessed August 26, 2018. http://www.theweek.co.uk/58343/may-day-2018-ancient-origins-strange-customs-and-modern-interpretations.; Chase, Eric. "The Brief Origins of May Day." The Brief Origins of May Day | Industrial Workers of the World. 1993. Accessed August 26, 2018. https://www.iww.org/history/library/misc/origins_of_mayday.

exercise
THE WORLD TREE WITHIN

Begin with the Breath exercise from chapter one. When you have reached a state of restful calm, proceed to the next step.

Focus your mind and your feelings on your spine. Feel it running from the base of your skull down to your tailbone. Feel the nerves that run through the spine and branch outward from it into the rest of your body.

Now place your focus on the base of the spine and your tailbone. Push your attention beneath you, pressing down into the ground under you. Visualize your focus moving through the earth below like roots pushing into the soil.

Continue going deeper and deeper, feeling the rocks and heat as you go. Press your visualization on until you reach the Earth's molten core. Feel the fiery heart pulsing in the depths of the Earth.

Bring your attention steadily back to yourself while keeping awareness of the heat in the Earth's core within you.

Shift your focus to the crown of your skull. Push your visualization upward into the sky, feeling your awareness grow like the trunk and branches of a great tree. As you go, feel the coolness of the wind and air around you.

Keep pushing your awareness until it goes beyond the limits of the atmosphere into the cold of the space beyond the sky's edge. Feel the deep, primordial chill of the stellar vacuum that lies beyond Earth's embrace.

While feeling the heat in the roots of your awareness and the cold at the outermost branches, pull both feelings into yourself as swiftly as possible. Feel these opposing forces move through the limits of your extended awareness as they race towards your body. As they move, pull the roots and branches of your awareness back into yourself.

Slam both energies together within yourself. Feel the raw energy, the opening of potential, and the re-enactment of the moment of creation within you. Let this feeling fill your physical body, your mind and your awareness. As you do this, perform one breath cycle.

When you have finished these breaths, sit with the new feeling inside you for a moment, open your eyes, and begin the work.

chapter five

CORE VALUES

The lives of the brave and noble are best,
Sorrows they seldom feed;
But the coward fear of all things feels,
And not gladly the greedy gives
HAVAMAL 48

Doing the right thing is an idea pretty much everyone can agree with. The place where it gets sticky is when people ask next, "What *is* the right thing?" People have been debating that answer for thousands of years. In the field of ethics, it is consistently taught that the manner in which the problem is approached is what truly matters. In the Way of Fire and Ice, the foundation for ethical philosophy is using the conduct and ideas of the Norse peoples to help answer the challenges of modern life.

This is, however, more challenging than it looks. There is no definitive list in the lore, like examples from other works such as the Old Testament, of what is and isn't always right. Instead, what you will find in the sagas is a lot of general advice and recommendations. The best-known example is the saga known as the Havamal. This saga's verses consistently urge the reader to think for yourself, always search for the most right path, and strive to be your best.

Based on this, Radical Norse Paganism is founded on nine core values which will help guide you toward the right path. These values are drawn from the advice in the Havamal and examples from other sagas. They are: Autonomy, Right Action, Weregild, Honor, Boldness, Wisdom, Hospitality, Generosity, and Solidarity. They are organized into three groups, known as the Fundamental Values, Personal Values, and Social Values to help explain how and where in life they are most likely to apply. All ethical philosophy for this practice flows from these ideas. Each of these principles is equally important, working as part of a broader whole. They are guidelines for conduct that give you tools for finding your way in life, rather than an exhaustive, highly detailed list of rules telling you exactly how to act.

Fundamental Values

The fundamental values are the foundation upon which all the other values rest. They are the heart of Radical Norse ethical philosophy. The Fundamental Values reflect the deepest truths of life, reality, and the core concepts that guide all of existence. Everything else in this practice flows from them. They are: Autonomy, Right Action, and Weregild.

Autonomy

All living beings are inherently autonomous, meaning they can make their own decisions, shape their lives, and live free within the Nine Worlds. All beings are born free and self-governing. Autonomy also means it is never right for the few to dominate the many, oppress others in the name of shoring up personal power or social systems, or for any to rule based on elevating specific race, ethnicity, caste, gender, sexuality, class, or vocation over all others. Doing so would trample on the autonomy of others, denying them the most core element of all life. Even the gods and Fate cannot deny this.

The best example of inherent autonomy in the lore is found in the creation of the first humans. As it says in the Voluspo:

> Then from the throng did three come forth,
> From the home of the gods, mighty and gracious;
> Two without fate on the land they found,
> Ask and Embla, empty of might.

Soul they had not, sense they had not,
Heat nor motion nor goodly hue;
Soul gave Odin, sense gave Hoenir,
Heat gave Lodur and goodly hue.[108]

What is most important from an ethical standpoint is that the gods do not give any decrees, commands, or laws to the first humans before or after giving these gifts. Even more importantly, the gods do not decree their Fate or give Luck and free will to Ask and Embla. This shows Fate, Luck, and free will are inherently a part of living, not gifts to be bestowed or taken away by any Power—they are essential to existence. Even the Norns, who have power over life and death, cannot deprive any being of their autonomy.

This idea of free will stands in contrast to other forms of spirituality like modern Christianity. In the Radical tradition, there is no deity handing down commandments, rules, or structures that must be obeyed. People are instead treated by the Powers as fully functional adults who can make their own life choices using what they have given humanity. If the gods cannot create or destroy anyone's autonomy, then no one has the right to arbitrarily deny others' autonomy. If any person or group is actively suppressing the autonomy of others, whether under their power or outside of their specific community, whatever actions are necessary must be taken to break their power and ensure such abuses can never be repeated.

You could conclude autonomy argues for total, unabridged freedom for every person to do as they please so long as they do not infringe on the autonomy of others. This is certainly one part of autonomy, but it is not all there is to understanding this principle. The role of society is just as important to autonomy as the individual. That humans organize communities of all kinds shows people cannot be truly free without others around to nurture, protect, and uphold each other's autonomy. Any society where everyone is living only for themselves is dominated by an endless war of all against all—genuine autonomy would be impossible.

This probably has you wondering how to ensure all forms of autonomy are respected. The key is to understanding and respecting consent, the clearest

108. Voluspo 17-18, Poetic Edda

expression of personal and communal autonomy. Through consent, you establish what actions, conditions, and systems of organization you do and do not welcome in your life. This means communities and lives founded on autonomy must respect every person's right to consent when it is granted, denied, or revoked. Consent is violated by disregarding the expressed desires of others, refusing to consider the desires of members of a community when decisions and actions will affect them, or compelling consent through force, threat of force, or deception.

The expression of consent and autonomy in a community setting is known as freedom of association. This is where individuals and communities choose whether they want to associate with specific people or other communities. Freedom of association is shown both by beginning and ceasing to associate with specific individuals or groups. Though all individuals and groups have the inherent right to choose who they associate with, some reasons for doing so are more ethically justified than others.

Refusing to associate with a person or group based on words, actions, and observed behavior that are harmful to others is justified. This aligns with the importance of actions to Norse-inspired philosophy. It is never justified to use free association to discriminate against others based on ethnicity, national origin, gender, race, sexuality, or ability. Such a decision is not based on a person's or groups actions and decisions but on features that are part of their ørlog. Such discrimination is unjustified and disregards the spirit of autonomy by hiding behind the letter.

Right Action

If the foundation of ethics is the inherent autonomy of all living beings, then Right Action is how you assess their conduct. In Radical Norse Paganism, the measure of a person's character is the sum of their words, actions, and the consequences of their decisions—not thoughts or feelings. The best summation of right action is this famous verse from the Havamal:

Cattle die, kinsmen die
And so dies oneself

But one thing I know never dies
Is the fame of the deeds of the dead[109]

Here the idea is expressed simply, directly, and powerfully. It combines the claim that a person's actions are the measure of their character with the belief that the memory of deeds will always outlast the life of the person who did them. As shown in this verse, deeds do not happen in isolation from the world. When you consider the whole of the Nine Worlds (described in chapter two), right action becomes more than just doing worthy deeds. The best way to summarize the interaction between Fate and Right Action is this statement: we are our deeds, and our fates are ours to make.

It works in two ways: all people everywhere are the sum of their deeds, consisting of all their words and actions. Hand-in-hand with it is that personal fate in life is yours to choose; and Fate is the sum of all the choices everyone has made. The second way it works is the idea that your actions are not just the product of your own decisions, ideas, and goals—they are shaped and influenced by the decisions, actions, and consequences of others' deeds. All fates are in every person's hands. It is therefore critical that you make the best choices possible, live the most ethical life you can, and be fully aware of the effect your choices have on others and the world around you.

Part of acting rightly means considering the impact of your words. As thought and feeling given form, words are incredibly powerful. The right words can inspire action, while the wrong ones can undermine deeds or even cause harm to others. No matter what form they take or medium they appear in, words are a different form of action. And like all other actions, they must be weighed based on what is said, how it is said, and the consequences of the words.

This raises the question of what place intention has in understanding right action. In this tradition, intent is shown by the manner in which someone executes an action. The best way to explain the idea is by examining different types of harm. When harm is done to self or others, there is a difference between deliberately damaging actions and those that are accidental or unintentional. Malicious intent has a calculated, specific end that is made clear through

109. Havamal 78, Poetic Edda

the action itself. Unintentional or accidental harm does not have such a deliberate, predictable outcome. Now, this doesn't mean that nonmalicious harm is less significant. It does, however, suggest any lack of harmful intent shown in an action should be considered when assessing deeds and their effects.

When put into practice, Right Action is directly at odds with the assumptions of modern consumer culture. When people are measured by what they do and have done, little room is left for the shallow materialist worth as measured by what one owns. A verse from the Havamal deals very directly with the problems of wealth:

Among Fitjung's sons saw I well-stocked folds,
Now they bear the beggar's staff;
Wealth is as swift as a winking eye,
Of friends the falsest it is.[110]

This idea is further supported by a later verse dealing with the question of material goods; it shows that to the ancients, clothes do not make the person:

Washed and fed to the council fare,
But care not too much for thy clothes;
Let none be ashamed of their shoes and hose,
Less still of the steed they ride.[111]

The value of work, which is the sum of many large and small deeds, changes from measuring how much money people make to what sort of work they do, the reason for doing it, how skilled they are and the impact their labor has on the world. Living life based on Right Action puts a different set of expectations on everyone than what much of modern society accepts as normal or praiseworthy.

110. Havamal 76, Poetic Edda

111. Havamal 61, Poetic Edda

Weregild

Weregild's foundation rests on Autonomy and Right Action. Weregild guides how to best resolve dispute, address harm, and make amends in a way that respects all people's inherent autonomy. The origins of this concept are in pre-Christian Scandinavian dispute resolution. The Scandinavian peoples lived in highly marginal environments where harm to people could put families and communities in danger by depriving them of the labor necessary for survival. This included false claims that could damage a person's reputation.

Weregild developed to prevent injury from escalating into a cycle of revenge and feuds. It consisted of material compensation or labor offered that was proportional to the harm done. If both parties found the proposed Weregild acceptable, the grievance was considered resolved as soon as compensation was delivered. If, however, Weregild was not offered or the amount was considered unacceptable, it was fully within the rights of the injured party to seek retribution on their own terms. This gave everyone involved incentive to seek and offer genuinely fair Weregild.

Ensuring Weregild was acceptable to all parties was achieved through transparent negotiations. Whatever Weregild was agreed on was presented, discussed, and resolved before and with input from the entire community. This was because any dispute requiring Weregild impacted the community of both parties and the community was expected to help enforce whatever terms were agreed on. The goal of any Weregild was always to ensure it did as much as possible to repair the harm done and was sufficiently steep to discourage repeating the same behavior.[112]

Weregild is as relevant in the present as it was in the past. The goal of Weregild in Radical Norse Paganism is reaching an agreement where some form of compensation, through material goods or actions that meets the injured party's needs, is justified in the eyes of the community, and is accepted by both parties as resolving any harm done. What works best for compensation is what can be reasonably delivered, addresses the core causes of the problem at hand, and considers if the incident is a first-time occurrence or part of a repeated

---

112. Robert Ferguson, *The Vikings: A History*, Penguin Books (London: 2009), 31–32, Gwyn Jones, *A History of the Vikings*, Oxford University Press (Oxford: 1984), 347-348, Else Roesdahl, *The Vikings*, Penguin Books (New York: 1987), 61.

pattern. It must also consider if the harm was accidental, the result of carelessness, or intentional.

If all parties have agreed to an acceptable resolution and compensation has been delivered, the dispute should be considered resolved. You should not revive a resolved dispute unless one of the parties is repeating the behaviors and actions that caused the original problem. This is why Weregild must address root causes as best as possible instead of simply dealing with the immediate consequences. The point is to stop a matter from escalating to a long-running feud of any sort by resolving the core causes in the most just, equitable, and decisive fashion possible.

That said, this does not mean Weregild should always be offered or accepted simply for the sake of peace. Anyone who cannot be trusted to hold to the terms of Weregild should not be offered it, and the same is true of those who refuse to respect the other party on a fundamental level. These behaviors cause injuries so severe that no amount of Weregild, save total exclusion or removal from a position of authority, could ever repair the damage done. It is also acceptable to refuse to deliver or accept Weregild if the other party is acting in bad faith, whether they have inflicted or claim injury. Generally speaking, an injured party should be given the benefit of the doubt until their actions show otherwise.

Though Weregild is a fundamental ethical principle, it should not be used for demanding forgiveness for its own sake. The letter and spirit of Weregild is equitable resolution, not forced peace founded on silence. True Weregild is the resolution of grievances through recompense that resolves the core problem. The absolution granted is a consequence of delivering recompense and is not the ultimate goal.

Personal Values

If the fundamental values provide the foundation for ethics, personal values address individual conduct. They are: Honor, Wisdom, and Boldness. These principles provide guidance for decisions and actions in daily life. They help show what sort of individual actions are most worthy.

Honor

If you are your deeds, then honor is the sum of your deeds. Many scholars who study the ancients call their form of honor a public virtue, meaning it was built on other people's opinions of you, yet in truth what makes up your reputation is your deeds. The sum of your actions show your integrity. The two exist in a mutually sustaining relationship. One verse, very similar to the one describing right action, best sums this up:

Cattle die, kinsmen die,
And so dies one's self;
But a noble name will never die;
If good renown one gets.[113]

The way honor creates reputation is through the impact of your deeds on the world. The consequences of deeds cause people to speak of what you did, remember them, and spread the word of what sort of person you are. Even the deeds only known to you shape your reputation, as these also change your circumstances and conditions, and leave an imprint on the world. This means you need to consider your deeds in light of your current reputation, what they can do to change it, and how they can maintain honor.

This is how honor is also integrity. What creates a worthy reputation are actions that are consistent with ethical behavior. This means building a worthy reputation requires being a person of integrity. Honor is more than a desire to ensure people say good things about you. It is the drive to ensure your deeds are the sort that cause people to praise you for worthy actions. The truly honorable make the most ethical choices possible as consistently and often as possible, regardless of the immediate benefits or cost this may have. Such integrity will outlast false or malicious claims and any rewards an unworthy action might bring.

Being honorable therefore means you should always emphasize doing worthy deeds over protecting image or saving face. Anyone who focuses on appearances becomes slaves to their ego, committing unworthy deeds to protect it. If people are criticizing your actions, that should be treated as an opportunity to

---

113. Havamal 77, Poetic Edda

do better and improve yourself. If people are making false claims, it is better to prove them wrong with actions rather than lash out (though it may be tempting).

Wisdom

Wisdom is spoken of often in the lore and is a central virtue in Radical Norse Paganism. The following verse sums up how critical it was and is:

A better burden may no one bear
For wanderings wide than wisdom;
It is better than wealth on unknown ways,
And in grief a refuge it gives.[114]

This begs the question: what is wisdom? The conventional definition fits with other commonly used understandings of the concept, showing wisdom is more than just possessing knowledge. Wisdom is having the ability to apply the knowledge you have in an effective fashion. It is also clear that in the sagas, wisdom includes possessing the necessary skills needed for acquiring more knowledge, determining what information is genuinely true or false, and assessing what sources are trustworthy.[115]

The beginning of the quest for wisdom is knowing your limits. This verse from the Havamal makes that quite clear:

A little sand has a little sea,
And small are the minds of all;
Though all people are not equal in wisdom,
Yet half-wise only are all.[116]

Though some are wiser than others, none are fully wise—not even the gods, thanks to the vastness of all reality and the limits of each person's ability to comprehend it. These limits should not discourage you from improving your capabilities and understanding. In the Havamal, hiding within your limits

114. Havamal 10, Poetic Edda

115. "Wisdom." Dictionary.com. Accessed March 29, 2018. http://www.dictionary.com/browse/wisdom?s=t.

116. Havamal 53, Poetic Edda

(or even worse, assuming your narrow focus or limited range and depth of knowledge is wise) is far from desirable:

The ignorant one thinks that all they know,
When they sit by themselves in a corner;
But never what answer to make they know,
When others with questions come.[117]

Through accepting these limits, you can better push yourself forward, improve, and become wiser. Embracing the intellectual humility that comes with knowing personal limits and the vastness of potential is the first, necessary step for growing your capabilities. Along with this urging is knowing how to probe information and find its worth:

Wise shall they seem who well can question,
And also answer well;
Nought is concealed that some may say
Among the children of humanity.[118]

Hand-in-hand with skepticism, self-knowledge and humility is discipline. Knowing what you can do carries the responsibility to act in a prudent fashion. The following verse brings this idea to the forefront:

Shun not the mead, but drink in measure;
Speak to the point or be still;
For rudeness none shall rightly blame you
If soon your bed you seek.[119]

The truly wise do not act recklessly. They think before acting, express their ideas in the most direct and easily understood fashion possible and know their limits, as shown here:

117. Havamal 26, Poetic Edda

118. Havamal 28, Poetic Edda

119. Havamal 19, Poetic Edda

The one who is prudent a measured use
Of the might they have will make;
They find when among the brave they fare
That the boldest they may not be.[120]

Prudence and discipline are good, but there are also times when it is necessary to take risks. Ultimately, wisdom is more than knowing facts and ideas, it is the capacity to assess their worth and determine the best course of action in a given situation based on what you can do and want to do.

Boldness

Boldness is one of the words most commonly associated with anything Norse. When first studying the Norse, many immediately are taken with the stories of glorious battle, epic conflicts, and the history of raiding and warfare. It is also clear from the sagas that bravery and boldness are praised:

The child of a king shall be silent and wise
And bold in battle as well;
Bravely and gladly a person shall go,
Till the day of their death is come.[121]

As shown above, boldness doesn't mean you are not afraid—it means taking necessary risks, seeking decisive solutions, and doing the right thing even if it means facing discomfort, danger, and conflict. The essence of this mentality is expressed in the Skirnismol when Skirnir, Freyr's manservant, is asked why he risks his life by entering Gerd's hall:

Boldness is better than complaints can be
For he whose feet must fare;
To a destined day has mine age been doomed,
And my life's span hereto laid.[122]

---

120. Havamal 64, Poetic Edda

121. Havamal 15, Poetic Edda

122. Skirnismol 13, Poetic Edda

Very clearly, taking risks and acting boldly does not mean deliberately putting yourself in harm's way needlessly or throwing your life away without purpose. Boldness does not justify stupidity. There are many instances where bold cunning is held up as praiseworthy. One excellent example is from the Fafnismol when Sigurdr goes to confront the dragon Fafnir. Instead of charging forth to face the dragon head-on in glorious battle, Sigurdr dug a ditch, hid in it, and killed Fafnir by stabbing the dragon in the belly with a spear.[123]

Throughout the lore, those who engage in bold action seek conclusive resolution to the problem at hand. Whether this is Odin, Vili, and Ve rising up and overthrowing Ymir or Sigurdr slaying Fafnir, the decisiveness of these actions is part of what makes them bold deeds.

The final element of boldness is the question of inaction. Not acting, regardless of how or when, is as much a deed as action. Refusing to act when you are morally obligated to do so shows a great deal about your character and is fiercely condemned in the lore, as best summed up in the following verse from the Havamal:

> The sluggard believes they shall live forever
> If the fight they face not
> But age shall not grant them the gift of peace
> Though spears may spare them.[124]

It is always better to do the right thing than do nothing. What that action is or should be is another matter, but doing nothing in times of crisis is never an option. Simply because you personally are not engaging in a conflict does not mean you will be spared by it or it won't affect you. You cannot remain neutral in matters of ethical importance. Failing to act enables unworthy deeds.

Social Values

Social values are the next step outward from the Fundamental and Personal values. They are Hospitality, Generosity, and Solidarity. These explain how people should act as members of a community and society. They provide guidance for

123. Opening Prose, Fafnismol, Poetic Edda

124. Havamal 16, Poetic Edda

the values a community should be founded on, as well as what should be expected of all involved.

Hospitality

Without any doubt, hospitality is the most well-known and thoroughly explained ethical principle for the ancient Norse peoples. Its origins are found in the harsh conditions the many societies of ancient Scandinavia faced. Anyone who found themselves stuck out in the open would face the fury of the Scandinavian wilderness, effectively a death sentence. To ensure survival, the custom of hospitality developed. Anyone in need of shelter who presented themselves at anyone's door was given food, a bed, and kept safe. In exchange, they were expected to provide labor or gifts for their hosts. These exchanges were acts of mutual aid, not crude transactions. The point was assistance, not profit or individual benefit, as this verse illustrates:

Curse not thy guest, nor show him thy gate,
Deal well with a person in want.[125]

The foundation of this principle is compassion for others. The conditions that created hospitality were experienced and feared by all who lived in those days. Turning your back on people suffering from such ubiquitous circumstances would have been a very cruel act. The following verse best shows hospitality's compassionate heart:

Better a house, though a hut it be,
A person is a master at home;
Their heart is bleeding who needs must beg
When food they fain would have.[126]

Many of the verses of the Havamal discuss the particulars of hospitality, with one of the first stating what should be provided to guests:

125. Havamal 135, Poetic Edda

126. Havamal 37, Poetic Edda

Fire they need who with frozen knees
Have come from the cold without;
Food and clothes must the farer have,
The one from the mountains come.[127]

In the present day, hospitality takes on many forms, ranging from providing guidance and shelter for travelers to giving aid to those in need. Even in its most literal form, how you give hospitality or request it should be tempered by the conditions you are facing. Hospitality urges you to consider how you can better improve your life and the lives of others through mutual assistance, reciprocal aid, and providing whatever you can spare for those in most need.

Generosity

Hospitality leads naturally into Generosity. If Hospitality is borne from compassion and mutual aid, then Generosity is the next logical step. The practive of generosity in ancient Norse society is influenced in part by how they lived. They had what would today be described as a gifting economy, where goods and commodities—ranging from fine swords to food and drink—were exchanged based on use-value and not for the purpose of maximizing profit. When you had more than you needed, the expectation was to share your bounty. Accordingly, the most esteemed people in the ancient Scandinavian world were praised for being generous with their wealth. The kenning "Ring-Giver" was highly respected, referring to anyone who gave freely of the wealth they had to others.

On more mundane levels are many examples from the Havamal that urge people to give of their bounty to others. One verse states clearly:

No great thing needs a person to give,
Oft little will purchase praise;
With half a loaf and a half-filled cup
A friend full fast I made.[128]

127. Havamal 3, Poetic Edda

128. Havamal 52, Poetic Edda

It's not necessary to give in massive, conspicuous ways to be a generous individual. Even if you cannot give of material goods, there are many other ways, such as wisdom and labor, to give to others. Such giving was also seen as a natural part of friendship and building enduring relationships, as shown here:

Friends shall gladden each other with arms and garments,
As each for themselves can see;
Gift-givers' friendships are longest found,
If fair their fates may be.[129]

This ancient Norse idea of Generosity is very much at odds with the modern idea that some of the most respected people are those who hoard vast treasures, use their wealth to live in unprecedented luxury, publicly revel in their excesses, and prioritize personal gain ahead of other concerns. Acts of charity and philanthropy, while laudable, are secondary, at best putting such actions worlds away from the open-handedness of the ancients. If anything, such rapacity shares a rather unflattering parallel in the lore.

Four solid examples of prioritizing greed at the expense of others exist in the lore. These are the great giant Ymir, the dragon Fafnir, Grendel, and the dragon that took Beowulf's life. Though the specifics of each case vary, what they all share is someone hoarding goods or space for themselves at the expense of others. Their greed is their most detested trait and the cause of their downfall.

Fafnir's case is the most direct example. He was originally a dwarf who, rather than share the gold given to him and his brother Regin by their father, took it all for himself. After stealing this great wealth, Fafnir transformed into a terrible dragon, feared by all other living beings. Greed quite literally made Fafnir into a hated monster.[130]

These examples give modern practitioners a lot to think about. If the ancients and the works they left behind show a different understanding of what wealth is for, that challenges us to reconsider how we live day-to-day and as a

---

129. Havamal 41, Poetic Edda

130. Prose between verses 11 and 12 and verses 14 and 15, Reginsmol, Poetic Edda

society. When the norms of life are at odds with ethical practice, you should seek out new forms of conduct that are in accord with such ideals.

Solidarity

Solidarity is the next step from Hospitality and Generosity. It means standing in unity with any you share affinity with, whether the bond is one of family, community, spirituality, work, study, recreation, or broader goals. Friendship, camaraderie, and shared company built on foundations of shared experience are celebrated in the lore. Such affinities are commended in the lore, such as in the following verse:

Young was I once, and wandered alone,
And nought of the road I knew;
Rich did I feel when a comrade I found,
For man is man's delight.[131]

Such bonds should be cherished, maintained, and kept up so long as those sharing such connections are worth defending. As is said later in the Havamal:

Be never the first to break with thy friend
The bond that holds you both;
Care eats the heart if thou canst not speak
To another all thy thought.[132]

Solidarity calls for all who hold such connections to stand together, fight for common interests, and resist those who would do harm to any part of their community. The best expression of this concept in the lore is found in this verse from the Havamal:

To their friend a person a friend shall prove,
To them and the friend of their friend;

131. Havamal 47, Poetic Edda

132. Havamal 121, Poetic Edda

But never a person shall friendship make
With one of their foe's friends.[133]

One of the greatest acts of selfless solidarity can be found in *Beowulf*, the famous Anglo-Saxon epic showing events that occurred in Denmark and Sweden, where the hero gives his reasons for traveling from his home in Sweden to the hall besieged by the monster Grendel in neighboring Denmark:

Then news of Grendel,
hard to ignore, reached me at home:
sailors brought stories of the plight you suffer
in this legendary hall, how it lies deserted,
empty and useless once the evening light
hides itself under heaven's dome.
So every elder and experienced councilman
among my people supported my resolve
to come here to you, King Hrothgar,
because all knew of my awesome strength.[134]

What dispels any notion his voyage was motivated by greed is this subsequent statement in which he gives his only demand in exchange for his help:

Is that you won't refuse me, who have come this far,
the privilege of purifying Heoret,
with my own men to help me, and nobody else.[135]

In these sections, Beowulf makes clear his entire motivation for journeying to the aid of Hrothgar's people—he heard of their plight and wanted to help them. That his only stated condition was to do the job himself with his own people instead of requesting any sort of compensation reinforces this. What makes this case even more potent is the point of affinity Beowulf speaks to

133. Havamal 43, Poetic Edda

134. *Beowulf* 409-418, translated by Seamus Heaney, W.W. Norton and Company (New York & London: 2000)

135. Beowulf 427-432

that is about shared humanity, one of the most inclusive forms of solidarity. This same sentiment is expressed very potently in the Havamal:

> If evil you see and evil you know
> Speak out against it and give your enemies no peace[136]

The real dilemma that arises with solidarity is who to stand with, what communities to be fully involved with, and when to walk away. It's clear the bonds of camaraderie, mutual support and assistance are essential for any community to function. This, however, does not mean anyone who is a part of such a community should be given a pass on unwelcome, dishonorable, or harmful actions against others. It is here the guidance offered by Right Action and Honor are appropriate for determining what communities are worth being part of. Communities are defined by more than shared experience and proximity. They depend on the values shared by their participants and how they are organized.

A Worthy Life

These principles are a guide for leading a good life. They are only a beginning and the specifics of how you live them out will be different from others. What matters is honoring the core values by doing your best to live them however you can. Ethics, as shown here, are more than just ideas given lip services. They are a way of understanding and the Norse give a clear path for all to follow, even though it is not always the easy one.

All these ethics, regardless of which element of life they address, guide you because no one lives as isolated islands removed from everyone else. All actions matter because of what they do to others and the world. Every step we take has effects both easy and difficult to foresee. The next exercise will aid your understanding of this by helping you reach a state of calm. By doing this it becomes much easier to reflect and consider your actions and the actions of others. It will also help you for deeper work with the runes and seiðr.

136. Havamal 127, Poetic Edda

exercise
CALMING THE SEA AND SKY

This exercise builds on prior work and is aimed at creating a state of receptive calm. It is important to emphasize the goal of this meditation is reach a state where you can put your focus on specific goals, states or ideas. This is different from other meditations aimed at creating an empty mind as the goal is to bring everything into holistic balance instead of denying or forcing out what is present.

Begin with the breathing exercise outlined in chapter pne. Perform as many breath cycles as necessary to reach a relaxed state before beginning the next step.

Once you are relaxed, close your eyes and visualize the open ocean with the sky above it. Let everything in your visualization begin to move on its own. Do not focus on creating waves, ripples from the wind, or motion in the sky—simply let it happen in a way that feels most natural.

When you feel everything is moving on its own you may begin with the next element of this meditation. This part is a bit tricky to realize, so take as much time as you need to get it right.

In the space you have visualized in your mind, allow your feelings and stresses seep in to very specific spaces. Let your thinking, worries and concerns be reflected in the sky as stormy weather. The more occupied your mind is, the more ferocious the storm in the sky should be.

As the sky becomes a mirror of your mind, let your feelings, emotions, and stresses to manifest in the oceans. The size, speed, and consistency of the waves and motion of the sea should match your distress, concerns, and feelings.

Allow these elements of your visualization to manifest uncontrolled. Let the mirrors of sea and sky take shape on their own; do not force their conditions to match your expectations. It should feel most appropriate when what you are visualizing matches your internal state.

It is now time to part the storm and calm the seas. Feel what is really driving the forces causing the storm. (There may be more than one root cause.) As you begin to process the causes of the storm, allow it to change the vision. As your thoughts become clear, let the clouds part, and as you better understand your emotions, let the seas calm. Continue this process until you are rewarded with a sunny sky, or, if you prefer, a starry night sky and calm waters.

This meditation is useful for other work but should never be seen or used as a replacement for long-term therapy and other such practices. If you find it helpful in such matters, use it with the understanding that it is not a replacement for seeking professional help. This exercise will be challenging at first but will become easier with practice.

chapter six

RUNELORE

I ween that I hung on the windy tree,
Hung there for nights full nine;
With the spear I was wounded, and offered I was
To Odin, myself to myself
HAVAMAL 139

Runes are one of the most unquestionably Norse things in existence. These ancient symbols have carried some of the ideas, beliefs, and core concepts of the Norse peoples across space and time. On even deeper levels they are symbols endowed with hidden knowledge and great power. Since time immemorial, people have used the runes to read the patterns of fate and create potent magical workings. They are a key part of modern Norse Pagan practice as a part of ritual work, mysticism, and art.

The story of the runes begins with Odin and his endless hunger for knowledge. The Many-Named god was restless in pursuit of answers to every question, no matter how far he had to go to find them. His endless journey brought him to his greatest act since overthrowing Ymir. This chase ended at the World Tree, the heart of reality.

When he arrived, he found the right spot, prepared a rope, impaled himself with his own spear, and hanged himself from the World Tree as a sacrifice of himself to himself. There he remained, caught between life and death, for nine days and nights without food, drink, or rest. On the final day, he looked down and saw strange shapes pulsing with power hidden in the roots. Screaming, he snatched up the very first runes. Odin then shared this new knowledge with the world, giving some to the gods, some to the spirits, and some to humanity.[137]

Historically speaking, the first runes, known as the Elder Futhark, appear in what is today Germany around the first century CE as a simple system of writing. They remained in use for centuries. As time passed and people moved, the runes changed. One form took shape in Scandinavia, known as the Younger Futhark. The other major form traveled with the Anglo-Saxon people, becoming the Anglo-Saxon Futhorc.[138]

Somewhere along the way, each rune acquired unique meanings to go with their names and sounds. These meanings were recorded in rune poems, three of which survive to the present day. These sources, along with the tireless work of runologists, are the heart of what is known about the runes. Along with the lore, such knowledge is the foundation for modern uses of the runes by Norse Pagans around the world.

There are two main ways, along with writing and art, the runes are used in modern Norse-derived practice: divination and magic. Both methods use the same meanings for the runes. There are people who use runes only for divination, only for magic, both, and neither—how you use the runes in your practice is entirely up to you.

Divination

Also known as rune-casting, divination is the most well-known use of the runes. Like all forms of divination, rune-casting is useful for reflecting on your current circumstances, viewing them from a new perspective, and gaining unexpected insights. Some see it as a reliable method for reading the currents of Fate. Regardless of your perspective, it is very effective for finding new perspectives.

Historically speaking, the oldest known example of rune-casting comes from the second century CE via the Roman historian Tacitus. He described peoples in ancient Germania divining their future by drawing lots with pieces

137. Havamal 138-140, Poetic Edda

138. Michael P. Barnes, *Runes: A Handbook*, Boydell Press (Woodbridge: 2012), 4–5, 9–10

of cut wood. The medieval Christian monk Rimbert, while preaching in Sweden, described a ceremony where Pagan Swedes performed divination by casting lots with wooden chips soaked in sacrificial blood. Runic divination as is commonly practiced today was first popularized in 1983 when Ralph Blum published *The Book of Runes*.[139]

If you need medical, legal, academic, psychiatric, or any other professional assistance, rune-casting can be a useful tool but is never a replacement for such services. It is also best to ask someone else to conduct divination for you if your question concerns a matter where you have very strong feelings about the outcome or if you are facing an especially difficult question. This is because it is very easy to impose what answers you want to hear onto the runes; having someone else do it for you avoids this problem.

You can make your own runes or, if you prefer or are just starting out, purchase a set. If you choose to carve your own, wood and bone are some of the most popular choices thanks to how easy they are to work with. Some prefer ceramic, metal, or even stone runes. The choice of material is a matter of personal preference. What matters is you use the material that works best for you and isn't too fragile or easily scratched. The runes should also have the same general shape—for example, all the runes in a set being shaped like discs or square tiles, so that you can't easily tell them apart by touch.

There are two ways to cast the runes, known as drawing and throwing the runes. In both forms, the rune-caster begins by putting all of the runes in a pouch. The caster then asks the questioner to place their hand in the pouch and shuffle the runes while thinking about their question. It is best to not ask what their question is until after casting and reading the runes because the caster can focus on interpreting the findings rather than trying to fit what they see to the questioner's desires.

When drawing runes, pull three runes from the pouch, one at a time without looking, and lay them out from left to right, reading them as past, present, and future. If there are any matters that need further explanation, you can draw a fourth rune and place it above the past, present, or future rune that is unclear. You can also lay out the runes in spreads and patterns used in tarot, substituting the cards for runes. Drawing the runes provides an orderly approach with some

139. Tacitus, *Germania* 10; *Vita Ansgari*, 26–30.

sense of consistency in readings, making it ideal for anyone who is new to rune casting.

Throwing the runes is a more intuitive approach that leaves a lot more to chance. In this form, after the questioner shuffles the runes in the pouch first. After they do so, the caster also shuffles the runes. After you have shuffled the runes, pull out as many as you feel should be in your hand without looking at them. Next, cup the runes in your hands, breathe onto them without looking to give the reading life, shake them like dice, and throw them onto a table, cloth, or other surface for reading. You then read the runes based on the patterns they make, where the runes fall, their proximity to each other, and the meanings of the runes themselves.

The shape the runes make and their relationships in space matter as much as what the runes themselves mean. This more intuitive style is less repeatable but can offer very profound, surprising insights. Throwing the runes is recommended for more experienced casters though if you feel like it's a good fit for you then feel free to start out with throwing the runes instead of drawing them.

Regardless of the method used, rune-casting gives the caster and questioner a useful tool for reflecting on their circumstances. The information they provide is helpful because it provokes you to consider possibilities or perspectives that you may have ignored. They can also inspire you to seek out different solutions or approaches to resolving the challenges you face. Even if a specific rune-casting gives you a highly positive reading, this is as much an opportunity to re-examine what is around you and what might have been taken for granted.

Magic

In Radical Norse Paganism, the runes are more than just symbols representing specific concepts. They are the notes of the music uniting the Nine Worlds, given form by Odin's sacrifice and their development over time. They are reflections of deeper, powerful concepts tied directly to the deepest workings of Fate and the societies who used them. When you use the runes in magic you are tapping into this deep well of meaning, unleashing forces with the power to change Fate.

There is a lot of evidence showing runes were used in ancient times for magical purposes. One of the best direct examples is from the Sigrdrifumal, where the Valkyrie Sigrdrifa tells the hero Sigurdr of different ways he can use runes to bring victory in battle, heal, and protect. In another example, the hero Egil Skallagrimson draws runes with his blood on a drinking horn to see if its contents are poisoned. Academic runologists also claim the meanings of the runes are evidence of magical use in ancient times, reinforcing other evidence showing their historical use for mystical purposes.[140]

There are three main forms of rune magic used in Radical Norse Paganism. These are drawing or carving runes onto objects, singing them, and bindrunes. Regardless of the method used, all runic workings draw their power from the meaning of the runes used. Runes can also be used, through these methods, to invoke the names of people, places, and Powers by spelling them out in runes.

Be careful when engaging in any kind of rune magic. The concepts you are invoking directly manipulate the forces of Fate. Your hamingja comes into play when you engage in any sort of runic magic, binding you to the working. This means you should beware the law of unintended consequences and any unexpected outcomes.

Always remember rune magic is not a replacement for engaging in all actions necessary for accomplishing your goals. A bindrune for protecting your home won't do much good if you don't lock the front door and performing galdr to get a better job won't get any results if you don't fill out some applications. Even though rune magic tilts the odds in your favor, you still need to place your bet and roll the dice.

In Radical Norse practice, you should always invoke fire and ice to charge a runic working. There are three ways to do this. The first is to use the method described in chapter four, which is just as effective for charging a space in preparation for a working as it is for ritual. The second method is good for workings on the fly: first, draw or visualize the runes isa and kenaz on the palms of your dominant and non-dominant hands, respectively, as you breathe in before clapping your hands together as you breathe out. You then use this energy to power a working. You can adapt this method using the base principles in a lot of ways, with it even being possible to get the same effect by drawing or visualizing the runes on a thumb and finger before snapping. The final approach,

140. Sigrdrifumal 5-10, Poetic Edda; Sturluson, Snorri, Bernard Scudder, and Svanhildur Óskarsdóttir. Egils Saga. Penguin Books, (New York: 2004), Chapter 44; Terje Spurkland, trans. by Betsy van der Hoek, *Norwegian Runes and Runic Inscriptions*, Boydell Press (Woodbridge: 2005), 11–12.

used for group workings and rituals, starts with dividing practitioners into two groups. One group chants "isa" while the other chants "kenaz" at the same time in a long, sustained tone.

The first and most basic method of magical use for runes is carving or drawing runes on objects. This imbues the object or place with the properties of the runes you inscribe. You can use this to invoke the power of one specific rune, several runes, or even use runes to call on a specific Power by inscribing its name in runes. You can also call on the power of the runes for a specific working or purpose, in the same way as inscribing them into an object, by drawing their shape in the air. When drawing runes, the order you draw or carve them in will influence how they manifest. A good first rune-carving is creating a set of divination runes. To do this, begin by laying out the material you will use for the divination runes, summon a charge, and then start carving.

The second form of runic magic is known as rune galdr, the art of the runic spell-song. To perform galdr, the first thing you need to do is take a deep breath in. Next you chant the name of the rune while visualizing its shape and concentrating on the purpose of the working. When you have finished chanting the rune's name, expel all remaining breath to release it into the world. Rune galdr can be as simple or complex as necessary, using whichever and as many or few runes as needed. That said, like drawing or carving runes, the order you sing the runes shapes how the working will unfold. You could, if you so choose, pair the galdr with a melody and make it into a song. Rune galdr can be combined with drawing or carving runes, creating bindrunes, trance and even some forms of seidr magic. This gives such workings additional potency. This versatility makes runic galdr a highly effective form of rune magic.

Bindrunes are the third form of runic magic. A bindrune is created by taking more than one rune (they can be from different runic alphabets), and combining them to make a single, new symbol. To make a bindrune, you first need to determine your intended purpose. Next, pick out the runes that will help achieve that purpose, such as using runes of stability, strength and endurance for a bindrune of protection. You then invoke fire and ice and start drawing the bindrune, using the chosen runes as the components for the design. If you want, you can galdr the runes you use as you draw the bindrune. When you are finished, take a deep breath in, place your drawing hand over the new bindrune, and expel all air from your lungs to release it into the world. Some examples are included on the next page. Here is an example of how to construct the Tyr's Arrow bindrune, which is used to banish injustice:

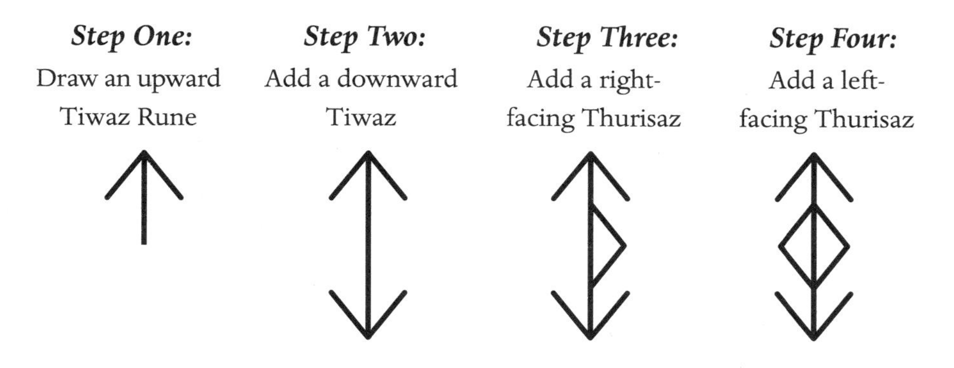

Tyr's Arrow, meant to banish injustice, created by the author

As this example shows, bindrunes can be made using the same rune more than once. In the case of Tyr's Arrow, the use of two bindrunes, Tiwaz and Thursiaz, twice each reinforces their energies. It also balances them, making the bindrune an equal mix of what each represents. Tyr's Arrow combines all of this into the greater purpose of a working meant to secure and support justice. It is guided by the powers of Tiwaz and bolstered by the overwhelming force of Thurisaz. This also shows how a bindrune is a working that draws power from the runes used to make it and becomes greater than the sum of its parts.

Bindrunes, like drawing or carving runes, can be inscribed onto an object to grant it the bindrune's power, drawn in the air or even summoned by runic galdr. Bindrunes are also be used to create personal or group symbols. Regardless, once a bindrune has been made it can be used by anyone who knows its shape and purpose. This means you can use already existing bindrunes for workings along with your own bindrunes.

There are many bindrune-like symbols that appear in many different sources. Two of the most famous are the Aegishjalmer, the Helm of Awe, which is said to inspire fear in enemies and strength in those who wore it, and the Vegsvisir, the Wanderer, that was said to help guide travelers. There are many other similar symbols that survive in Icelandic grimoires, with *The Sorcerer's Screed* as the most famous collection of such symbols.

Examples of Bindrunes

The Aegishalmar, the Helm of Awe, thought to inspire terror in the user's enemies

The Revealing Eye, meant to uncover hidden truths and dispel lies and deception, created by the author

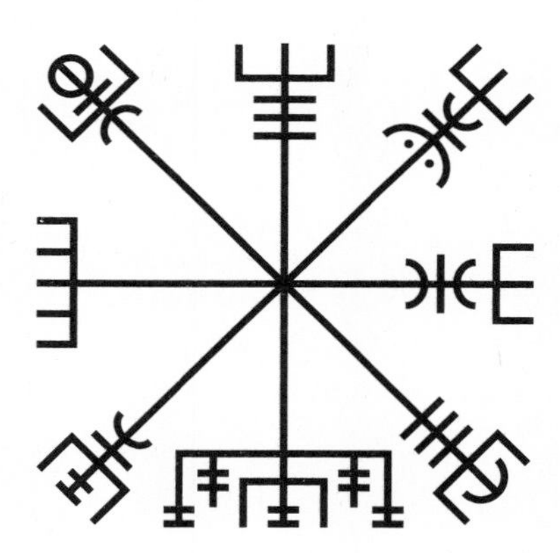

The Vegsvisir, the Wanderer that granted guidance for those who traveled or were lost

The Unmoving Bar, meant to secure a room against intrusion, created by the author

Tyr's Arrow, meant to banish injustice, created by the author

The Elder Futhark

Symbol	Name	Sound	Meaning
ᚠ	Fehu	F	Wealth
ᚢ	Uruz	U	Wild Ox, Auroch
ᚦ	Thurisaz	Th	Giant
ᚨ	Ansuz	A	god
ᚱ	Raido	R	Riding, Ride
ᚲ	Kenaz	K	Torch
ᚷ	Gebo	G	Gift
ᚹ	Wunjo	W	Joy
ᚺ	Haglaz	H	Hail
ᚾ	Naudiz	N	Need, Affliction
ᛁ	Isa	I	Ice
ᛃ	Jeran	J	Harvest
ᛇ	Ihwaz	Ae	Yew

Symbol	Name	Sound	Meaning
ᛈ	Perthro	P	Vessel
ᛉ	Algiz	Z	Elk
ᛊ	Sowilo	S	Sun
ᛏ	Tiwaz	T	Tyr
ᛒ	Berkanan	B	Birch
ᛖ	Ehwaz	E	Horse
ᛗ	Mannaz	M	Human
ᛚ	Laguz	L	Water
ᛜ	Ingwaz	Ng	Ing, Fertility
ᛟ	Othilan	O	Inheritance
ᛞ	Dagaz	D	Day

The Elder Futhark 141

The Elder Futhark is one of the most commonly used of the futharks thanks to its age, being popularized by authors like Ralph Blum, and how directly the runes correspond to most of the modern Latin-style alphabet. The names and meanings of each of these runes were determined by academic runologists through comparing the meanings described for the Younger and Anglo-Saxon Futhorc in their surviving rune poems.[142]

Fehu—Cattle, Liquid Wealth

Fehu is the rune of wealth. In all the rune poems, wealth is portrayed as a source of comfort *and* a cause of discord. Fehu as the rune of cattle represents liquid and portable wealth rather than invested or non-liquid wealth like property.

141. Meanings for the Elder Futhark are from Barnes, 27.

142. Barnes, 157.

Uruz—Auroch, Strength, Labor

Uruz is the rune of the auroch, the prehistoric ancestor of modern cows. The auroch was larger, stronger, and more vicious than domesticated cattle, tying it to strength. It is also tied to labor, as the descendants of the aurochs were used in ancient times as beasts of burden.

Thurisaz—Giants, Danger, Overpowering Might

Thurisaz is the rune of the giant. In the rune poems, the meaning taken is one of the great power, danger, and fear inspired by giants. Giants are also powerful beings, suggesting this is a rune of overwhelming might with the risk of great danger.

Ansuz—Speech, Odin

Ansuz is the Odin rune and the rune of speech. The ties to Odin are shown in the Norwegian and Icelandic poems while speech is present in those and the Anglo-Saxon poem. When used, it can represent Odin, the power of speech, and impact of words.

Raidō—Journey, Travel

Raido is the rune of riding, traveling and the journey itself. The poems reference all these aspects, making Raido a potent symbol of movement through the world. It can represent journeys of all kinds, physical and otherwise.

Kenaz—Fire, Light, Ill-Tidings

Kenaz is a more complex rune. In the Norwegian and Icelandic poems, it is the rune of the boil, a symptom of serious illness. In the Anglo-Saxon poem it is the rune of the torch, light, and flame. What meaning Kenaz takes depends heavily on how and where it is used.

Gebō—Gifts, Exchange

Gebo is the rune of the gift, but its meaning is different from the modern concept. In the ancient world, gift-giving was seen as part of a reciprocal exchange where any who receive gifts were expected to give in exchange. This makes Gebo a rune of exchange, where a gift requires a gift in turn.

Wunjō—Joy, Pleasure, Lust

Wunjo is the rune of joy and pleasure. It also has overtones of lust in some poems, tying it to joy and pleasure, but it can also inspire greed and possessiveness. Wunjo's meaning is therefore dependent on context and circumstances.

Haglaz—Chaos, Upheaval, Opportunity

Haglaz is the rune of the hailstone. It has implications of disaster, chaos, and upheaval. However, the disruption of Haglaz brings the potential for future growth. Whether it is an omen of growth through struggle or destruction depends on how it appears.

Naudiz—Binding, Fate, Necessity

Naudiz is the rune of necessity and fate, with connotations of binding or deep ties. Which meaning it carries depends on how it appears in readings or magical uses. Regardless of which aspect is present, Naudiz should always be heeded.

Isa—Ice, Order, Stasis

Isa is the rune of ice. It represents all that ice is, from a more static form of water to a slow-moving bringer of change. Isa's meaning depends on how you see it appear, with possible meanings including preservation, stagnation, and slow change. It can also have connotations of an unexpected path or new opening as suggested in the Norwegian and Icelandic rune poems.

Jēran—Year, Harvest

Jeran is the rune of a good year and harvest. It represents work coming to fruition, the results of earlier work. Based on the good year meaning, this is a generally positive rune, though it is key to remember what you plant is what you will pluck.

Ihwaz—The Center, Endurance, the Yew

Ihwaz is the rune of the yew tree. In the poems the yew is referred to as being tough, difficult to burn and green in winter. Ihwaz is a rune of endurance and a strongly rooted center, suggesting a point of strength and the qualities needed to persevere.

Perthro—Vessel

Perthro's meaning is not directly given but is hinted at in the Anglo-Saxon rune poem. It refers to Perthro as a source of amusement for the great and something warriors sit around in a hall, suggesting it represents a vessel for food or drink. In this sense, Perthro could mean potential and the vessel that carries it.

Algiz—Barrier, Hidden Danger

Algiz is the rune of the elk-sedge, a type of grass that grows in swamps and marshes. In the Anglo-Saxon poem the elk-sedge cuts anyone who touches it. This suggests the rune algiz represents something seemingly safe that is actually harmful but also something that can be a barrier, depending on context and use.

Sōwilō—Sun

Sowilo is the rune of the sun. In the rune poems, the sun is the light of the world, a source of comfort to travelers and bringer of warmth. Sowilo is a hopeful rune and bringer of good tidings. It represents the power the sun holds in our lives.

Tīwaz—Tyr, Justice

Tiwaz is the rune of Tyr, the god of Justice. In the Norwegian and Icelandic poems, he is explicitly named, while in the Anglo-Saxon poem Tyr, named as Tiw, is called the guiding star. Tiwaz represents all of what Tyr is as a source of guidance and inspiration. It also represents justice in all its forms, whether that is achieved through law or other means.

Berkanan—Birch, Hope, Renewal

Berkanan is the rune of the birch, a tree that is noted in the rune poems for its fresh appearance and green leaves. It carries with it renewal and new growth. It represents the potential for new life, new possibilities and new beginnings to spring forth.

Ehwaz—Cooperation, Horse, Movement

Ehwaz is the rune of the horse. Horses were a means of travel, and according to the Anglo-Saxon poem, a source of comfort and joy for their riders. This also suggests Ehwaz is a rune of cooperation, as horse and rider must work together to move ahead.

Mannaz—Community, Humanity

Mannaz is the rune of humanity. In all of the rune poems the related runes describe the greatest joy of all is sharing space and time with other people. Mannaz represents humanity collectively and the shared communities that make us most human.

Laguz—Water

Laguz is the rune of water and the vastness of the ocean. The poems carry connotations of great mystery and the awe-inspiring power of a great unknown. Water also causes change and is itself changeable.

Ingwaz—Fertility, Seed

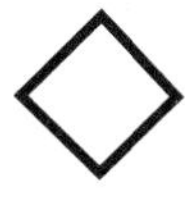

Ingwaz is the rune of Ing, one of the names of Freyr, who is god of fertility. For this reason, runologists believe the rune represents fertility. It is also a rune of potential and new beginnings.

Othilan—Inheritance, Legacy, Property

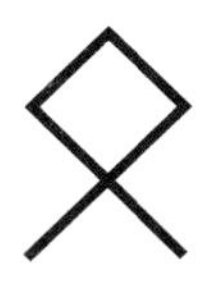

Othilan is the rune of heritage, possessions and property. It represents what is passed on from those who come before you and what you leave behind. Othilan can mean the stability these things provide as well as their impact. Which of these potential meanings it holds depends on the context in which it appears or is invoked.

Dagaz—Dawn, Day, Revelations

Dagaz is the rune of day. It carries with it the coming of light, new beginnings, and potential. Dagaz also emphasizes the light day brings. It can be interpreted as new revelations or epiphanies along with the more literal meaning of a new day.

The Younger Futhark

Symbol	Name	Sound	Meaning
ᚠ	Fe	F	Wealth
ᚢ	Ur	U	Iron/Rain
ᚦ	Thurs	Th	Giant
ᚬ	Oss	A	god
ᚱ	Reid	R	Ride
ᚴ	Kaun	K	Ulcer, Boil
ᚼ	Hagall	H	Hail
ᚾ	Naudr	N	Need
ᛁ	Iss	I	Ice
ᛅ	Ar	A	Plenty
ᛋ	Sol	S	Sun

Symbol	Name	Sound	Meaning
ᛏ	Tyr	T	Tyr
ᛒ	Bjarkan	B	Birch
ᛘ	Madr	M	Man/Human
ᛚ	Logr	L	Sea
ᛦ	Yr	R	Yew

The Younger Futhark 143

The meanings of the Younger Futhark are known thanks to the surviving Norwegian and Iceland rune poems. Though they provide direct, clear meanings for what each rune likely meant, each poem offers a different perspective on these meanings. The meanings are also not as straightforward because both poems, particularly the Norwegian one, freely use kennings to convey meaning, suggesting there were additional layers or implications those composing the poem would have clearly understood.

Fé—Cattle, Liquid Wealth, Jealousy

In the Younger Futhark, Fe as wealth is treated in a very cautious light. In the Younger Futhark wealth is a creator of discord and potentially a source of comfort or security. If Fe emerges or is used, be careful with the context, as there's more than meets the eye with this rune.

Ur—Iron, Rain

Here Ur, as rain or iron, has a very different meaning from the Elder and Anglo-Saxon Futharks. It is called rain in the Icelandic poem, iron in the Norwegian poem, and in both places is treated with caution. Rain at the wrong time can ruin a harvest, and bad iron can bring death to the user. Ur must be used with respect for its double-edged power.

143. All Younger Futhark rune meanings are taken from *Runic and Heroic Poems of the Old Teutonic Peoples*, edited by Bruce Dickens, Cambridge University Press (Cambridge: 1915), 24-33

Thurs—Giants, Overwhelming Power

Like the Elder Futhark, Thurs is the rune of the giant. In the Younger Futhark, giants are seen as dangerous and harmful to people. They are also beings of great power with great means to cause harm. Thurs must be treated with the same care as Thurisaz, whether it appears in a reading or is used in a working.

Oss—Estuary, Odin, Openings

Oss, like Ur, has two different meanings in the Younger Futhark. In the Norwegian poem, Oss is the rune of the estuary, a rivermouth that opens into the sea. In the Icelandic poem, it is associated with the god Odin. Between the two, it represents a place where things flow out into the world or Odin as a bringer of knowledge.

Reid—Travel

Reid is the rune of travel and journeying. As the rune of riding, it also carries an extra emphasis of a speedy journey (at least in the Icelandic poem), and calls attention to the burden it places on the steed. Reid can represent travel in every sense, including the abstract.

Kaun—Disease, Harm, the Ulcer

In the Younger Futhark, Kaun is the rune of the ulcer. It is clearly described as a symptom of worse diseases that bring a bitter end for its victim. It is a warning sign, an indication of a source of harm, or an omen of malice.

Hagall—Destruction, Hail, New Possibility

Hagall is the rune of hail and new potential. Both poems call it the cold grain, showing that while hailstones can bring destruction, they also carry within them the seed of new growth. This makes Hagall a rune of ending and beginning.

Naudr—Binding, Frustration, Obstacles

In the Younger Futhark, Naudr is the rune of binding, restriction, and the grief they bring. It represents restraining obstacles, whether imposed by yourself or others, signaling the existence of chains in need of breaking or invoking their essence.

Iss—Ice, Order, Stasis

Iss, like in the Elder Futhark, is the rune of ice. It represents both the steady, grinding change of glaciers and ice's ability to lock things in place. It also, as is suggested in both poems, represents the potential opportunities that ice can open up, similar to how a frozen lake or river can provide a new road for travelers.

Ar—Abundance, Generosity

Ar, as the rune of plenty, stands in stark contrast to Fe. Where Fe in the Younger Futhark warns of the strife caused by wealth. Ar is more positive. What sets Ar apart is the emphasis on sharing abundance generously with others. Ar invokes and represents plenty while also reminding us that bounty should be shared, not hoarded.

Sól—Sun

Sol is the rune of the sun. In the Younger Futhark is special emphasis on its role as a bringer of light and warmth, suggesting it is a rune full of potential and transformative power.

Týr—Justice, Tyr

Tyr is the rune of the god bearing the same name. In the Younger Futhark, this rune is unquestionably his, making it associated with all he represents. This rune suggests the presence of the One-Handed God in what is at work and can bring all forms of justice.

Bjarkan—Birch, Renewal

Bjarkan is the rune of the birch in the Younger Futhark. In these poems, the birch's greenery and freshness is emphasized, showing it is a rune of new possibility and growth.

Madr—Community, Humanity

Madr is the Younger Futhark rune of humanity. In the poems, it describes the greatest joy comes from the company of others. Humanity, under Madr, is realized through community with others. Its appearance or invocation carries the same power.

Logr—Water

Logr is the Younger Futhark rune of water. In the poems, water's movements are the focus, whether it is in the shape of a stream, waterfall, or geyser. This shows water as a changeable, dynamic force. Logr carries the same power in readings and invocation.

Yr—Bow, Endurance, Yew

Yr is the Younger Futhark rune of the yew tree. In the Norwegian poem, Yew is the greenest of trees in the depths of winter, showing its endurance. The Icelandic poem speaks of using yew for making bows. This shows Yr is enduring, flexible, and potent, representing many possibilities when invoked or appearing in a reading.

The Anglo-Saxon Futhorc

Symbol	Name	Sound	Meaning
ᚠ	feoh	f	Wealth
ᚢ	ūr	u	Aurochs
ᚦ	thorn	th	Thorn
ᚩ	ōs	o	god
ᚱ	rād	r	Ride
ᚳ	cēn	c	Torch

Symbol	Name	Sound	Meaning
ᚷ	gyfu	g	Gift
ᚹ	ƿynn	ƿ, w	Mirth
ᚻ	hægl	h	Hail
ᚾ	nȳd	n	Need
ᛁ	īs	i	Ice
ᛄ	gēr	j	Year, harvest
ᛇ	ēoh	eo	Yew
ᛈ	peord	p	Vessel
ᛉ	eolh	x	Hidden danger, barrier
ᛊ	sigel	s	Sun
ᛏ	tīƿ	t	Glory
ᛒ	beorc	b	Birch
ᛖ	eh	e	Horse
ᛗ	mann	m	Man
ᛚ	lagu	l	Water
ᛝ	Ing	ŋ	Ing (a hero)
ᛟ	ēdel	œ	Ethel (estate)
ᛞ	dæg	d	Day
ᚪ	āc	a	Oak
ᚫ	æsc	æ	Ash-tree
ᚣ	ȳr	y	Bow
ᛡ	īor	ia, io	Eel
ᛠ	ēar	ea	Grave

The Anglo-Saxon Futhorc 144

144. All Anglo-Saxon Futhark rune meanings are taken from the translation by R.I. Page, *An Introduction to English Runes*, Boydell Press (Woodbridge: 1999), 65-76

The names and meanings of the Anglo-Saxon Futhorc come from a single surviving poem. The Anglo-Saxon Futhorc poem is more detailed in descriptions of the runes. It also shows much more explicit Christian influences. Even so, the similarities between what the Anglo-Saxon runes represent and those in the Younger Futhark suggest their meanings are based on pre-Christian ideas.

Feoh—Cattle, Wealth

Feoh, the Anglo-Saxon Futhark rune for wealth, is a straightforward representation of material, liquid wealth. The rune poem urges the reader to be generous with their wealth, giving it freely to others. Feoh carries the same power when read or invoked.

Ur—Auroch, Endurance and Strength

Ur, like in the Elder Futhark, is the rune of the auroch. It is described as fierce and powerful, showing great strength and endurance. Ur carries the same power and meaning, showing the strength of steady labor when read and invoked.

Thorn—Thorn, Potential Danger

Thorn is the rune of the thorn in the Anglo-Saxon Futhark. Thorn is said to be very sharp, harmful, and dangerous to others because of this. In this understanding, Thorn has a clear sense of harm attached to it, suggesting this rune should be seen as a warning of potential harm.

Os—Mouth, Speech

Os is the rune of the mouth and speech. In the Anglo-Saxon poem, it is a source of wisdom, comfort, and joy for all. This shows Os has the power to sway others and cause change or harm, as all speech and words do. It shows the need of words when read or embody their power when invoked.

Rād—Riding, Travel

Rad, like Raido, is the rune of travel and riding. Here it also carries the message that journeys may seem easy at first but have their own challenges. In a reading, Rad shows travel of some sort lies ahead. When invoked, it can carry the wanderer forward.

Cēn—Fire, Torch

Cen is the rune of the torch. It represents light and flame harnessed to improve people's lives. It is more controlled than raw fire but still carries the potential for destruction. The same is true when Cen is read or invoked.

Gyfu—Generosity, Gifts

Gyfu is the rune of the gift and generosity. In the Anglo-Saxon Futhorc, giving to others and sharing your bounty are praised. Giving in turn requires gifts in exchange, showing the pattern of a gift for a gift. When invoked, Gyfu calls up the wisdom of exchange; when read, it shows exchange may be necessary to reach the desired result.

Wynn—Bliss, Joy

Wynn is the rune of bliss. It is a positive rune that defines what is necessary to have joy. The poem says eliminating suffering and creating prosperity are necessary for creating the ideal conditions for bliss. When read or invoked, Wynn could refer to the coming of such circumstances, or the need to create them, and it brings the power to do so.

Hægl—Destruction, Hail, Renewal

Haegl is the rune of hail. In the Anglo-Saxon Futhorc, it is referred to as a grain along with vivid descriptions of how it whirls around violently in the sky. In reading and invocation, it carries the double meaning of the destruction hail can bring along with the potential for new growth.

Nyd—Adversity, Need

Nyd is the rune of need and adversity. Like in the Younger Futhark, it is clearly seen as an obstacle to a better life. However, in contrast to the Younger Futhark, it also suggests such adversity makes a person better in the long run. When invoked or read, Nyd warns of such difficulties while reminding us that they are often chances for us to grow.

Is—Cold, Frost, Ice

Is is the rune of Ice. In the Anglo-Saxon Futhorc, most of the emphasis is on cold and its fair appearance. Like Isa, Is carries with it all of what ice means while also showing the cold that brings stillness as the core of its essence. When read or invoked, Is reminds us of ice's static power and the creeping cold that brings it.

Ger—Harvest, the Year

Ger is the rune of the year and the harvest. It represents the abundance and prosperity that comes from a year's labors. Suggesting Christian influences, it also emphasizes the role of God in providing this. The implication is that fate has a very deep impact on our work through the year, and we should be mindful of it when Ger is read or invoked.

Eoh—Center, Stability, Yew

Eoh is the rune of the yew tree. In the Anglo-Saxon Futhorc, the main focus is on how strongly it holds in the earth and improves the land where it stands. When read or invoked, Eoh shows the power of a strong center that can enrich all around it.

Peorth—Vessel

Peorth is vague in its meaning, though based on the poem it appears to represent some sort of vessel that holds food or drink in a hall. Based on what is known (and keeping in mind the scholars' debate on this rune's meaning), Peorth carries the power of both great potential and a container for holding it when read or invoked.

Eolh—Barrier, Elk Sedge, Hidden Danger

Eolh is the rune of the elk-sedge, a type of grass found in marshlands. In the Anglo-Saxon Futhorc, it is clearly depicted as potentially harmful in spite of its innocent appearance. When read, Eolh offers a warning; when invoked, it can be used to ward off danger with hidden defenses.

Sigel—Guidance, Sun

Sigel is the rune of the sun. It is shown as a source of light, joy, and hope for those journeying on the sea. In the Anglo-Saxon Futhorc, Sigel is both the sun's power and a source of guidance when read or invoked.

Tiw—The North Star

Unlike in the other futharks, Tiw is not associated with Tyr in the Anglo-Saxon Futhorc. It is instead described as a source of guidance that lives in the sky, a fixed point of reference, and useful to those who lead. In this way, Tiw is a point of reference, either literal or abstract, when read or invoked.

Beorc—Beginnings, Birch, Vitality

Beorc is the rune of the birch. In the Anglo-Saxon Futhorc, it refers to birch's beauty and vitality. Beorc represents such potential, growth, and new beginnings when it appears in a reading.

Eh—Horse, Partnership

Eh is the rune of the horse. It is described here as a joy to riders and a source of comfort for travelers. It is more than just a means for journeying, suggesting one should heed what helps you move through life and the world. These meanings are present in Eh when it is invoked or read.

Mann—Humanity

Mann is the rune of humanity. Like in the other futharks, the emphasis here is how we are at our most human when we are participating in a healthy, supportive, and nurturing community. When read, it suggests all things tied to humanity and community. When invoked, it can bring out what makes these possible.

Lagu—Ocean, Water

Lagu is the rune of water, with emphasis on the ocean. In the Anglo-Saxon Futhorc, Lagu carries more potential of danger, fear, and uncertainty. If Lagu is invoked or read, it has all of the potential, uncertainty, and risk that comes with the vast power of the ocean depths

Ing—The Hero

Ing is the rune of a great hero. In the Anglo-Saxon Futhorc, it is associated with a person who came to the East-Danes before departing again by sea. Ing, when read, may suggest the coming of times that make heroes or be invoked to bring these qualities forward.

Edel—Estate, Inheritance, Legacy

Edel is the rune of the estate and inheritance. It is the fruits of your forebears' labor as well as what you leave behind. Edel is property and the process through which it is accumulated, passed on and influences people's lives. If it is invoked or read, it reminds us of what came before and what comes from our actions.

Dæg—Beginnings, Dawn, Day

Daeg is the rune of day. In the Anglo-Saxon Futhorc, it focuses on hope and new possibilities. Daeg can be invoked to bring forth this power and, when read, suggests a new beginning is coming.

Ac—Oak, Stability, Support, Sustenance

Ac is the rune of the oak tree. The poem discusses how oaks provide food for pigs, shelter, and are strong enough to withstand the fury of sea storms. When read, it could mean there is a new source of support coming or that such strength will be needed. When invoked, the oak's power is called upon.

Aesc—Ash, Endurance

Aesc is the rune of the ash tree. The ash tree is described as tall, precious to humans, a valuable source of wood, and very tough. Aesc represents endurance and toughness when read or invoked, giving strength or suggesting endurance will be needed soon.

Yr—Bow, Tools

Yr is the rune of the bow. It is described as a source of joy and honor while also being useful equipment on a journey. This is likely because in ancient times bows were used to hunt for food. Yr represents reliable instruments, both in needing and having them, when read, and when invoked, what such tools give to their user.

Iar—Crossing Boundaries, Eel

Iar is the rune of the eel. In the poem, the eel is described as a river dweller that survives by capturing land-based prey. In readings, Iar can suggest a need to leave your comfort zone to get what you need to survive or thrive. When invoked, it can also help give the means to reach beyond your limits and press into unfamiliar territory.

Ear—Death, Endings, Grave

Ear is the rune of the grave. In the poem, the grave is a thing most dreaded, as it is the place of the greatest ending. It also is the home of the dead. These aspects make it a very potent rune. When read, it suggests a powerful, earth-shattering ending is coming, or to heed the dead's wisdom; when invoked, it can call such power into the world.

Symbols of Power

The runes represent elements of the mentality of the Norse peoples. They provide insights into what they held dear, how they viewed the world and what was important. They also, for the modern practitioner, provide useful tools for art and mystical purposes. The magic of runes is the magic of words, ideas and concepts given form. They offer a way for understanding these deeper concepts, how they are shaped, and what they mean.

The next exercise is meant to help you internalize their meaning, wrestle with it, and understand your own perceptions of the concepts each rune represents. As written, the following exercise is meant to be done with one rune at a time. That doesn't mean you can't do it more than once, and you may feel called to do so. Whatever insights you gain from this exercise should be supplemented with study of the runes based on credible, academic sources.

exercise

BREATHING THE RUNES

This exercise is for getting a deeper understanding of each rune, their meanings, and their applications.

Begin with three breath cycles to calm the body.

After finishing your three breaths, do the Calming the Sea and Sky exercise. When the waters are calm and the sky is clear, you may proceed with the next step.

Close your eyes and draw the rune in your mind. When it is completed, do one breath cycle. As you breathe, feel the energy of the breath enter the rune. Do not force any particular form for how this manifests in the rune; let the rune respond in whatever way feels right.

Begin a second breath cycle. With this breath cycle, let your mind be filled with whatever words, images, sounds or feelings you most associate with the rune. Let whatever emerges be what comes most naturally and easily, rather than fitting any preconceived image of what should be. The results may be surprising to you.

Breathe in to a count of nine while keeping whatever emerged during the previous step in your mind. As you breathe out say the rune's name to a count of nine. As you do so, feel whatever you have associated with that rune flow out with your speech.

Begin a third breath cycle. With this cycle, like the first breath cycle in this exercise, feel the energy of your breath fill the rune again.

Breathe in to a count of nine, then, as you breathe out, say the rune's name to a count of nine. As you do this, visualize the rune leaving your mind and flowing out from you with your breath. Spend some time sitting with the feelings, images, sounds, and other associations the rune brought up for you.

chapter seven

THE ART OF SEIÐR

Then Odin rode to the eastern door,
There, he knew well, was the wise-woman's grave;
Magic he spoke and mighty charms,
Till spell-bound she rose, and in death she spoke
BALDRS DRAUMAR 4

Seiðr is a uniquely Norse form of mysticism. Scholars discuss seiðr in many different terms. Some call it witchcraft, others a form of spirit work, and some a form of sorcery. Some seiðworkers had the power to divine the future and uncover hidden knowledge. Others could speak to the dead. On the battlefield, seiðworkers clouded their foes' judgment, binding their courage and will to fight. There are even accounts of seiðworkers conjuring storms, healing the sick, shapeshifting, and performing other acts best described as magical.[145]

Even with the fragmented information we have, it is clear seiðr was very important in the ancient world. Odin was said to be a seiðworker and two whole sagas, the Voluspo and the Baldrs Draumar, show his power over the

145. H.R. Ellis Davidson, *Gods and Myths of Northern Europe*, Penguin Books (New York: 1964), 117–121; Jenny Blain, *Nine Worlds of Seid-Magic: Ecstasy and Neo-Shamanism in North European Paganism*, Routledge (London & New York: 2002), 114; Davidson *The Road to Hel* 154–155; Price, 64.

dead to compel answers from the Nameless Seeress. Odin is not even the most skilled of the gods in this art, with Freyja named as his teacher and an expert in seiðr. Frigga is also said to be skilled in seiðr, with the art being a possible source of her great knowledge of many hidden things.[146]

Scholars have long argued where seiðr came from. One prevailing theory is seiðr came from the Saami peoples of northern Scandinavia. This argument, described by Stefanie V. Schnurbein, claims cultural exchanges between Norse and Saami groups lead to Saami techniques being transmitted to the rest of Scandinavia. Jenny Blain argues this is likely, asserting the process was probably one where the techniques, ideas and methods of the Saami were integrated into existing Norse practices. Neil Price also offers support for this theory, providing specific examples of documented overlap between Saami and Norse seiðr practices, including ancient accounts of Saami performing seiðr. This suggests the stories of the Vanir teaching seiðr to the Aesir may also be a cultural memory of this process.[147]

Seiðr was also a transgressive art, seen in ancient times as more associated with women than men. Odin was named by chronicler Snorri Sturluson as *ergi*, a very loaded Old Norse word associated with being the receptive sexual partner or engaging in traditionally feminine sexual practice because of his learning seiðr. Scholars have observed a similar stigma was attached to seidworkers as other mystical workers, such as witches, in later times. This has led to many associating the art with queer sexuality and practices. Even so, there are examples of men practicing seiðr, suggesting the stigma attached may in part be due to the biases of Christian chroniclers like Snorri and Victorian-era translators who amplified existing attitudes to match their own assumptions.[148]

Seiðr today consists of three main forms. They are utiseta, sorcery and spae. All are conducted in an ecstatic state as discussed earlier in Chapter Four. There are a few additional resources you can consult in Appendix I on modern seiðr. This chapter is a general introduction to this art. Those who wish to

---

146. Davidson *Gods and Myths of Northern Europe* 48, 119–121.

147. Stefanie V. Schnurbein, "Shamanism in the Old Norse Tradition: A Theory between Ideological Camps", *History of Religions*, Vol. 43, No. 2 (November 2003), 117–120; Blain 135-136; Price, 48.

148. Blain 17–19, 114–115.

learn more should seek instruction from experienced practitioners in seiðr or other similar disciplines like mediumship and trance possession.

Understanding the Self

The Self, in Norse practice, is seen very differently from the conventional division of body, mind, and soul. In Radical Norse Paganism, as inspired by the ancients, the Self is made of four parts. These are your physical form, known as hamr, your mind, which is called hugr, your spiritual shadow or subconscious that is named fylgja, and your luck, which is referred to as hamingja. Understanding how they collectively make you who you are and what they do is essential for seiðr and can help you better know yourself.

Hamr (pronounced *HAM-er*) is your physical form. The root of hamr is your body but that is not all there is to hamr. Hamr is your whole form, including how you present yourself, how you dress, the way you move, and your body language. The ancients believed the hamr could be changed and called this art shapeshifting. Berserkers were said to be shapeshifters who took on the abilities of different animals, usually bears or wolves, to gain their strength and ferocity before going into battle. On the surface, the idea of changing physical form may sound fantastical or ludicrous. Upon digging deeper, however, there is a far more profound truth. How everyone acts, appears and dresses are things you control that change how people react to you. Adopting different garb and mannerisms, like wearing a suit and speaking in jargon or putting on a mask, is as much an act of shapeshifting as when the berserkers took up their famous bearskins. Hamr is more than flesh and blood; it is everything that makes up how you move in the world and how people perceive you.[149]

Hugr (pronounced *HOO-ger*) is your mind. It is thought, consciousness, and awareness. Through your hugr you can understand and shape the world around you. In the ancient world it was said those with a strong mind could directly influence the world with their thoughts. This might sound highly esoteric, but the powers of mind provide you with the means to understand, perceive and direct your efforts to cause change. Hugr can also give you the

149. Bettina Sejbjerg Sommer, "The Norse Concept of Luck", *Scandinavian Studies,* Vol. 79 No. 3 (Fall: 2007), 282; Davidson, *Gods and Myths of Northern Europe* 67–68; Price, 244–246.

words, creativity, and inspiration to put ideas in motion. When you know your own hugr you can better influence on the world around you.[150]

Fylgja (pronounced *FILL-ge-yah*; the plural, fylgjur, is pronounced *FILL -ge-yur*) is your spiritual shadow. It is your subconsciousness, a reflection of your hidden desires, and an extension of your Self. You could see your fylgja as the voice in the back of your head that questions what you are doing, urges you to question what is in front of you, or decides to play some catchy jingle in your brain for three hours just because. As much as it might sound like a troublemaker and distraction, when you are in tune with your fylgja it serves as a powerful ally. The fylgja may catch things that you miss or overlook. During workings, this shadow self can take on the shape of an animal, moving around and acting independently of you as a guardian or a guide. The ancients believed highly skilled seiðworkers could use their fylgja to carry their hugr out to watch over others or deliver a working. Being in tune with your fylgja gives you both a better understanding of who you are, the world around you, and serves as a powerful ally.[151]

Hamingja (pronounced *HA-ming-ya*) is Luck. How your hamingja interacts with Fate is explained earlier in chapter two, but it is mentioned again here for its part in how it works as a component that makes up your Self. As your capacity to change the world, Hamingja can be gained or lost through your actions; you could consider it the sum of all your knowledge, tools, capabilities, and influence in the world. What makes hamingja different from simply seeing it as the sum of these things is that hamingja is a part of your Self just as much as your body or mind. Just as these capabilities can be loaned out or used to support others, you can give some of your hamingja to others and strengthen their Luck. The ancients believed that if a person's hamingja was especially strong, it could pass on to relatives, be reborn in a new form, and be called on by others after its owner died. As your means to influence the world around you, hamingja is your Self's metaphysical muscle.[152]

Understanding the parts of the Self will give you greater insights into who you are and can unlock your true potential. Each is a part of the greater whole

---

150. Sommer, 279–280; Davidson, *Gods and Myths of Northern Europe,* 120; Price, 244–246.

151. Blain, 65; Davidson, *Gods and Myths of Northern Europ,e* 118–119; Sommer, 282.

152. Davidson, *The Road to Hel,* 132–133; Sommer, 279, 282.

that is you. Understanding each on their own terms brings deeper understanding and self-knowledge. Thinking on how they all come together and complement each other will bring you closer to living as a whole, complete Self. Even if you never practice any of the forms of seiðr, understanding the four-part Self brings its own wisdom. If you do pursue the mystic arts, each is used in the three forms of seiðr in their own unique, powerful ways built on this self-awareness.

Utiseta

Utiseta is the most personal and safest of the three forms of seiðr. The word means "sitting out" and comes from the Old Norse expression *seti uti til frodleiks*, "sitting out for wisdom." Utiseta is both a form of meditation and a mystical art used for answering challenging questions. The most famous example of utiseta from the ancient world is where the Icelandic lawspeaker Thorgeirr went "under the cloak" to resolve the growing divide between Christian and Pagan Icelanders in 1000 CE. Thorgeirr was respected by all parties as fair-minded and sought out a solution through sitting out:[153]

> . . . then Thorgeirr lay down, and spread his cloak over him, and he lay all day, and the night after, saying no word. And the next morning he sat up and called people to the Law Rock.[154]

For the Norse, utiseta was an accepted way of gaining hidden or inaccessible knowledge. There were many places the information came from, with much speculation as to what the source of knowledge was. In most cases, utiseta moves you into a space where you can more directly contemplate the patterns of Fate, giving deeper understanding of potential cause and effect. However, there are other uses of utiseta in the ancient sources. One common application of this form by vǫlur was getting information from the dead by sitting out on grave-mounds. You can also use utiseta for journeying to the other

153. Blain, 60–61.

154. Ibid.

Nine Worlds or for speaking with local spirits and receiving guidance directly from the Powers.[155]

As a mostly solitary form of seiðr, utiseta can be learned and practiced by anyone on their own. The foundation of utiseta, like all other forms of seiðr, rest on working in an ecstatic state and understanding the parts of the Self. During utiseta, your hugr goes into the Nine Worlds, reaches out to spirits or taps into fate, and is protected by your fylgja. During utiseta anything you experience is filtered by your mind and experiences into the easiest form for you to understand. What you see in utiseta and how you interpret it will always be different from what others see, making understanding a highly personal process.

If you want to practice utiseta, the best place to start is by doing regular meditations as discussed in chapter four. The exercises in this book will help you build your meditative skills. Regular practice cultivates the discipline, focus and controlled shift into ecstatic states necessary for utiseta. When you are comfortable in your ecstatic practice, you can then attempt your first utiseta journey. The exercise at the end of this chapter, Going to the Well, is a good format to follow for your first time. Once you have finished your journey or have encountered something that's more than you can handle, it's really easy to end the journey. You do this by focusing on your hamr and its physical surroundings.

When you have finished a journey, take some time to ground yourself back in the physical world. You can do this by having something to drink or eat, going for a walk, or using the Spatial Awareness exercise. This helps bring you back into reality and is essential for a healthy understanding of utiseta.

You should always balance any insights gained through utiseta with other information regarding any questions you are exploring while on your journey. Utiseta provides new or unconventional perspectives that can help provide solutions, but utiseta alone is never enough. It is best used along with other forms of divination, outside research, investigation, and critical analysis. Like all skills, your first attempts at utiseta may be challenging but will become easier with practice and discipline. As you get more comfortable with utiseta, you can, if you choose, easily add it into your daily practice.

155. Blain, 60–63; Davidson, *The Road to Hel,* 144–145.

Sorcery

Sorcery is the second form of seiðr. Sorcery in seiðr is the art of using the parts of your Self to directly manipulate Fate and change the world around you. In many sources, both ancient and modern, the term seiðr refers to this specific use of power as well as utiseta and spae. To make things even more confusing, some call it witchcraft, wizardry, magic, and energy work. This book uses the term sorcery for second form seiðr because this is one of the commonly accepted translations of the word seiðr and to avoid any confusion. Regardless of the specific term you use, sorcery is very different from utiseta and spae because unlike these forms of seiðr, the point of sorcery to cause direct change instead of gathering information. The ancients believed you could use it for everything from cursing enemies to banishing hostile spirits, curing illness, and even conjuring thunderstorms.[156]

There is little surviving documentation describing exactly how Norse sorcery was done. Most of what exists comes from Scandinavian folk practices and customs. How you do sorcery will be different from how others do it. What matters is any methods used are ones you genuinely understand, have not appropriated without permission or proper training, and work best for you. One common choice is using different forms of rune magic, like galdr or bindrunes, as a part of seiðr workings. Even with all the variety of how you do it, sorcery generally has three types of workings that are commonly practiced by seiðworkers. These are spirit work, shape-changing, and direct sorcery.

Sorcery uses all four of the parts of the Self to cause change in the world. In sorcery, your hamingja is the metaphysical muscle that gives power to your workings. If your hamingja is the oomph that gives the working power, then your hugr is the tool you use to direct your workings. Your fylgja acts as a guide and protector, providing advice and safety during the working while your hamr is a medium that can be altered by sorcery. One way you can think of how the parts of the Self work is to think of sorcery like singing. Hugr is your voice shaping the music that is the working, hamingja your lungs giving breath to the song, fylgja the muse whispering in your ear, and Fate (or, if you are practicing shapeshifting, hamr) is the air that carries it into the world.

156. Blain, 16, 114.

No matter what you are doing or what your goal is, you should be careful with sorcery. All these methods bind your parts of your Self in the workings in a very intimate way that can impact your life in unpredictable and unexpected ways. The best way to protect yourself from unintended consequences is to be very precise in what you are doing, consider the possible impacts of your working, and be as careful as possible. Regardless of what you do, sorcery is not a replacement for doing the necessary work to make your goals happen. A working for getting a better job or removing an obstacle cannot bring these changes into your life if you don't act to make them reality. Sorcery, like rune-magic, may tilt the odds in your favor but can't make life happen for you.

Spirit-work is a straightforward form of seiðr. Interacting with spirits is a quite common form of seiðr for modern practitioners in most Norse Pagan traditions, including this one. Seiðworkers may seek out spirits for guidance, information and sometimes ask for their help. Petitioning spirits for information or assistance is the safest form of sorcery because you are reaching out to different spirits and bargaining with them instead of directly using your own hamingja to directly change Fate. These bargains usually include making oaths, giving the spirit specific offerings or performing tasks on the spirit's behalf. Even though spirit work is safer than direct sorcery, it is not risk-free. Many practitioners have encountered hostile spirits who were difficult to work with or actively tried to hurt the practitioner. In such cases, your best defenses are your fylgja, protective bindrunes, or workings combined with pulling yourself back, as described under utiseta. Be assured that spirit work is relatively safe even with these dangers; it allows you to build on existing relationships you have with local spirits and can deepen these relationships.[157]

Shape-changing is the art of changing your hamr. There are many ways you can do this; the most mundane include changing your clothes and how you speak. When you are engaging in sorcerous shape-changing, you take this foundation to the next level. Visualization and action conducted in an ecstatic state make it easier to focus specifically on more subtle changes like body language, mannerisms, and movement. The most radical changes come from focusing on specific elements of other beings, such as bears or wolves, as was the case with berserkers, and acting them out during ecstatic states. In some ways,

157. Blain, 63–65.

shape-changing is very similar to the processes used by actors to get inside the head of a part or role so they can give a better performance. Shape-changing happens on many levels, from the obvious different garb to the subtle difference in tone and body language.

The third method of sorcery is direct sorcery. This form is where you use elements of your Self to cause change in the world. This work is the riskiest form of seiðr as these workings very intimately tie your Self into the working, the changes to Fate, and the consequences unleashed. Like all other forms of sorcery, direct sorcery is best done in an ecstatic state. In this state you will use a combination of visualization, proxy objects, chants, poems, and whatever else helps you focus your Self for manifesting a specific change. It cannot be said enough that you should exercise caution and restraint when performing direct sorcery. The earlier warnings of unintended consequences and outcomes are in full force here. Like all other forms of sorcery, a direct working is not enough on its own to make the changes you desire come into the world. Be careful, precise, and—above all else—ethical in your uses of direct sorcery.

Spae

Spae is a form of seiðr where the practitioner, known as a spaeworker, becomes a channel, giving their voice to one of the Powers so they may speak through the spaeworker. Spaeworkers were figures of awe and fear in ancient society. Their arts set them apart from society, yet their skills were frequently sought. A description of the spaewoman of Greenland in the Saga of Erik the Red shows the importance of spaeworkers for the Norse peoples:

> He invited, therefore, the spae-queen to his house, and prepared for her a hearty welcome, as was the custom wherever a reception was accorded a woman of this kind. A high seat was prepared for her, and a cushion laid thereon in which were poultry-feathers. Now, when she came in the evening, accompanied by the man who had been sent to meet her, she was dressed in such wise that she had a blue mantle over her, with strings for the neck, and it was inlaid with gems quite down to the skirt. On her neck she had glass beads. On her head she had a black hood of lambskin,

> lined with ermine. A staff she had in her hand, with a knob thereon; it was ornamented with brass, and inlaid with gems round about the knob. Around her she wore a girdle of soft hair, and therein was a large skin-bag, in which she kept the talismans needful to her in her wisdom. She wore hairy calf-skin shoes on her feet, with long and strong-looking thongs to them, and great knobs of latten at the ends. On her hands she had gloves of ermine-skin, and they were white and hairy within.[158]

The garments of the spaewomen show she is very wealthy and treated with great respect. Thorkell, the host, goes out of his way to make his home as welcoming as possible. He sets out a cushioned seat for her and the feast in her honor is a very impressive spread with many rich dishes.

Spae is a possessory form of spiritual work. In some cases, the spaeworker is directly under the control of the Power called on for the working. Other cases may have the spaeworker act as an intermediary who receives messages from the specific Power, conveys questions from others and delivers that Power's answer. Regardless, there are two big differences between spae and other forms of seiðr: Spae is always a form of possessory work or mediumship, and spae, unlike sorcery or utiseta, is always a communal practice. Spae sessions have questioners who approach the spaeworker seeking answers and the spaeworker provides answers as best as possible.[159]

If you are interested in learning spae, the best way to do it is finding in-person, hands-on training from people who are experienced spaeworkers or have done similar work like mediumship. Apprentices studying spae under a trained spaeworker learn the craft by working in support roles for their teacher. In these positions they help bring the spaeworker back from deep trances, guide all who approach the spaeworker and assist in creating an ecstatic state for the spaeworker with song and music. This was as true in ancient times as it is in the present day.[160]

---

158. Chapter 4, *The Saga of Erik the Red*, translated by J. Sephton.

159. Blain, 63, 66–67.

160. Blain 33, 35–36.

Like all other forms of seiðr, spaeworkers do their practice in an ecstatic state. This opens their minds to different sources of information, processing sensations, and obtaining insights. During spae, practitioners have their focus divided between the physical and spiritual. This divided attention is another reason why spaeworkers have assistants or apprentices supporting them in the work.[161]

If you want further information, seek out in-person training and attend a few spae sessions. Spae should **never** be done alone or learned out of a book. There have been instances where improperly, incompletely, or self-taught spaeworkers have experienced involuntary possession. Some use spae to blame possessory entities for engaging in harmful behaviors. Properly trained spaeworkers know how to reassert control during possessory work, prevent involuntary experiences and affirm what is ethical behavior. For these reasons you should not study spae as a solitary practitioner and all uses of spae should always be conducted with other experienced spaeworkers. The information in this section is enough to give you an idea of what spae is. If spae is something you want to do, always study it in person with an experienced, proven spaeworker or someone who has proven skill in related disciplines like mediumship or possessory trance. Spae is not for everyone, and it is very common for Norse Pagans to practice the other forms of seiðr without ever doing spae.

Work of the Self

Seiðr is a deep, powerful art whose tools offer great potential for insights and change to their users. Many modern practitioners have used its skills to deepen their relationship with the Powers. Others have refrained from using seiðr while still seeking out the insights of those skilled in its ways. It can be deeply uncomfortable for some, but any distress can also bring greater understanding of the Self and the world. Whether you choose to practice seiðr, or which forms you prefer, is entirely up to you and what you are comfortable with.

The exercise at the end of this chapter is an introduction to utiseta. You should practice the other exercises in this book regularly before attempting it, as Going to the Wells effectively depends on developing other key skills. Regular, daily practice will help you hone the necessary discipline and focus for

---

161. Blain 33, 36–37.

effective utiseta. When ready, you may begin this exercise and take your first big step into a much larger world.

exercise
GOING TO THE WELLS

Begin by finding a calm, undisturbed place for doing the working. Make sure there are no potential distractions when you first practice this exercise. With experience, this can be done in places like public parks or even in a busy crowd. Even so, when you first engage in Walking the World Tree, it should be in a calm, undisturbed place.

Conduct the Breath exercise in chapter one. Complete as many breath cycles as you feel are necessary until your heart reaches a resting state.

Once you have reached a resting state, begin the Sea and Sky exercise. When you are doing Going to the Wells make sure you continue the Sea and Sky exercise until the sea is smooth as glass and the sky is completely clear. When engaging in utiseta, it is critical you are as calm and relaxed as possible. This makes you more receptive to what may come during the work. After you have completed the Sea and Sky exercise, perform the World Tree Within exercise from chapter four. After you have completed this exercise and held the extremes of void and core within, you may proceed to the next step.

Feel the version of the World Tree that has just been running through you. Imagine you are now on the Tree, holding onto the trunk and its branches.

Visualize yourself climbing down the Tree until you reach where the trunk meets the soil Yggdrasil is planted in.

Walk along the base until you see a great, open pool before you. This is the Well of Urdr. In the lore it is said those who wish to drink from it must sacrifice something in exchange, but you will not be doing this for the purposes of this exercise.

Gaze deep into the Well. Let whatever images surface run through your mind. Pay attention to what you see but do not try to analyze. Allow what emerges from the Well to flow freely through you.

With practice, it is possible to approach the Well seeking guidance for specific questions or problems by fixing them in your mind as you climb the tree. Such an approach should be conducted later with time and experience. While you are starting out, focus on reaching the Well and taking in what you see.

When you feel you have seen enough, imagine yourself stepping away from the Well. Feel your body again, take a deep breath, and awaken. Think on what you experienced and its potential meaning.

chapter eight

FINDING COMMUNITY

All wretched is no one, though never so sick;
Some from their children have joy,
Some win it from kinsmen,
and some from their wealth,
And some from worthy works.
HAVAMAL 69

For many Norse Pagans, solitary practice is more than enough to meet their spiritual needs. This is, in fact, the norm for most Norse Pagans. Even so, you may reach a point in your journey where you want to practice with other Norse Pagans. This chapter will help you find what you are seeking. It is important to remember that while many follow several different forms of Norse Paganism, simply latching on to any community that exists is not the wisest approach. What is important when seeking out community is knowing how to distinguish between healthy, nurturing groups, dysfunctional and abusive ones, and those who use Norse Paganism as a façade for concealing hatred and cowardice.

When getting started, you shouldn't restrict yourself just to Norse Pagan groups. It's quite common for Norse Pagans to find each other through broader Pagan groups who welcome followers of all traditions. Do not be discouraged if you do not find any groups who are a good fit for you. Your goal when seeking community should always be finding what enriches your practice, not to being part of a group for its own sake.

Finding Community

There are many challenges in finding a community. Most Pagan groups operate on shoestring budgets, are run by volunteers, and are usually on the fringes of modern society. In some places Pagans are forced underground by active persecution, fear of backlash at home or on the job. The handful of groups with the resources to openly advertise their presence are very much the exception. Thankfully there are many groups who may fit your needs, making the search a question of knowing where to look and what exactly to look for.

Where to Look

A good place to start looking for community is the closest Pagan, metaphysical, or New Age store. Even if your local store isn't quite what you are looking for, the owners usually have some information on what groups are active, who to talk to, and what is going on. Groups also tend to post flyers in these stores, knowing such businesses tend to attract people who are interested in different forms of Pagan practice. You can make similar contacts at Renaissance Faires, as these are often popular with some Pagans and many Pagan vendors often attend these events to sell their wares.

Another good starting point is searching for local Pagan groups on the Internet. They might be using sites like Meetup.com or Facebook to get the word out. Active groups who are interested in accepting new members usually have some sort of easily accessible information online. If they have contact information, reach out and ask your questions about the group before attending any of their events. Remember, these groups do not have to be Norse Pagan to be worth contacting or working with. There may be people in these communities who are also interested in Norse practice or know of nearby Norse groups.

One option in some places are Pagan Pride festivals. Pagan Pride began in the United States, taking direct inspiration from Gay Pride festivals, and they have spread around the world. Though Pagan Pride isn't everywhere, it is present in many places; usually Pagan Pride Day is celebrated in late September. If there is an active Pagan Pride group in your area, they are a great place for finding other Pagans. More information on Pagan Pride festivals can be found at www.paganpride.org.

There are also several online communities who mostly exist in cyberspace. This doesn't make them any less valid, but it does influence what they can and cannot do. Online groups can be very useful resources for getting information, finding local community, networking, and talking through different elements of practice. They do not, due to their nature, usually offer anything like in-person ritual. They also tend to have the same problems other web groups face. Some are excellent quality discussion spaces, while others are a nonstop virtual cage match. The benefit of online groups is that they are much easier to find than in-person communities.

Another option is contacting a national Norse Pagan organization, of which there are many around the world. These organizations usually have information on local or regional activities and often hold their own events. If you are interested in contacting a national organization, you should do some research on them first. All of these groups, especially if they've been around for some time, have their own cliques, usually prioritize the desires of long-standing members over the needs of newer people, and may have unresolved problems that could be a deal-breaker for you. If the organization active in your country doesn't have a local group close to you in practice, they aren't much different from being part of an online community.

What to Look For

There are several questions you should be asking when searching for community. Some of these are easily answered by doing some simple research, asking members and other groups who have heard of them. The most important questions are:

- Do they have a strong, clear nondiscrimination statement affirming they are an inclusive group and bigotry is not tolerated?
- Are they holding regular public or private events?
- Do they offer resources for independent learning, hold study groups or provide training of any kind?

- Do they provide clear, easily accessible information on how their group makes decisions and accepts new members?
- Do all members have a say in making decisions or is everything determined by a small clique or even one individual?

Other questions can only be answered by interacting with community groups and attending their events. These questions are just as important and will help you figure out if you should work with them:

- Is the group supportive of its members, providing comfort for those in need and compassionately correcting mistakes made by new people?
- Do their actions show official processes for making decisions and resolving disputes are consistently followed?
- Do they consistently hold members, including people in positions of power, accountable when they break community rules or norms? Are their accountability processes consistently applied and enforced?
- Is the practice they offer engaging for you? Do you believe it will help deepen your spiritual practice and enrich your life?

All these questions and any personal concerns should be considered before approaching or staying with an existing group. If a group answers all such questions to your satisfaction, it is worth staying with them and helping build them up. If they do not, it is best to move on. As enriching as being a member of a spiritual organization can be, it isn't worth your time, energy, or effort to be a part of one for its own sake. Do what is best for meeting your needs first, even if that means staying solitary, seeking out a less-known group that is a better fit, or starting your own.

Living in Community

Once you've found a healthy, sustaining community, what comes next is being an active, supportive member. The best advice is to be yourself, act in the most ethical way possible, and work to improve your community. Doing these things is not always easy, and sometimes it is best to step back, take a break, and focus on taking care of yourself first. The needs of community never go ahead of taking care of yourself. Being effective for a community means being at your best, and supportive communities will always recognize this.

If you have the chance to take on a larger role in any community, think long and hard before taking on such responsibility. Most of such work is voluntary and an act of service to others. Before taking on any larger duties, you need to ask yourself if you have the knowledge, training, and capacity to do the job. If you don't, you'll need to determine what you need so you can serve effectively and the best way to get the skills or resources you need.

If there are serious problems in your community, do not shy away from addressing them. Points of tension and conflict are best resolved by resolving them directly when they first become a problem. Ignoring them, letting them fester, and saying nothing in the hopes of keeping the peace nearly always backfires horribly, guaranteeing the situation will get worse. Always bring such concerns to the attention of the community through the accepted, established channels for dispute resolution first before pursuing other means of resolving any problems or grievances. Weregild, as discussed in chapter five, is a useful guide for how to resolve such problems, as are the dispute resolution processes discussed in chapter nine.

Tackling Harm in Community

When the problem at hand is getting people hurt, making the community unsafe for its members, or power is being abused to the point where attempts to resolve the problem through accepted channels are rejected, direct action becomes necessary. The best way to prepare for direct action is by reaching out to others in the same community who feel similarly and collectively discussing the shared concern. This builds a base for further work, such as raising awareness, convincing others in the community, or exerting pressure on those in positions of authority to provide redress. Always focus on the ultimate end goal and set your collective course based on what is the best, most sustainable way of achieving that result.

Remember that it is much easier to justify direct action if all attempts to resolve a problem through normal channels have either failed or concerns have been rejected outright. This is why you should try seeking resolution through established processes before escalating to direct action. Repair what can be fixed and replace anything that can't. Sometimes it can be hard knowing what is fixable and what isn't. The best advice here is to let your ethical compass be your guide.

If a group is a total a dumpster fire, don't stick around long enough to get burned. Groups who only pay lip service to confronting deep challenges, act indecisively in resolving them, try to please everyone while serving no one's needs, protect people in power whose actions cause harm, and prioritize rehabilitating very toxic people over the safety of the whole community should be left to die. Staying in a dysfunctional community does nothing to address serious problems, and it makes the situation worse by convincing community members they must be doing something right. It may sound counterintuitive, but when people are actively denying a community or organization's problems, they'll use the presence of good, ethical people to reinforce their denial.

If you encounter abusive or incredibly dysfunctional groups, your two main priorities should be getting out as quickly and cleanly as possible and documenting everything. Getting out and taking care of your needs should always be your first priority. The sooner you get out of an abusive situation, the sooner you can start your recovery. Getting out quickly may help reduce the damage you suffer. If there are people who are also suffering harm from such groups, you can help them too: keep lines of communication open and do what you can, but never at the expense of your own safety.

In the process of removing yourself from an abusive group, document everything, find other witnesses, and when you have a persuasive amount of material, get the word out to the broader community. Dysfunctional and abusive groups depend on others not knowing about their serious problems or denying such problems exist. Exposing them greatly limits their power. That said, it is unfortunately very common for people to deny even the most credible claims of abuse, downplay accusations by appealing to civility or ineffective processes, dismiss all evidence, or even work to discredit any accusers. The grim truth is that even though many people claim to abhor abusive, bigoted, and controlling behaviors, much of society (Paganism included) usually puts defending the powerful and influential ahead of justice for their victims. It is therefore necessary to get as much rock-solid, unquestionable evidence as you can and as much support as possible before you call such people out. As is the case with getting out of abusive groups, make sure your safety will not be jeopardized before you act.

Understanding Fascism

The most serious problem facing modern Norse Paganism is the neo-Volkisch movement and their fascist allies. In the past they exercised considerable power and influence and were actively protected by other elements of the community. Thankfully, more people are becoming comfortable with what they really believe, standing up to them, and actively repelling them from Pagan spaces, organizations, and communities. The best example of the Norse Pagan community collectively doing this is Declaration 127. In September of 2016, just shy of a hundred and eighty Norse Pagan groups, ranging in size from local fellowships to international organizations, jointly denounced the Asatru Folk Assembly for promoting neo-Volkisch ideology, declaring the AFA was no longer welcome in their spaces.[162]

Even so, many neo-Volkisch believe they have the sole right to dictate who can practice Norse Paganism. The modern fascist movement uses them as tools to advance their agenda, treating the neo-Volkisch as disposable pawns. As aggressive as they are, the neo-Volkisch and their fascist friends are not unstoppable. The first step in addressing the challenges posed by fascism is to know what fascism is and how it works in Norse Paganism.

What is Fascism?

Fascism, as influential as it has been in the past and is becoming in the present, is a poorly understood concept. The word is frequently misused and misunderstood. The best, most complete definition of fascism comes from Robert Paxton's book *The Anatomy of Fascism*:

- a sense of overwhelming crisis beyond the reach of any traditional solutions
- the primacy of the group, toward which one has duties superior to every right, whether individual or universal, and the subordination of the individual to it

162. Declaration 127 can be found at the following link: www.declaration127.com.

- the belief that one's group is a victim, a sentiment that justifies any action, without legal or moral limits, against its enemies, both internal and external
- dread of the group's decline under the corrosive effects of individualistic liberalism, class conflict, and alien influences
- the need for closer integration of a purer community, by consent if possible, or by exclusionary violence if necessary
- the need for authority by natural chiefs (always male), culminating in a national chieftain who alone is capable of incarnating the group's historical destiny
- the superiority of the leader's instincts over abstract and universal reason
- the beauty of violence and the efficacy of will, when they are devoted to the group's success
- the right of the chosen people to dominate others without restraint from any kind of human or divine law, right being decided by the sole criterion of the group's prowess within a Darwinian struggle[163]

Based on this widely accepted definition, there is no doubt the neo-Volkisch tick every single one of these boxes. An excellent source with proof is Circle Ansuz, who did a thorough article on the Asatru Folk Assembly.[164] According to independent reporter Shane Burley, their allies in the modern fascist movement fit the mold just as neatly, regardless of if they call themselves alt-right, Identitarians, or white nationalists.[165]

The fascists' ultimate goal is very straightforward: create a society where the only people who are allowed to exist are white fascists. According to Burley, this is commonly referred to as a "white ethnostate," a society where anyone who doesn't qualify in the eyes of fascists as white, conform to traditional

---

163. Robert Paxton, *The Anatomy of Fascism*, Vintage Books (New York: 2004), 219–220.
164. The Circle Ansuz investigation into the AFA and Stephen McNallen can be found at circleansuz.wordpress.com
165. Shane Burley, *Fascism Today: What It Is and How to End It*, AK Press (Chico, CA: 2017), 21–27.

gender roles, and adhere to fascist ideology will be eliminated. Robert Paxton makes it totally clear that fascists believe anyone deemed a "race enemy" is utterly irredeemable and must be exterminated.[166]

The truth, however, is that even the achievement of the ideal white ethnostate would not bring an end to the bloodletting. Former neo-Nazi TJ Leyden, who was in the movement for more than twenty years, had this epiphany in a conversation with a fellow Neo-Nazi he discussed in an interview with the Southern Poverty Law Center. His realization was a key part of what pushed him to leave:

> In 1996, when I was at the Aryan Nations Congress [in Hayden Lake, Idaho], I started listening to everybody and I felt like, "God, this is pathetic." I asked the guy sitting next to me, "If we wake up tomorrow and the race war is over and we've won, what are we going to do next?"
>
> And he said, "Oh, come on, T.J., you know we're going to start with hair color next, dude."
>
> I laughed at it, but when I drove home, 800 miles, that question and answer kept popping into my head. I thought that kid was so right. Next it'll be you have black hair so you can't be white, or you have brown eyes so somebody in your past must have been black, or you wear glasses so you have a genetic defect.[167]

If all of these horrible goals are not reason enough to oppose fascists and their neo-Volkisch lackeys, consider what would happen to Paganism if they won. Most of the alt-right and modern fascist movement are highly militant Christians, some of whom openly shout the Crusader battle cry, "Deus vult." Those who aren't, are militant atheists. Most of the groups they recruit from are dominated by hard-line Christians. If fascists ever took power, then

166. Burley, 58; Paxton, 213.

167. "Former Skinhead T.J. Leyden Tells His Story." Southern Poverty Law Center. https://www.splcenter.org/fighting-hate/intelligence-report/1998/former-skinhead-tj-leyden-tells-his-story.

Pagans—including the neo-Volkisch—would be very high on the list of undesirables in need of purging.[168]

The ideals of fascism are completely at odds with anything resembling ethical conduct for a Norse Pagan. They twist the Powers and sacred symbols into hateful mockeries for hiding their true faces. The objectives of modern fascism are a direct threat to our community's existence. Building inclusive communities and creating a world with no room for what sustains fascism is the only viable solution for Norse Paganism and all of society. To do this effectively, you must understand how they operate and the concrete steps your community can take to win.

The Fascist Creep

A common strategy modern fascists use is a combination of deception, code words, and veiled rhetoric. Alexander Reid Ross calls this the fascist creep, describing it as an organizing and propaganda strategy where fascist groups co-opt the rhetoric of opposing groups, call for alliances that "transcend politics," and corrupt otherwise non-fascist ideas and symbols into vehicles for advancing fascist power. Fascists will always claim what they advocate is the "natural order of things" so they can better snare the unwary and uneducated with their rhetoric.[169]

Former neo-Nazi Christian Picciolini, co-founder of Life After Hate, confirms this main approach: "Look like your neighbor, your dentist, your attorney, your teacher, your nurse, and take the message of the ideology and polish it just to make it a little bit more palatable." These deliberate acts to normalize fascism are all part of furthering their agenda. The neo-Volkisch do the same with Norse Paganism, dressing up their hate in a stolen spiritual cloak so they can falsely claim anyone opposing them are the real bigots. Claiming their highly destructive beliefs are just another political or spiritual position makes recruits more comfortable and helps them gain ground.[170]

---

168. Brian D. McLaren, "Charlottesville: 'Alt-Right' Has Created Alt-Christianity." Time. August 25, 2017. http://time.com/4915161/charlottesville-alt-right-alt-christianity/.

169. Alexander Reid Ross, *Against the Fascist Creep*, AK Press (Chico, CA: 2017), 12–16.

170. "Former Skinhead on the Threat of White Supremacist Violence in the U.S." WBUR. August 30, 2017. http://www.wbur.org/hereandnow/2017/08/30/life-after-hate-white-supremacy.

How the neo-Volkisch mainstream their ideas is very similar to the tactics used by the alt-right. This isn't surprising, as there is a long history between neo-Volkisch organizations and the groups who created the alt-right. The work of Alexander Reid Ross, Shane Burley, and Circle Ansuz confirm this deep relationship. As discussed earlier in this chapter, aggressive denial is one key component of this strategy, but it isn't the only one. Mainstreaming also uses deceptive narratives, framing devices, and messaging to obscure the truth of their goals.[171] Some of the most common methods are described in a series of YouTube videos from Innuendo Studios titled "The AltRight Playbook."[172] One of the best messaging strategies to counter their approach is consistently responding to the neo-Volkisch with, "This is not normal," before clearly explaining how and why.

Another key element of the fascist creep is the manner in which they seize power. There is no example in history, as Paxton shows, of fascists taking power outright on their own. They always gain positions of authority by forming alliances with people in existing institutions that see benefits from either actively working with or not opposing the fascists. In return, the fascists cooperate with their new allies by targeting mutual enemies before turning on any allies they feel cannot be trusted.[173]

This was just as true in Norse Paganism. The main form of this cooperation was an unwritten pact of silence that was the norm for much of the community from the 1980s until the creation of Declaration 127 in September 2016. Supporters of the unwritten pact, which included many organizations in North America and local or regional groups elsewhere, refused to speak out against neo-Volkisch groups. Anyone who refused to abide by the pact was denounced as a trouble-maker, accused of "breaking the frith," harassed, and even cast out from participating. It was also not unusual for critics of the neo-Volkisch or people they perceived as ideological and racial enemies to suffer harassment and threats of violence by the neo-Volkisch while pact supporters said nothing.

---

171. Ross, 194–207; Burley, 132–133; "Stephen McNallen and Racialist Asatru Part 2: The Roots of Racialized Religion." Circle Ansuz. September 10, 2013. https://circleansuz.wordpress.com/2013/08/26/stephen-mcnallen-part-two/.

172. "The AltRight Playbook." https://youtu.be/4xGawJIseNY.

173. Paxton, 96–105.

Some even excused and defended the neo-Volkisch as just another form of Paganism instead of calling it what it is. The growth of the neo-Volkisch movement was due both to their own organizing methods and the complicity of other Pagans who didn't want to cause trouble, saw no problem with neo-Volkisch beliefs, or quietly agreed with them. These actions created the perfect conditions for the neo-Volkisch to thrive. This is why it is absolutely essential for anyone who supports inclusive practice to draw a firm line around their communities—made of ideas, organization, and truly inclusive practice that says to the neo-Volkisch, "You shall not pass!"

It is worth noting that the tactics used to maintain the pact were almost exactly the same as those used by groups to silence accusations of abuse. It also was quite common for groups who upheld the pact to deal with other serious problems, like abuses by leadership or long-time members, in the exact same way. This shouldn't be as surprising as it sounds. If the response to the biggest problem in Norse Paganism is only enforced silence, it makes perfect sense that it should be resolved in the exact same manner.

Identifying the Neo-Volkisch

When looking for community you will need to watch out for neo-Volkisch groups so you can avoid them. These groups have the twin problems of promoting destructive ideas and being incredibly abusive, unhealthy, and focused on serving the needs of their leaders instead of their members. A consistent warning sign in all cases is the lack of a clear non-discrimination statement. Some groups turn this on its head by claiming they don't discriminate based on political ideologies while saying nothing about race, gender, sexuality, or national origin, which effectively means the same thing as the absence of a non-discrimination statement. Some make themselves really obvious by sporting swastikas and SS runes, spouting anti-Semitic rhetoric, denying the Holocaust, advocating violence against members of marginalized groups, or anyone they claim is a communist (which in practice always means anyone they don't like, disagree with, or who actively oppose their ideas), posting Alt-Right memes, and other unquestionably Nazi stuff.

Other groups are far more dangerous because they go to great lengths to disguise their true ideals behind flowery language, misrepresented information, and fake science. When confronted on the truth of their actions, the more deceptive neo-Volkisch groups claim to be the real victims, say their accusers are being rude, argue that they don't hate other people, they only "love their race," or attempt to change the topic by falsely claiming their bigotry is exactly the same as what Native Americans, Shinto practitioners, and modern Judaism all do. They will encourage people to read more obscure fascist philosophers, with Julius Evola, Alain de Benoist, and Miguel Serrano as the most popular examples. They also promote material from fascist publishing houses like Runestone Publishing, Counter-Currents Publishing, Arktos Media Group, and Red Ice Radio.

Such evasiveness and aggressive approaches are key elements of their recruiting and organizing strategy. PhilosophyTube has an excellent video called "White Supremacist Propaganda vs Truth" exploring how the propaganda tactics used by many neo-Volkisch groups and organizers work which can be found at the link in the footnote below.[174] YouTube channel Angie Speaks also has an excellent video on esotericism, the occult, and fascism.[175] Three of the symbols most commonly used by less obvious neo-Volkisch groups are the Black Sun, the Odal Rune, and the Wolfsangel, which are less-known Nazi symbols.

---

174. https://www.youtube.com/watch?v=267w2rSnB-Y.

175. https://www.youtube.com/watch?v=DJWFpocUvWc.

Commonly Used Neo-Volkisch Symbols

The Black Sun/Schwarzesonne, also known as a Sun Wheel/Sonnenrad. First known instance of this design was for decorating the SS headquarters at Wewelsburg Castle

The Odal Rune, also referred to as Othala by the neo-Volkisch. This specific design was first used as a unit badge for a Waffen-SS Division.

The Wolfsangel, also appears turned on its side and incorporated into other symbols. First instances were based on medieval German wolf traps, used as a part of unit badges by Wehrmacht and Waffen-SS combat units

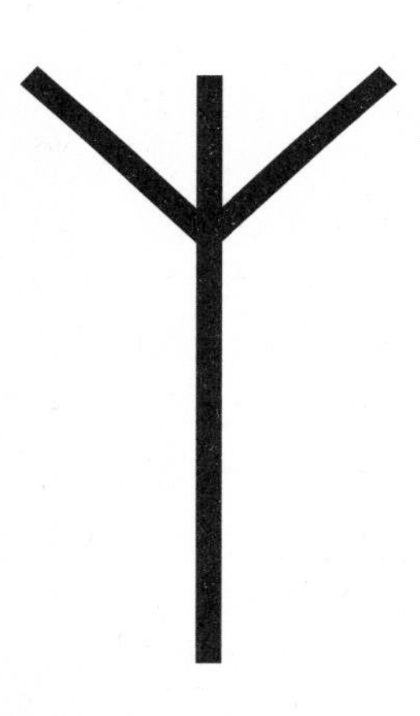

The Life Rune, the commonly used white nationalist name for the rune known as Algiz, Eohl, and Madr. First known use by a fascist group was National Vanguard in the United States

Even if a group is just using these symbols or repeating neo-Volkisch ideas with no awareness or concern for what they mean, you should avoid them. Such groups are used by the neo-Volkisch as recruiting grounds for gathering information on potential targets and as front groups. For more information, the YouTube channel Contrapoints has an excellent video called "Decrypting the AltRight" on the deceptive tactics that are commonly used by the neo-Volkisch movement.[176]

The Search for Belonging

Community presents many challenges for Norse Pagan practitioners, but also offers many rewards. If you believe your practice is best served by joining a community, it is important to know what you want and what potential communities can offer you. Confronting problems in community is also a key part of the experience. Whether those problems are as simple as strong disagreements or as complex as repelling fascist influence, they are always best handled directly, decisively, and without hesitation.

The next exercise is meant to help you better understand what it is you want from a community. It can be done both for when you are seeking out community and if you are trying to organize one. You may find it useful to repeat it from time to time, updating it as your priorities and conditions change.

exercise

COMMUNITY EXPECTATIONS

This exercise requires a piece of paper and a pen or pencil, though you can also type this up on a word processor.

Start by drawing a line down the center of the paper. At the top of the page write "Goals" on one side and "Fulfillment" on the other side.

Start writing down, in whatever order they come to you, what your hopes are from an existing or potential community. These can be as broad as "Safety" and "Comfort" or as specific as "Training in Seiðr," "Festivals," and "Social Nights."

176. https://www.youtube.com/watch?v=Sx4BVGPkdzk.

Once you have a good-sized list or have run out of ideas or space on the page, move over to the "Fulfillment" side. This column is for writing down how you think those goals would be best realized. Fulfillment, in this case, represents what that community could or will do to satisfy your hopes for it. For one example, if a goal is training in seiðr, then one form of fulfillment could be organizing a study group or seeking out a teacher.

Take as much time as you need when writing out the fulfillment options. If new hopes come to mind from writing down or discussing possible fulfillment, then add those to the hope column.

Keep going until you have some form of fulfillment for every hope you have written. If you are doing this activity with a group, be sure everyone has a chance to comment on each hope and agree on the form of fulfillment proposed for it.

When you have finished, keep this paper in a place where you won't lose it. If you are doing this exercise with a group, make sure everyone who participated gets a copy.

Consult what you've written when approaching a new community to remind yourself of what you expect from them, as well as when building a community group. Which items must absolutely be present in a community to meet your hopes is entirely up to you. The list you now have is a guide for better understanding what you are seeking from community.

chapter nine

BUILDING COMMUNITY

Then sought the gods their assembly-seats,
The holy ones, and council held,
Whether the gods should tribute give,
Or to all alike should worship belong.
VOLUSPO 24

There may come a time in your journey when you feel the best way forward is starting your own spiritual community. This chapter provides some initial tools for building your own community. When it comes to community organizing you should always be open to adopting methods, ideas or practices proven to be effective by the experiences of others. One source that is especially helpful for this subject is Starhawk's *The Empowerment Manual: A Guide for Collaborative Groups*. There are many more written by community organizers, activists, and others that might guide your community in its development.

The backbone of communal practice in Radical Norse Paganism is local groups known as fellowships. These in-person groups meet regularly, conduct their own rituals (public or private), hold study sessions, have social nights, and do whatever else the members like to do in the belief that it is part of their spiritual practice. Fellowships, at their best, are a blend of spiritual group and chosen family. They offer support, instruction, solace, and a place for Norse Pagans to practice their spirituality among like-minded people.

Sometimes groups of neighboring fellowships band together in alliances known as *Things* (pronounced *tings*), the name for the popular assemblies of the ancient Norse peoples. Things provide member-fellowships with more resources, support, and information than any individual fellowship could muster on their own. Things are not that common, but as more fellowships develop, the question of regional organization becomes more pressing, making them the best existing answer. This type of organization is inspired by the East Coast Thing event, which takes place yearly in the northeastern United States.

Fellowships and things are not the only kinds of community out there for Norse Pagans. In many places there are pan-Pagan groups where members come from different practices, traditions, and forms of Pagan spirituality. Some of these are regional alliances of many different Pagan groups. There are also online groups which in many ways work a lot like most other internet groups, with a Norse Pagan or generally Pagan focus. There are many Norse Pagans who are perfectly comfortable with these different arrangements. Several fellowships have been born from people who met through these groups, making them a viable option for many Norse Pagans looking to build community.

Forging Ties That Bind

The first thing your community should always do is set and maintain realistic goals. Always keep focused on what your community wants to do, must do, and can do. Nothing hurts a community more than trying to do too much, too fast, without enough people or resources to do it all. At the absolute minimum, your community should be holding as many regular rituals and social get-togethers for its members as it feels are necessary, communicating effectively, educating all current and potential members, and resolving conflicts equitably. Only worry about taking on more after these core functions are working smoothly and you have enough people to handle additional projects or services.

Your community should also include a very strong inclusivity and hospitality statement. These statements make it clear your group is genuinely inclusive in practice. Here is an example of an inclusivity statement which you are free to use in whole or in part for writing your own:

> We are an inclusive community. We believe practicing this form of Norse Paganism is open to all individuals who feel it is valid, fulfilling, and speaks to them regardless of race, national origin, gender, sexuality, gender identity, physical or mental ability. We believe discrimination for any of those reasons is antithetical to the practice of Norse Paganism. We do not associate with, support, or agree with any groups or individuals who deny the right of others to practice Norse Paganism freely based on any of these grounds. Any individuals, groups, or organizations who believe those forms of discrimination are fundamental to practicing Norse Paganism are not welcome at any of our events, rites, or gatherings so long as they hold such beliefs.

Structure

The first real question, once you have your core group of people together, is how you are going to organize your fellowship. The obvious answer many groups tend to fall into is people take charge, lead by example, and delegate as needed. This sort of top-down, charismatic approach has a lot of drawbacks, namely that it puts most of the burden of organizing and community-building on the people at the top. Such groups also turn off many new members when they realize they'll have little actual input. It also burns out the people in charge very quickly, greatly limiting the group's effectiveness.

A better approach is what Starhawk calls collaborative organizing, which is different from a top-down or charismatic model because the group is organized as a circle of equals. Decisions are made collectively by all members. Another term for this approach is participatory democracy, a method of governance where community members take a direct role in setting policy, choosing who will implement it, and have the power to directly hold those endowed with such responsibility accountable. This model has been proven effective at every level, from small study groups and community organizations to cities like Porto Alegre, Brazil which has over a million inhabitants.[177]

As modern as this solution may sound, it has historical and spiritual foundations for Norse Pagans. The most famous example was the Icelandic Althing, where the people came together in a great assembly to make laws and settle disputes without kings. The sagas of the Heimskringla include several examples of similar assemblies in Norway and Sweden that had the power to make or break ruling kings. There's one example from Sweden where a thing threatened to depose and kill a king because he tried to force the people to keep fighting an unpopular, unnecessary war. Even the gods, according to the Voluspo, created Midgard by deciding all things in council, and when Ragnarok comes they will gather to debate the best course of action one last time.[178]

All these ideas are soil for growing a healthy community. Starhawk recommends making this happen by bringing everyone involved together to discuss their priorities and preferred methods. Prospective community members should draw up a set of governing agreements laying out how often formal meetings happen, how many members need to be present for decisions made at a meeting to be legitimate, how decisions are made, channels of communication, dispute resolution, delegating responsibility, and the manner in which new people are brought in to the group. Governing rules should be broad, only subject to change through unanimous consensus or a supermajority of all members, and cover the core functions of the group. They should be written down, accessible to all members, and available to the public on request or posted in a visible place such as a website or social media page.[179]

When it comes to the question of making decisions, a highly effective model is a blend of majority vote and consensus. In this approach, decisions

---

177. Starhawk, *The Empowerment Manual: A Guide for Collaborative Groups*, New Society Publishers (Gabriola Island, Canada: 2011), 5–6; Enriqueta Aragones and Santiago Sanchez-Pages, "A theory of participatory democracy based on the real case of Porto Alegre," *European Economic Review*, September 21 2008, http://www.iae.csic.es/investigatorsMaterial/a12231123057archivoPdf88451.pdf.

178. Robert Ferguson, *The Vikings: A History*, Penguin Books (London: 2009), 164–167; The Frosta-Thing, "Saga of Hakon the Good," *Heimskringla*, translated by Samuel Laing; Thorgny's Speech, "Saga of Olaf Haraldson," *Heimskringla*, translated by Samuel Laing; Voluspo 6, 9, 24–25, 48.

179. Starhawk, 38–41.

for most matters are resolved by a pre-determined majority, usually two thirds or three quarters of all members, while all members retain a special kind of vote known as a block. A block is where any member, or for larger organizations a group of members, declare they cannot support the current proposal as it stands and will leave the group if it passes without addressing their concerns. If there is a block, the proposal cannot be implemented as written until the concern is resolved or, if it cannot be resolved through genuine good faith efforts, the blockers leave the group. This method ensures that serious objections are addressed while guaranteeing decisions are made in a timely fashion, combining the best of majority vote and consensus decision-making systems.

The final structural question is what standards people need to meet to join your community. Even the most well-intentioned and informed person still needs time to learn how a community works, its norms and expectations. This is why education is critical for all healthy communities. Prospective members should be mentored by an existing member in how the community works, regularly attend community events for a set period such as between six months and a year, and participate regularly in study groups. Only after prospective members have done all of this is when community members should discuss and vote on if they should become a member in good standing, giving them a vote on community affairs, and be delegated responsibilities.

Running Meetings

Having agreed on processes is only the first step for organizing community. It is also important to learn the skills of facilitating meetings and discussions so that things run smoothly. The first part of this process is ensuring meeting dates, times, and locations are posted to agreed-on communication channels well in advance of the meeting, preferably a week at the minimum for a non-emergency meeting, and all meetings start on time.

The first item on any meeting's agenda is nominating a lawspeaker to facilitate the meeting, a note-taker, a time-keeper, and someone to keep track of who is speaking next, who is also known as a stack-taker. All these positions should be approved by consensus. The lawspeaker then either reads off the meeting's agenda, if it was already agreed on at a previous meeting or worked out through approved communication channels, or facilitates the necessary discussions for setting one. They should include time for any items people add to the agenda.

The job of the lawspeaker as facilitator is ensuring all voices are heard and given a fair hearing. Lawspeakers abstain from voting and offering their opinions on whatever is being discussed, sacrificing their voice in service of ensuring all voices are heard. What they can do to achieve this is ask clarifying questions when needed, summarize existing proposals including any amendments offered by members, supervise votes, administer oaths, and keep everything moving smoothly according to agreed on processes. Facilitation is a big responsibility and is necessary for effective meetings.

The stack-taker tracks who is up next to speak and gives priority to those who speak the least often. People should indicate their desire to speak by quietly raising their hands. A time-keeper watches the clock. If the group has agreed that each person should only have a set amount of time to speak when it is their turn (two minutes is a common choice), they keep track of each speaker's time. The note-taker's job is to keep simple notes of the agenda, who ran the meeting, what was discussed, and what decisions were made and ensures the final meeting notes are distributed to all members. If you want more information, Seeds for Change has an excellent guide on running meetings.[180]

Delegation

There are always specific jobs that need to be carried out on behalf of the community. The best way to handle this is delegation. When a community decides a specific job or set of tasks need to happen they choose people, either an individual or if necessary a team known as a working group, who are delegated the necessary authority for carrying out the day-to-day work and making necessary on-the-spot decisions. One example of delegation is choosing a team to manage an upcoming ritual.

Transparency and accountability are essential for delegation to work. Anyone that is delegated power by their community, whether an individual or group, must make regular reports on what they've done and the outcomes of their actions to their community. The community always has the power to limit or change what delegates can do through direct vote. If the community

180. Seeds for Change. https://www.seedsforchange.org.uk/shortfacilitation.

feels the people in positions of responsibility have abused the community's trust they may remove that power through a vote of no-confidence. Communities must always have the power to collectively revoke delegated power for any reason they feel is justified at any time.

Anyone seeking to hold such a delegated position must remember the core of these duties is to serve, not rule. The power you are endowed with is not yours. It has been lent to you and decisions you make while holding it impact the whole community. Starhawk says, "An empowering leader rarely uses Command mode. Most of the time, she leads by example and persuasion." She further says delegates should always work to empower others, pass on their skills, and prepare successors both to grow the community's knowledge and take care of their own needs while also recognizing, "All of this is, of course, the ideal. We can strive for it, but most of us will fall short in one way or another. An empowering leader makes mistakes."[181]

Communication

Having a consistent, reliable channel for internal communications is essential for maintaining a healthy community. There are several different ways this can be done, ranging from something as simple as a phone tree and text message groups to online forums, chat servers like IRC or Discord, email lists, and social media groups. Regardless of the medium your community uses, it is essential that it is clear what channel is used for announcing events, meetings, and distributing notes, and that the method used is consistent, reliable, and secure.

When setting up your communications network, it is important for your community to establish clear ground rules, clearly state expectations, and explicitly state what is appropriate to post. This is important because having clear expectations for how people should treat each other on internal communication channels encourages productive conversation and helps people feel welcome. Communication channels that do not have rules on what is relevant or appropriate behavior tend to end up jammed with just about everything imaginable, making them useless for actual organizing. You will need to delegate people either individually or as a working group to enforce these expectations.

181. Starhawk, 138–139.

Privacy and security are especially important for these channels. Spirituality is a very sensitive, personal subject for many people, so having a secure, private space encourages people to open up and participate. It also helps discussion stay on topic by keeping out disruptive and actively malicious people. Private, secure channels for official internal communications also give people the space to freely discuss community matters in a productive fashion. Many effective organizations have handled day-to-day problems by effectively cultivating a readily available communications network that is accessible to all members.

Along with the mechanics of setting up communications, it is important people feel free to speak up. The flipside is being open to what they want from community. Act with empathy toward all in your community as best as possible, genuinely listen to others, and engage with what they say. Collaborative groups thrive when everyone is given space to speak, be heard, and discuss in good faith.

Conflict Resolution

All groups and communities will inevitably experience conflict of some kind or another. After all, communities are made up of people who each have their own thoughts, goals, feelings, perspectives, and biases. What is presented in this section is mostly an introduction to some ideas and techniques. For a more complete understanding, it is highly recommended you read *The Empowerment Manual,* which goes into much greater depth on conflict resolution. Starhawk's work is the main guide for this section.

Starhawk argues there are two ways a community could view conflict. The first is where everything is an all-or-nothing, "right must prevail" sort of model ending in absolute victory—and lots of burned-out people. The second is where tensions and conflicts draw attention to existing problems, providing a community with the opportunity to learn, improve itself, and emerge stronger from the experience. As tempting as it may be to always fight and be right, the more sustainable path—especially in building a spiritual practice—is one of growth from tension rather than smothering or silencing it.[182]

Bruce Tuckman, an influential psychologist, has done much work on group dynamics, noting that there are four stages of group development: forming,

182. Starhawk, 160.

storming, norming, and performing, All are useful in understanding different sorts of conflicts and why they pop up. According to Tuckman, conflict of a sort is pretty much inevitable during the first three stages. During the forming stage, people are sorting out goals, systems, and getting to trust each other, leading to clashes based on different perspectives. The storming stage, unsurprisingly, is where it can get most intense as differing views and solutions clash. Norming, when the overall direction sorted out in the previous stages is being refined, is about smoothing things out, though some conflicts can still emerge.[183]

Growing through and from conflict depends on developing effective means for resolving it as equitably and amicably as possible. The key, according to Starhawk, is remembering that "... conflicts are often Good vs Good, and framing them in that way can help us resolve them creatively." This, she argues, is because, "We are acculterated to view conflict as Good vs. Evil." Another factor may be miscommunication, leading to misunderstandings and confusion.[184]

The best way to resolve such conflicts is offering mediation. There are many books (including Starhawk's) with excellent information on the details and skills needed to be an effective mediator. What matters is that all parties feel they are being heard, the mediator is genuinely fair-minded, seen as such by all involved, and shouldn't be involved in the conflict or have a strong opinion either way beyond a desire to resolve the problem amicably. Mediation also has existing precedent from the ancient Norse peoples. For them the goal for resolving any dispute is to reach the most equitable arrangement possible and only call for punishment if one person had clearly done injury to another.

Any agreements that come from mediation should be mutual for all people involved and the mediator should follow up with them after the fact. If the problem is one that involves the broader community, such as one involving the actions of a person with delegated responsibility, any settlement should be voted on by the community. Offers or requests for weregild should also be considered during mediation and terms of any weregild should be clearly agreed on before the end of a mediation session if it is requested.

---

183. Team Building. "Forming—Storming—Norming—Performing." Tuckman; Forming —Storming—Norming—Perfoming, https://www.teambuilding.co.uk/theory/Forming-Storming-Norming-Performing.html.

184. Starhawk 162, 164–165.

There are, however, some cases where one side of an argument is genuinely in the wrong. These are shown by the person or people involved consistently acting in ways causing people to feel devalued, disrespected, or unsafe. The best thing to do is remove them from the community. Such situations put the safety and hospitality of the community at risk. In these cases, it may be best to limit the harmful person's responsibilities, suspend them from group activities, or even remove them from the community entirely. This is both the best practical solution in such cases and is directly derived from the Norse practice of exiling repeat, dangerous, or otherwise totally irredeemable people, effectively exiling from the community and the protection of its laws.

If an exile ever tries to return, they must demonstrate that they have genuinely changed their behavior. Any decision to make them members in good standing should take much longer than normal to give them time to prove they've turned over a new leaf. Such a decision must be discussed with the community, with extra weight given to the voices of the people most affected by the exile's actions. In cases where the autonomy of the people harmed and ensuring genuine hospitality is always more important than the exile's desire to associate with a specific community. Requiring weregild from an exile as a precondition for returning to the fold is entirely appropriate and encouraged.

In cases where people are serial sexual harassers or assaulters, active bigots, physically violent, or consistently act in bad faith the best—and often only—solution is permanent exile. Just as there are times when no amount of weregild can make up for harm done, there are actions that cannot be forgiven and risks that should never be taken. The safety of your community is always more important than one person's desire for redemption or acceptance.

Education

Education is essential for building any functional, sustainable community. It consists of two equally important components. The first is teaching people spiritual practices, the lore and the ideas behind modern Paganism. The second is instructing people in the norms, practices, expectations, and decision-making processes of their community. Regardless of what you are teaching, the basics of effective instruction remain the same. Anyone who wants to teach others should first study educational theory and work with skilled teachers before doing so themselves.

Conventionally speaking there are three main styles of learning known as auditory, visual and kinesthetic. Auditory learners absorb information best through listening to what others say, lecture, tone of voice, discussion, and talking things through. Visual students learn best from observing the material and work best with diagrams, charts, videos, and hand-outs. Kinesthetic learners understand material by direct interaction with the subject, preferring hands-on exercises, physical activities and demonstrations to reading or lecture. Most students tend to favor one of these methods all tend to use a combination of all these methods. Teachers should use a variety of instructional techniques to engage all students as fully as possible and adapt to what works best for the subject being taught.[185]

These frameworks are just the beginning. All effective teachers must also learn and practice several necessary behaviors. Teachers must show patience and compassion for difficulties faced by students in understanding material. New concepts are not easy to understand, and those steeped in the practice can easily forget struggles of the past in understanding things you now take for granted. Even so, don't be afraid to push students a bit with clearly communicated expectations and goals. This may sound contradictory, but both elements must be kept in balance, shifting between one and the other as needed.[186]

When teaching, use as much ordinary, everyday language as you can; avoid jargon and technical terms when describing concepts or ideas. When used poorly and often, jargon tends to intimidate students—it reinforces their ignorance instead of inspiring their desire to learn. Excessive use of jargon locks people out of conversations, creates resentment, and fosters elitism. If you must use a specific technical term, make sure you clearly define it, use it as little as possible, and ensure everyone understands what it means. This doesn't mean you should water down the content. What is key is realizing people will better understand what you are teaching if you present the material in terms

185. "The VAK Learning System." Southwestern Community College. https://www.southwesterncc.edu/sites/default/files/VAK_Learning_Styles.pdf.

186. "10 Tips on Becoming a More Effective Teacher." Inclusion Lab. http://blog.brookespublishing.com/10-tips-on-becoming-a-more-effective-teacher/; Sarah Marsh, "Effective Teaching: 10 Tips on What Works and What Doesn't." *The Guardian*. October 31, 2014. https://www.theguardian.com/teacher-network/teacher-blog/2014/oct/31/effective-teaching-10-tips.

and frameworks that are easy to follow.[187] When planning study sessions, always use the most credible, proven, and qualified sources possible. Using credible sources helps build the students' trust in the teachers, spreads solid information, and builds everyone's understanding by giving them the tools to continue their own study. It also helps show students how to evaluate the credibility, knowledge, and usefulness of sources and think critically. Teachers should continually improve their own knowledge so they can better serve current and future students.[188]

These practices are effective in the immediate study space, but education does not start and stop there. Your goal, as a teacher, is empowering your students to learn and grow on their own. As a teacher, you should provide materials for students to conduct self-directed learning outside of study sessions. Doing so provides learners with the means for continuing the process on their own, inspires them to pursue independent study, and enriches their practice.[189]

Required Subjects

There are three topics every group should cover: spiritual education, community education, and inclusivity education. Each has its own quirks, challenges, and importance. The teaching techniques discussed earlier are all effective tools for educating people in each of these subjects.

Essential for building any Pagan group, spiritual education covers teaching the lore of Norse Pagan practice, providing the tools for developing personal practice, training in the sacred roles, conducting group ritual, and training in

---

187. The Secret Teacher, "Secret Teacher: Jargon Is Ruining Our Children's Education." The Guardian. August 09, 2014. https://www.theguardian.com/teacher-network/teacher-blog/2014/aug/09/secret-teacher-jargon-education-pupils; "Don't Confuse Jargon with Rigor." *Education Next*, January 23, 2015. https://www.educationnext.org/dont-confuse-jargon-rigor/; Kristi Hedges, "Five Communication Traits That Turn People Off." *Forbes* June 25, 2014. https://www.forbes.com/sites/work-in-progress/2014/06/25/five-communication-traits-that-turn-people-off/#2f14ce7f4b28.

188. BBC. "Master the Classroom: The Power of Teacher Credibility." http://www.bbcactive.com/BBCActiveIdeasandResources/ThePowerofTeacherCredibility.aspx; Marsh, "Effective Teaching."

189. "Supplementary Learning and Teaching Materials." Unesco IIEP Learning Portal. https://learningportal.iiep.unesco.org/en/issue-briefs/improve-learning/curriculum-and-materials/supplementary-learning-and-teaching.

the mystic arts of Norse Paganism (like seiðr and runelore) for any who are interested. Spiritual education depends on providing opportunities for direct, practical experience and working models for building individual students' understanding. Everything from hands-on workshops to free-flowing discussion are highly effective for this topic.

Community education goes hand-in-hand with spiritual education: where spiritual work focuses on developing a deeper understanding of Norse Pagan practice, community education helps people understand how their new community works. The goal is teaching people how to be fully autonomous, active members of community. Fully educated community members better know how to contribute, develop proposals and implement them, and enhance the experience for all participants. Community education includes everything from teaching expected norms to having newer members sit in on community decision-making and dispute resolution processes.

Inclusivity education is for helping people understand how to treat each other, particularly people from groups who suffer from discrimination and marginalization in society, with dignity and respect. Inclusivity education is best done explicitly and implicitly. Explicit inclusivity education is where you teach people how to build a genuinely inclusive community, understand concepts like privilege, and truly respect all other people in the community. Implicit inclusivity education is weaving respectful conduct into all other aspects of your community, showing people how to be inclusive by positive example.

Inclusivity education requires great patience and understanding. Always remember people sometimes make mistakes while acting in good faith. When asked for further reading or research, always recommend specific works instead of telling them vaguely to seek out information for themselves. Always remember that it is never the responsibility of a person from a marginalized group to handle another person's education, especially since people from those groups have often experienced serious trauma, including physical assault or fundamental violations of their autonomy. It is, however, always the responsibility of the community to ensure everyone receives effective inclusivity education.

Study Groups and Apprenticeships

There are two formats you should use for educating members of your community. These are study groups and apprenticeships. Study groups are good for providing necessary information to groups of people on spirituality, community, and inclusivity. Apprenticeships are best used by those who hold sacred roles or support roles to train others in necessary skills, teach the mystic arts, and provide in-depth instruction on topics previously covered in study groups.

Organizing a study group is easier than it seems but it does take work to run a successful one. The first step is working out potential study group members' availability, use that to arrange a regular time, place, and day based on what works best for everyone, and agree on a regular system for communicating information related to the study group. Next, determine the major elements, themes and topics that need to be covered in the study group. Assign a session to each of these elements and provide all study group participants with the complete schedule. Prepare a consistent agenda for each session outlining it, what preparations participants need to do prior to each session, and send it to all participants at least a few days before the session will take place. Always organize the segments of your sessions based on the ten-minute rule.[190]

During study sessions it is important you do your best to get everyone involved. A good way to make this easier is starting your first session with an icebreaking activity like a round of introductions or a name game. This helps get people comfortable with each other. If there are people who speak less frequently, try calling on them or asking for their opinions before asking for input from people who speak more frequently. If they are consistently not speaking up in study sessions, set aside time outside of sessions to find out why and work out solutions to help them feel more welcome. The same is true of people who speak so often it becomes disruptive or is discouraging other people from participating. The University of British Columbia has an excellent guide on organizing study groups at https://science.ubc.ca/students/blog/study-groups.

The dynamics of apprenticeships are very different. Unlike study groups, apprenticeships are a one-on-one relationship between teacher and apprentice. These relationships encourage more personalized, specific instruction and feedback for both parties. Instruction sessions should always be one-on-one meetings between teacher and apprentice even if the teacher has taken on mul-

---

190. "Starting and Managing a Study Group." Western Sydney University. February 2017. https://www.westernsydney.edu.au/__data/assets/pdf_file/0005/1082795/Starting_and_managing_a_study_group.pdf.

tiple apprentices. The goal of an apprenticeship is raising the apprentice's skill to a level where they can do the work of the role they're training for on their own, expand their understanding of the skills they've studied, and, if they are so inclined, train their own apprentices when they are ready to.

Before initiating an apprenticeship, the apprentice and teacher should have a serious discussion of what both are expecting, if the teacher has the skills for meeting the apprentice's desires, if the apprentice has enough of a grasp of the subject to do more advanced work, and if both feel they are a good fit for each other. Once this has been worked out, both parties should write up a formal contract. This contract must be sealed with an oath sworn by both parties and witnessed by at least two other members in good standing of their community. This contract should outline expectations, obligations, an opt-out clause for both parties, define acceptable conduct, including prohibiting the teacher and apprentice from entering a romantic or sexual relationship with each other during the period of instruction, and any other concerns that need to be spelled out. Both parties and the witnesses must receive a copy of the written contract.

An apprenticeship is a long-term, ongoing relationship. On average, apprenticeships for skilled trades take at least a year with some lasting as long as six. Apprenticeship in Norse Paganism should be treated similarly by teachers; a year-long process is the norm. Quick results are not the point—the goal of apprenticeship is to train people to a level where they can apply their skills effectively and independently of their teacher. Teachers should exercise patience with their apprentices based on the understanding that such training takes time and hands-on experience.[191]

Outreach

Once your group has finished working out the decision-making structure, have clear communication systems, transparent conflict resolution, and effective education, reaching out to the general public is the next logical step. Outreach is a lot of work but is well worth the effort when done right. The challenge is

191. "How Long Is Apprenticeship Training Typically?" Learn.org . https://learn.org/articles/How_Long_is_Apprenticeship_Training_Typically.html; "How to Train an Apprentice—Business Voice." CBI. http://www.cbi.org.uk/businessvoice/latest/how-to-train-an-apprentice/.

clearly communicating what your group is about and handling many different factors beyond your community's control. It is important to learn from your mistakes and the experiences of others when developing your outreach methods.

Outreach begins with being present. It means making an effort regarding the work of the hospitality team at public events to attending pan-Pagan networking events, festivals, and Interfaith events. It means genuinely listening to people, engaging with them, and showing compassion where appropriate. It also means being the best person and representation of Radical Norse Paganism that you can be. What you do, rightly or wrongly, in such situations reflects on your community, including anywhere on the internet. Always remember this when engaging in outreach and if you hold a known position of responsibility.

A very common outreach activity by Pagans is holding a pub moot. This is where your group hosts a public social night at a popular pub, café, club, or other similar and easily accessible venue. If your pub moot is happening at a popular location, make sure to book space in advance. Pub moots are a great way to encourage people to come out, meet others, and relax. The best pub moots are usually unstructured, starting off with a round of introductions and some sort of icebreaker conversation before letting things develop organically.

The next step for outreach is creating your own publicly available media. This used to be a difficult, expensive process, with everything from flyers and zines to posters and building up word of mouth as the tools of the trade. The internet and social media have made this quite easy in terms of cost and materials, and tools like social media and websites make it much easier to reach the public. In the present day the best places to start are on social media with Twitter, Facebook fan pages, Instagram, and independent networks like Mastodon.

Most of the content posted from your social media outlets should be official announcements, links to useful information including blogs produced by your group or its members, any relevant videos or photos, and promotional materials like memes. Make sure you post regularly, ideally at least once a day, so followers will have always have new material. Crosspost the same materials across multiple platforms, like posting pictures of your fellowship doing an outdoor ritual to the Facebook fan page, Twitter, and Instagram, as such cross-posting helps build visibility and promote consistency in messaging.

If your community has the expertise and resources to run one, a website is the next logical step forward for your outreach strategy. Whether they are free blogs hosted on sites like Wordpress or independently owned by your community, official websites provide the public with a readily available source of information and a consistent place for posting all material. If your community has a website and a blog, always post any new updates to your social media outlets. Your site should also have your community's governing agreements and contact information. Websites are not totally necessary, but they can be a major boost for your community's outreach and media presence if you have the means to support one.

One problem your community's media outlets will likely face are trolls. These trolls aren't the ones discussed in chapter two, though they're very similar in some ways. For those who are unfamiliar, trolls are people on the internet who either enjoy riling other people up or actively driving people away from a specific page or site. They do this by harassing their targeted social media and site by posting offensive material, making false claims, insults, and worse in the comments sections or on the site directly. Trolls aren't really interested in genuine debates or discussion; earnest engagement with them is pointless.

The best thing to do with trolls—whether they're out to cause trouble for their own amusement or because they are actively hostile—is ban them and delete their posts. Moderation of this kind can be time consuming, but it is always better to smash the trolls than waste time or energy debating them. To paraphrase a popular internet meme, trying to argue with trolls is like playing chess with a pigeon: no matter how good you are, they're just going crap on the board and strut around like they won anyway.

Essential to your media strategy is the art of messaging. There are many books, blogs, and podcasts on the topic that describe what works best. The foundation of it is understanding the power of story. Storytelling and narrative are without a doubt the oldest form of human communication. Everything we talk about, no matter how it reaches us, is put in the form of a story, whether chatting about what happened at the shop down the street or discussing advanced quantum mechanics. Messaging is thus the art of telling the best, most concise, consistent, and persuasive story.[192]

In all cases, the foundation of messaging must be the truth. Honesty and authenticity have greater power than spin, deception or lying either actively or by omission. Another key part of narrative is actively affirming your vision. Talk up the positives of your ideas and activities while avoiding negatives as much as possible to help keep people focused on what you are talking about instead of what you are opposed to. "We don't" statements implicitly encourage people to think about the bad thing; instead you should say something like, "Here is what we do and support; it is different from the bad thing you are talking about, and here is why what we do is important to us while also being different from / opposed to the bad thing." Always keep messaging simple, consistent with your values, and to the point, whether it's a blog describing practices, an event announcement, or a public statement.

All media strategy and uses must be a community decision. This should include delegating the responsibility of managing your community's publicly visible media outlets to a specific individual or working group. These delegates are responsible for executing the specifics of media strategy, reporting on the results to the broader community, and providing suggestions for consideration. Your messaging framework, guidelines for content, and the exact words of any official statements should always be determined by the community and not the media delegates. Their job, like all delegates, is to carry out the will of the community and not to make such decisions for them.

Dealing with the press—including television, radio, and newspapers as well as independent news and community blogs—is different from handling your own media. The most important thing to remember is that all press, no matter who writes for them or what their audience is, has bias in some way or another. Most are passively biased toward getting as many hits, views, and papers sold as possible, so it's common for articles to play up spectacle, outrage, and controversy at the expense of truth. Others are actively biased, promoting a specific view or perspective to the point that they will obscure or leave out critical facts to make it happen.

192. Brian Boyd, *On the Origin of Stories: Evolution, Cognition and Fiction*, Harvard University Press (Cambridge: 2009), 1–3.

The best way to deal with media bias is to have your community decide what your key message is before a possible interaction with the press, whether they show up to an event you are participating in or ask for an interview or comment on a recent event. The key message should be simple and delivered with a single, consistent point. Make sure everyone knows and agrees on the message for the press. Anyone interacting with the press should take every opportunity possible to reinforce the point. That way, no matter how much a press outlet may distort what is said, that point will get through one way or the other.

Once you have decided on your message, decide who is the most effective in delivering it. From there, the designated representatives should be the only people actively interacting with the press to both prevent confusion and keep the message consistent. Press representatives need to stay focused on the message, avoid going off on tangents, and be calm throughout any press interaction. Anyone who is not a designated press representative should deliver the same, collectively approved points. If you are not a press representative and are asked for further comment or clarification, you should direct the press to ask the designated press representatives for more information.

Group Ritual

Communal practice builds on the foundation laid by personal practice. The same tools used for developing effective personal practice are the core of effective group practice. That said, there are key differences, dynamics, and elements that are unique to group ritual that come from getting groups of people to work together in a cooperative fashion. Reaching ecstatic states and facilitating meaningful spiritual experiences in a group environment involves different challenges than solitary practice faces. Even so, the methods used in your personal practice, like meditation, creating sacred space, and using dance or music, are relatively easy to adapt to communal practice. When in doubt, above all else, keep things as simple as possible. Effective group ritual should be engaging and transformative for all participants.

The Ritual Team

Every group ritual needs a team to run it. The ritual team is made up of all the people with specific ritual functions and tasks. This includes specific and sacred roles as well as necessary support positions. Regardless of what position you have in the ritual team, everyone needs to put in work before, during, and after. No one is too important to avoid getting their hands dirty, whether it means washing dishes, unloading a truck, or setting up equipment. Being in the ritual team means doing what you must to create a meaningful spiritual experience for all participants, which means taking part in all elements of making sure this happens whether they are glamorous or mundane.

Sacred Roles

In this form of Norse Paganism are three specific roles necessary for group rituals: Goðar, Vǫlur, and Skald. All are equal partners, fulfilling specialized duties that support each other and the ritual participants. If you want to take on any of these roles, you should seek training in the work and tasks associated with a role. There is nothing wrong with seeking guidance from teachers outside of this practice, or even Norse Paganism, so long as their ethics are in line with yours. Anyone in service to others should always aspire to be the best they possibly can be, doing whatever they can to improve their skills.

All sacred roles are positions of service to community before anything else. Taking up a sacred role includes the responsibility of acting as a facilitator for creating the best experience possible for all ritual participants and practitioners. Anyone who abuses their positions by engaging in gate-keeping, refusing to share critical knowledge, placing themselves between participants and the Powers, or using their sacred roles to exert power over others is unfit to hold their position. Anyone performing a sacred role is a guide for other practitioners, not a ruler or the sole interpreter of the will of the Powers.

Goðar

Goðar (pronounced *GO-thar*) are responsible for running rituals. Male Goðar are referred to as Goði (pronounced *GO-thee*), female Goðar are gyðja (pronounced *GI*-thee-ya) and they are referred to as Goðar when discussing more than one or referring to a person who does not identify as masculine or feminine. They guide the flow of a group ritual, facilitate group offerings in blot, and do all work necessary to organize and carry out rituals. There might be multiple people in an active community who take on this role. Some communities rotate performing the role between trained and willing members.

Goðar are like priests and priestesses in other Pagan practices. Along with running rituals goðar provide counseling, support, and care for any ritual participants in need. They also keep an eye on the overall situation to ensure people are safe, engaged, and having their needs met. In Radical Norse Paganism, group rituals, the goðar invoke and thank the gods.

Historically, the role comes from Iceland. Before the island converted to Christianity, it was divided into several groups who elected a goðar to hold sacrifices and enforce the law. These individuals were the chosen representatives of the people who oversaw communal events and were responsible for hosting them.[193]

Vǫlur

Vǫlur (pronounced *VO*-lur) specialize in the mystical aspects of ritual. A male vǫlur is referred to as a vitki (pronounced *VEET-kee*), a female Vǫlur is referred to as a vǫlva (pronounced *VOL*-va), and the word vǫlur is used to refer to more than one or to a person who does not identify as masculine or feminine. People in this role study the mystic arts of modern Norse practice; they use those arts to develop their understanding of the Powers and reach ecstatic states both individually and in groups.

Outside of ritual, vǫlur study the arts of seiðr and runelore, commune with the Powers, and explore deeper mysteries. They share this knowledge with their community and show others how to achieve such insights, making sure such practices are passed on. In Radical Norse Paganism group rituals, the vǫ lur invoke and thank the spirits.

In the ancient world, vǫlur lived in a respected yet outside status. As the bridges between worlds, they stood at the crossroads of reality. They were respected and sometimes a little feared for their abilities, but always valued. They were often assisted by vǫlur in training. These assistants helped regulate ecstatic states, watched for potentially hostile influences or energetic shifts and guided vǫlur back from deep seiðr work. One of the most well-known tools of

193. J. L Byock (1986). "Governmental order in early medieval Iceland." *Viator*, 17, 19, 32–34.

a vǫlur was their staff; many vǫlur used it as a tool for anchoring themselves during deep trance states and directing their energies.[194]

Skald

Skalds are the keepers of lore, story, and song for ritual and their community. All skalds are referred to as a skald, when discussing them individually, or skalds when discussing more than one. During rituals they tell tales, share knowledge, and inspire participants with stories meant for the moment and ceremony. The skald's job is to use tales of the gods, the ancestors, history, more current events, or even of their own making to teach, offer insights, and inspire action.

Outside of ritual skalds are artists, performers, and scholars. What makes a skald distinct from other performers is their tales, songs, and performances are rooted in a deep understanding of the lore and its significance in the modern world. In Radical Norse Paganism group rituals, the skalds invoke and thank the dead.

In the ancient world, skalds held a critical role: as the tellers of stories and singers of songs, they were the primary means for passing on information between and within communities. People with good fame were hailed and celebrated by the skalds, while doers of ill-deeds were condemned. This role of giving praise and shame was central to the skald and their duty to community. The best skalds carry the wisdom of history and deliver it in engaging ways so all may learn from the experiences of others.[195]

Supporting Roles

Supporting roles are just as critical to group ritual as the sacred roles. Support roles handle the logistical challenges in planning and executing a group ritual. What supporting roles are necessary depends on the specific ritual and what is involved. These could include kitchen volunteers who make sure food

---

194. Sue Brunning, "A 'DIVINATION STAFF' FROM VIKING-AGE NORWAY: AT THE BRITISH MUSEUM", *Acta Archaeologica,* Vol. 87, Issue 1 (December 2016), 193–195.

195. Hannah Burrows, "Rhyme and reason: lawspeaker-poets in medieval Iceland." *Scandinavian Studies* 81, no. 2 (2009): 215-216; Lotta Fernstål (2007) "Spoken words: equality and dynamics within a group of women skalds in the third century AD," Skovgårde, Denmark, *World Archaeology*, 39:2, 272–274.

prep happens and dishes are cleaned, equipment specialists like audio-visual technicians, and, in some cases, people to handle physical security. For larger rituals, support roles are organized into designated teams based on the specific function each support role covers. Supporting roles are just as vital for making communal ritual possible as the sacred roles, and people fulfilling these duties must always be honored for their work.

One thing every group ritual must have is hospitality. Whether it is handled by an individual or a team of volunteers, the person in charge of hospitality is responsible for making sure all participants feel welcome, know what is going to happen, and offer instructions for how they can directly participate. Anyone engaging in hospitality support should make sure every person entering the ritual space is greeted and all questions or concerns are answered before the ritual begins. Hospitality people are also responsible for dealing with—and if necessary, removing—participants who are too disruptive or are making others present feel unwelcome or unsafe.

Types of Group Ritual

The best way to categorize group rituals is by the ritual's size and purpose, mostly because there are different factors to consider based on how many people are involved. Purpose is also critical, as it helps shape what needs to happen in the ritual as well as its size. Based on size, rituals can be defined as private, public, and mass rituals. Purpose is much broader and covers everything from devotional rituals to holiday rituals, weddings, funerals, coming-of-age rituals, and naming ceremonies for children.

A private ritual is usually smaller in scale, as such rituals are invite-only. Sometimes they can be much larger, but this is uncommon. Planning private rituals can be easier and more specific than other rituals because the number of attendees is determined in advance. Likewise, the dedicated ritual team can be smaller, and it is easier to give specific tasks to participants.

Public rituals are open and advertised to the public. As such, they usually take place in public places, and the group organizing it is understood to be representing the practice to the public. Public rituals require larger ritual teams, as they must handle all the necessary preparations such as welcoming in new people, handling any media who may be present, and, in some cases, outside groups.

Usually, ritual teams for public rituals have more than one person handling each of the sacred roles, with other volunteers handling other functions.

Though they share several of the same challenges and needs as public rituals, mass rituals are a category of their own. A good rule of thumb for determining whether your event is a mass ritual is if you are expecting at least thirty participants (not including the ritual team) to attend. The challenges of handling so many people require different planning from smaller public rituals. Ritual teams need to be much larger, have people assigned to handling more functional duties outside of the three sacred roles, and ritual activities need to be planned based on mass participation and finding ways to involve much larger groups than usual.

Guided Trance

One skill that is necessary for group ecstatic practice is guiding others through a trance state. The basics in chapter four provide a solid foundation for reaching a simple ecstatic state. Guided trance builds on this earlier foundation. In guided trance, the vǫlur takes on the role of guide for the rest of the group. They should also be supported by an assistant, known as a warder, who focuses on seeing how people are doing or reacting to the trance. Warding is often assigned to apprentice vǫlur and anyone else undergoing such training, but can also be done by anyone with sufficient experience in trance and ecstatic work. Larger group trances often have several warders.

The trance guide, along with any warders, must remain out of a trance state while feeling the vibe in the room and how people are responding to ecstatic triggers. Effective guides operate with one foot in each world, leading from a place of understanding what the trance participants are experiencing. Doing so takes discipline and practice; if you are interested in working as a trance guide, you should study the deeper trance methods of seiðr before practicing this halfway state. Accordingly, warding is usually assigned to vǫlur in training as it helps introduce them to this state.

The next skill for guided trance is clear descriptions. Trance is a state where the mind is open to many different possibilities, which makes participants somewhat suggestible and open to many pathways. Vague descriptions may confuse people, lead to inconsistent experiences, or invite unexpected results. Using simpler meditations when you are first starting out, such as the exercises in this book, is a good way to practice these skills. Once you are comfortable with these meditations, try writing out your own in advance, practicing them on your own and testing them with a small, experienced team before using them in group ritual.

When it is time to end the trance journey, it is important to guide people back slowly. Do the steps of the journey in reverse, taking more time to draw people back out than you did to plunge them in. You and your warder should be keeping an eye on people's reactions, particularly if they are showing any physical or emotional responses to the experience. When everyone is out of trance, check in with the group and ask about their experience.

If anyone had strong responses, they should be spoken to one-on-one, either with the warder taking them aside or making time after you have finished helping the group decompress. Helping people decompress is very important to having a healthy, sustainable trance experience.

Organizing Group and Community Rituals

When planning a ritual, you should include as many participation opportunities as possible. Providing engaging activities for ritual participants helps bring people together and makes ritual more fulfilling and empowering for all involved. If there is anything the whole group can be part of—such as an invocation or setting the space—then go for active participation and inclusion over leaving them out as a passive audience.

In some cases (usually well-organized communities), it is possible to have access to or possess a sacred space known as a hall. A hall is an indoor space used by groups for communal rituals. They can be permanently dedicated spaces owned by community members, a room in a private home, or rented rooms used for a specific ritual. A hall may contain multiple shrines along with space for many people to participate in sacred practice.

Always remember the ten-minute rule for setting the length of ritual segments, whether the segment is a skald telling a story, a vǫlur team doing trance work, or generally introducing the ritual and telling people what to expect: this rule is based on substantial research that has shown most people are able to keep focus on any one thing or topic for about ten minutes unless they are re-engaged in some way. A famous example of this rule in use is with TED Talks, where each talk, supported visuals, and other presentation aids must be no more than eighteen minutes long. While it is possible to stretch the amount of time you can keep people's attention (especially if you engage them in several different ways beyond talking), it is best for less participatory sections of a group ritual to be no longer than ten minutes each.[196]

It is also a good idea to break up these sections as much as possible. For example, if you are going to have a skald tell a tale from the lore, you should probably put a group chant before the story and follow it up with a round of people giving offerings to the Powers. Scheduling more than two different passive spectator segments back-to-back is a great way for people to tune out and make ritual incredibly boring.

Rituals are also community-building events and opportunities for socializing. You should set aside some space for people to hang out before things get started, which also gives time for latecomers to arrive, as well as to chat afterwards. This also gives space for people to process what happened in the ritual, especially if it was more intense.

Make sure to schedule time before and after the ritual for any setup and packing that needs to happen. There should be volunteers whose job is to make sure this happens, however, it is always a good idea to ask participants to help. Ritual setup should be completed before the participants arrive. The only real exception is if you have food that should be served hot. Such dishes can be kept warm so they will be ready when it's time to eat.

As with solitary practice, sacred space is set by invoking the powers of fire and ice to call on the primordial forces that created reality as we know it. Symbolically re-creating this moment clears the way for the work of the sacred to begin. The easiest and most reliable method for doing this in a group environment is to use collective chanting. Divide the participants into two roughly equal-sized groups. Have one group chant Kenaz, the fire rune, while having the other group chant Isa, the ice rune, at the same time. You can do this as a

---

196. Charlotte Hill, "Most Humans Have an Attention Span of about 10 Minutes, after That They Will Revert to Daydreaming." Psych2Go. September 09, 2014. https://psych2go.net/most-humans-have-an-attention-span-of-about-10-minutes-after-that-they-will-revert-to-daydreaming/; Carmine Gallo, "TED Talks Are Wildly Addictive For Three Powerful Scientific Reasons." *Forbes*, March 05, 2014. https://www.forbes.com/sites/carminegallo/2014/02/25/ted-talks-are-wildly-addictive-for-three-powerful-scientific-reasons/#22912e426b6a.

single, prolonged tone or through steady repetition of the runes' names. You could also have each group perform a simple, pre-written chant that invokes the powers of the fire and ice runes, incorporates music like drumming, or includes simple dance moves. Regardless of the method used, what matters most is making sure everyone present is participating in the process and that the powers of fire and ice are invoked at the same time.

Creating Engaging Rituals

Just as solitary ritual builds relationship and understanding of the Powers, group ritual does the same for all participants. It is critical that all participants in group rituals are as engaged, involved, and active as possible, lest your ritual become nothing more than a performance that excludes everyone who is not at the center of the action. There are several ways to bring people in; your methods will depend on the goals of the ritual, your group's skills, and the participants.

The easiest activities are music and chanting. Whether performed using instruments, the human voice, or played from a recording, music has been used in spiritual practice by societies across time and space. The widespread use of music in spiritual acts across many different cultures shows how effective it is in creating ecstatic states. In the case of the pre-Christian Norse peoples, there are records of skalds singing spell-songs and using poetry forms like *ljodhattar* for invocations. You can incorporate music using everything from acoustic instruments accompanied by chants, to recordings of bands blasting the right music from amps and speakers.

Regardless of the specifics, there are a few key points to remember when using music or chanting as a ritual tool. Any musical elements should be intended to get people involved in what is happening. The best way to do this is to keep chants and songs as simple, easy to teach, and repeatable as possible. A member of the ritual team, usually the skald, should teach the chants to be used to all participants before any ritual chanting begins. They should then lead all participants in the chant.

There are also specific ways of conducting chants that are effective for bringing people in. Call and response and singing in rounds are two popular, effective tools for creating highly participatory group chants. One effective approach, widely used in Reclaiming Witchcraft, is a group tone or humming together to bring everyone in sync.

If you are using musical instruments, always include parts that are simple and easy for people to join in, such as parts that keep the rhythm, i.e., drums, simple percussion instruments, or even clapping and stomping. This doesn't mean you can't include more complex elements, such as an elegant guitar melody or harmonies played on flutes, but things of that nature should rest on a foundation of simple, easy-to-teach parts performed by all participants. If you use participatory music like chanting, then a member of the ritual team (usually a skald) should teach participants the group part and lead it. This person should not be the same person responsible for leading the chant.

Dance is another method for getting people involved. The dances you use should be chosen based on what is easiest for people to learn and join, whatever the ritual team is most familiar with, and whatever achieves the desired result—it can be anything from folk dances to a mosh pit. As with music and chant, the most important thing here is that the dance is easy to teach, learn, and gets as many people involved as possible. Members of the ritual team should show all the participants how the dance is done beforehand and also lead the dance. If you are incorporating music and dance in the same ritual, the best way to handle it is having a pre-determined group of people handle the music so more participants can focus on dancing or have people who are less comfortable dancing play supporting music parts. It is best to use larger group dances, as they bring people together better than separating a large group into smaller chunks.

A more performance-based method you could use is skaldic recitation. A skaldic recitation is when a skald tells a story, recites poetry, or engages in a poetry battle (known as a flyting) with another skald. On the surface this seems simple, but there is a lot more to an effective recitation than simply speaking verse or rattling off a story. Delivering information to participants in a ritual is actually the bare minimum of what a skaldic recitation should be. An effective recitation pulls all the participants in, engages them on as many levels as possible, and inspires a strong reaction from the listeners.

There are some reliable techniques for making a recitation engaging for the participants. The most important is for the skald to decide, in cooperation with the ritual team, is what is the desired reaction from the participants. Any skald engaging in any sort of recitation needs to earn the participants' attention. To go in assuming you already have it will usually leave people bored and tuned out. If there is a competitive aspect, such as a poetry battle or a storytelling competition, the outcome should be determined by the participants instead of members of the ritual team. Good ways for learning effective techniques for skaldic recitation are going to poetry slams, live storytelling, studying improvisation, and watching effective public speakers. Above all else, skaldic recitation is a performance; anyone reciting must remember they have to earn every second of the participants' attention, energy, and focus.

Another effective tool is ritual drama. The most important element of ritual drama is determining what the ride is for the participants. Along with the obvious elements of plot, characters, and conflict, every story has some sort of journey invoked in those watching it unfold. This can be intellectual, emotional, moral, a combination of some, or all of the above. Professional theatre director and Reclaiming Witch Patricia says that what's important is:

> [t]he distinction between theatre and ritual is intention and audience / celebrant participation. Although theatre and ritual drama are both are ideally acts of transformation, ritual drama sets a high bar. Every act of theatre needs to earn its keep by always keeping the audience's experience in mind, the audience's ride. This is more true of ritual drama where the best intentions of performers, well-chosen archetypes and plots must ask how the next section moves the participants, called audience or spectators in straight theatre. Failure to do this may result in a well-intentioned history pageant reminiscent of Sunday school nativities.

Unlike other forms of engagement, ritual drama requires a lot of advance preparation. Stories need to be scripted in language that is engaging and easy to understand. Actors need to be recruited and rehearse until the story is second nature for them. The heart of any ritual drama is starting with the core intention of the drama and building outward from there.

Ritual drama can be very powerful when done effectively, but it also risks leaving most of the participants out of the action, reducing them to passive spectators. Thankfully, there are specific forms of drama that offer ideas for how to keep participants engaged in the action instead of sitting on the side-lines. Street theatre is one place to look for ideas with special mention going to forms that break the fourth wall and invite spectators to participate. The works of William Shakespeare also provide examples of direct audience engagement, especially when performed by experienced Shakespearian companies. The works and theories of playwright Berthold Brecht also provide a handy guide for creating engaging drama.

Patricia recommends studying the Greek dramas and Christian mystery plays from the Middle Ages as templates because "they have a clear objective or teaching and use popular theatre tropes such as the everyman, the chorus, masks and symbolic props/costume, antagonist vs. protagonist, that are easily recognizable in any culture." Regardless of what you use for inspiration, make the time to see a few performances in person or consult someone with theatrical experience before writing and staging a ritual drama.

ritual
SAMPLE GROUP RITUAL OUTLINE

Setup

As much time as needed, generally 15 to 30 minutes

This is the time when the ritual team arrives, conducts any work for physically preparing the space to be used for public ritual, sets up any altars or shrines, and lays out space for any food and drink. If there's any food preparation that needs to take place on site, this is the time to do it.

Doors Open

Doors open is the time you have told people to arrive by before the ritual begins. You should give yourself enough time while planning to make sure all setup will be finished by doors open.

Meet and Mingle
30 minutes at most

This is time for people to show up, lay out any food in the designated area if the event is a potluck, socialize, find space to sit or lay out their things if the ritual is taking place outdoors, and for any latecomers to arrive. This period should be no more than thirty minutes, especially if your group does regular public rituals. If this period goes on for too long, people get bored and you implicitly communicate that it's alright to be consistently late to events. This can cause frustration for other participants, especially if they are operating on tight schedules, have limited energy, or have other time-related concerns. Keeping things punctual is a good practice, and the opening meet and mingle portion tends to be one of the most likely places for time to run over.

Meet and mingle should not be used as time for completing unfinished setup, as this makes the ritual team look unprepared. It is totally alright to cut this portion short if people seem ready to get started and all expected participants have arrived.

If you are expecting new people to be arriving at the ritual, please make sure there are members of the ritual team or your group who are there to greet them, help them feel welcome, answer any questions, and explain how things work. Please be friendly, hospitable, listen to them, and address any concerns they may have. Nothing turns new people off more or guarantees they'll never come back than failing to engage with them or helping them feel like they belong. Be kind, and where reasonable, give them the benefit of the doubt.

Introduce Your Group, Statement of Principles, Ritual Intent, and Sequence of Events
5 minutes at most

The goðar introduces the group to everyone, whether you are an ad hoc ritual team, a regularly meeting fellowship, or whatever else the case may be. Read your group's principles of unity and hospitality statement. More information on how to write these and what they should include is covered in the chapter on community organizing. Explain the sequence of events for the ritual, how people are expected to participate in each section, and what is involved.

Set Space
5 to 10 minutes

The goðar takes the lead, beginning by invoking the powers of fire and ice, followed by members of the ritual team inviting the Powers to participate. Always make sure to ask permission of the local spirits to use the space for ritual and invite the local dead before invoking any other Powers. You can make this portion participatory by including a simple chant recited by the whole group, some drumming or background music and possibly some kind of simple movement all people can participate in. If there are other things your group does to set space, such as lighting incense, walking the space, or anything similar, now is the time to do it.

Shift Consciousness
10 to 15 minutes

The purpose of this section is to get the participants more engaged, active, and into an altered state of consciousness. It is usually best to begin with a guided group meditation led by the vǫlur, which can be based on the World Tree Within meditation. After this is finished, the skald should lead the group in more energetic drumming, dancing, or chanting to help ramp up their energy. The chants used should be ones that are most appropriate for the ritual's purpose. It is usually best to begin with steady, even chant and beat before moving to faster, more energetic ones. The skald should play this by ear, read the participants' mood, and get everyone to a point where they are energized but not tired.

Ritual Activity
10 to 20 minutes

This is the section where the focal action of the ritual takes place. If there is a specific activity associated with the purpose of the ritual, such as a game, a symbolic action, seiðr, ritual drama or a skaldic recitation, this is the time to do it. Make this activity as engaging as possible. For ritual dramas and skaldic recitation, please follow the guidelines provided earlier in this chapter on how to perform these activities in an engaging fashion. Whatever the activity, the goðar will be responsible for facilitating as necessary in addition to whatever other functions are handled by the other members of the ritual team.

Blot
10 minutes

The goðar leads the blot (outlined in chapter four). If you are conducting a large group ritual where passing around a plate of shared offerings or drinking horns would be time-consuming or logistically challenging, the ritual team should set out portions of the food or drink and distribute them to all practitioners before the goðar performs the blot invocation.

Take the Omen
5 to 10 minutes[197]

The vǫlur asks the Powers for guidance and performs divination for the group. Depending on the group and those involved, this could be a rune-casting, as discussed in Chapter Six, where the results are read to the entire group. It could also be utiseta or spae seiðr, as discussed in chapter seven, if the vǫlur is trained in either of these arts and feels comfortable doing so.

---

197. This section is inspired by a similar practice common to ADF Druidry.

Thank the Powers and Participants
5 minutes

The ritual team thanks the Powers for their presence, those working in supporting roles for their labor and the participants for coming to the ritual.

Decompress
10 to 20 minutes

This is time for everyone to socialize post-ritual, enjoy the food and drink provided, and come back from the altered state brought on by ritual activity. This is also time where the ritual team should address any questions from participants who need help processing anything that happened during the ritual. This time goes on for as long as needed or until it is time to leave if you are in a time-sensitive space, such as a rented room or a private home where the hosts have given a specific, necessary end time.

Clean-up

The ritual team, along with any additional volunteers, cleans everything up. Please always leave whatever space you used better off than you found it. No matter where you are holding a ritual, always leave no trace.

Confronting Fascism

One type of work all Norse Pagan communities need to participate in is confronting fascism and driving it out from our communities, whether those are our spiritual communities or the places we live or work. Confronting fascists is necessary for building truly safe, inclusive communities and attracting more inclusively-minded people. On a grand scale, the problem of fascism can only truly be defeated by removing the conditions in society that enable and encourage its growth. The work of pushing it out of your local community, confronting fascist actions, and building alliances with anti-fascists are all steps needed to accomplish this goal.

There are many compelling reasons to confront and remove fascism, but the most important are moral and practical. Morally speaking, everything fascists, fascism, and their neo-Volkisch allies stand for is completely at odds with Radical Norse Paganism and the sources other Norse Pagan traditions use for inspiration. Standing between fascists and their intended victims in whatever way you can is the right thing to do. Practically speaking, fascists present a clear and present danger to anyone who does not submit to them. Anyone they call undesirable or degenerate are not even treated as people, and they face threats, physical and psychological harm, or even deadly violence. And to be clear, even those who have lashed themselves to the fascist yoke are not safe from their own brutality. Letting fascist groups operate unchallenged puts people in danger. This cannot be tolerated and must be confronted on every level possible.

Securing Community

The foundation of securing community is knowing how fascists operate. A lot of the basics in identifying them are in the earlier sections on the neo-Volkisch and understanding fascism in chapter eight. Those guidelines are useful for anyone seeking safe, genuinely inclusive community, but keeping fascists out of existing communities requires an additional set of skills. These skills are based on knowing the general patterns fascist groups tend to follow: passive fascists, active fascists, and entryists.

Passives are either people who repeat neo-Volkisch and fascist ideas from a place of ignorance and misinformation, or sympathize with fascist ideas but are not actively organizing, promoting, or advancing them. It is important to point out that people of this persuasion are not exactly the same as those who may have conservative political opinions. Passive fascists, unlike people with conservative or other right-wing political beliefs, promote covert and overt fascist material online and in person. Some are members of fascist groups but may be in denial of the group's true nature, clinging to claims of shared heritage as a defense. Inclusivity statements are useful for attracting the misinformed who are seeking genuine community and deterring passives who are more entrenched in fascist ideas.

Some passives can be educated and won over with work. Usually, their support for fascism is thanks to unexamined ideas or bad information, so any who respond well to discussion, engagement, and the offering of new sources are worth working with. Those who are consistently defensive or become more overt in their positions are not. Regardless of whether or not they are receptive to engagement, winning over passives is never more important than the safety of your community. Engagement with passive fascists must be discussed collectively and handled on a case-by-case basis. Above all, remember that the neo-Volkisch are a small but vocal minority within Norse Paganism; winning over one passive is never worth alienating many more already inclusively-minded people or losing existing community members.

Actives are members of unquestionably fascist organizations and more overt neo-Volkisch groups. They promote overt and covert fascist material, defend known fascists and neo-Volkisch ideologues, use coded racist language (an act known as dogwhistling), actively argue in bad faith, and participate in fascist actions. Some have a history of violence. Many harass inclusive practitioners, discredit Norse Paganism through their actions, recruit the unwary and already discontent, and work to create a world where everything they call degenerate or impure is destroyed. Despite their threats, they often refuse to engage with or have anything to do with openly inclusive groups, making clear and consistently enforced inclusivity statements a highly effective tool for keeping them out.

The best way to deal with active fascists is to identify them, remove them from the community, and warn all other community groups about them. Having active fascists in an inclusive group undermines that group's credibility, emboldens other active fascists, and *will* push good people out. Rehabilitation is best handled by organizations like Life After Hate, Small Steps Consulting, and other groups who specialize in helping active fascists leave fascism. This type of work should not be handled by your community; actives who want out should be referred to or seek out rehabilitation groups. If local groups of this type see a role you or your community can play in their rehabilitation, then feel free to take part; know that above all, it is always best to leave the heavy lifting to the people best equipped to handle it.

Entryists are the most insidious fascists thanks to their deliberately deceptive methods. According to Alexander Reid Ross, entryism is a political strategy where fascists conceal their true beliefs, join non-fascist groups or subcultures, move into positions of influence, and change them from within to havens for fascism. Entryists actively pursue positions of power and responsibility, shield their true goals with a veil of plausible deniability, and use coded bigoted language or misrepresented facts when presenting fascist ideas until they feel safe to act openly. If an entryist is identified, they should be immediately expelled and publicly denounced.[198]

Despite the problems defeating entryism (it can easily inspire paranoia, for example), it is easier to expel than you would think. Transparent, democratic methods of decision-making that involve as many community members as possible make it very difficult for entryists to reach positions that can be abused. Having key functions, like managing social media, handled by working groups further dilutes any power an entryist individual could wield. Votes of no confidence provide an easy mechanism for removing them from such roles. Entryism is another reason for community groups to only take on tasks they already have the people to handle and not overextend themselves. Overextension inspires desperation to fill empty slots, creating opportunities for entryists to gain power.

Hand-in-hand with structural barriers are education and equitable conflict resolution systems. Educating people cultivates shared values and ensures people know what to watch for. This makes entryists stand out like sore thumbs when they break out their sugar-coated propaganda. Effective, transparent, and honest conflict resolutions also help deter and detect entryists. Such mechanisms, when cultivated and maintained in a consistent fashion, foster an environment where people feel free to discuss their concerns with other members or group leaders, something else that helps identify entryists early on. Decisively removing them through these systems discourages other entryists from attempting to infiltrate a specific community.

When it comes to preempting or defeating organized fascist activity in your community, it is recommended you study works on strategy like Sun Tzu's *The Art of War,* Machiavelli's *The Prince,* and Carl von Clauswitz's *On War* along with reading works on anti-fascism, some of which are listed in Further Reading. These can provide insights on what to expect from fascists, as they often apply the methods discussed in these and other texts. Knowing what to expect

198. Ross, 141–142.

and how underhanded tactics work makes you better prepared for defeating them through more honest, sustainable methods.

Working with Antifa

The most critical work for securing the Norse Pagan community is participating in the broader struggle against fascism. The most visible way of doing this is participating openly as Norse Pagans in public protests opposing fascist rallies. This is necessary for confronting fascism in the battleground of popular opinion, defeating them decisively, and combating their attempts to hijack our practices. If you are engaging in direct action, go with a group, plan ahead, and study the materials on anti-fascism in the Further Reading section. Securing your community and direct confrontation are only the beginning of taking the fight to the fascists. The next essential step is building alliances with the Antifa movement.

One of the most valuable allies any community can have in confronting fascists and the neo-Volkisch is the antifascist movement, often shortened to "Antifa." Antifa's goal is best summed up in two words: "never again!" According to Mark Bray, Antifa are more than just people who are morally opposed to fascism. They are activists committed to using direct action to disrupt and defeat all attempts by fascists to organize as a movement. Antifa are not a single organization but instead a decentralized movement made up of local groups who adhere to similar principles and share information. Bray claims most Antifa believe grassroots action is a far better solution than government-directed censorship and suppression, as history has many examples of state-sponsored censorship ending badly.[199]

Many assume involvement with Antifa means street brawling with fascists. While these visible actions tend to draw a lot of media attention, they are only the tip of a very large iceberg. According to Shane Burley, the bulk of Antifa work is careful investigation, raising awareness, shutting down fascist media platforms and sources of funding, and denying fascists access to venues, commonly known as no platforming or deplatforming.[200] Bray's research confirms

---

199. Mark Bray, *Antifa: The Anti-Fascist Handbook*, Melville House (Brooklyn: 2017), xv–xvii.

200. Bray, 168; Burley, 202–207.

these strategies work, showing most Antifa work is focused on information gathering and public education.

Antifa is therefore a valuable ally for inclusive communities. Antifa often have vital information for Norse Pagans, both for keeping communities safe and knowing which fascist or neo-Volkisch groups are active near them. Radical Norse Pagans can help Antifa by educating them on the ins and outs of local communities, providing information on known neo-Volkisch groups, and helping steer Antifa toward active fascists in the Pagan community. This also helps in other ways, as many Antifa usually engage in other forms of activism, making them potential ambassadors to broader society. Above all else, for Norse Pagans, fascism is the antithesis of everything we stand for and we should fight to end the threat they pose to the world. This makes any Norse Pagans who agree natural allies of the Antifa movement.[201]

Due to the nature of their work and the risks they take building such relationships, isn't as simple as finding the nearest Antifa group, dropping them a line, and offering to chat over a cup of coffee. Many Antifa groups are very security conscious and hesitant to meet with people they've never worked with before. There is also the problem of fascists creating false anti-fascist pages, the fake Boston Antifa web presence being a notorious example to harvest the personal data of would-be Antifa and other activists.[202]

The best way to get started is reaching out to proven anti-fascist websites or magazines, several of which are in the Further Reading section. They usually know who can be trusted and have people willing to set up an initial meeting. From these beginnings you can build an enduring relationship, earn the trust of anti-fascists, and effectively oppose fascists in Paganism. Installing secure messaging apps like Signal and getting a free encrypted email account with ProtonMail are highly recommended tools for making contact with Antifa. Here are some common anti-fascist symbols that are widely used in the Antifa movement and identify a group as anti-fascist. They appear on their own and are often incorporated into broader designs.

---

201. Burley, 202.

202. "Eugene, OR Alt-Right Trolls Behind 'Boston Antifa' Exposed." It's Going Down. March 30, 2017. https://itsgoingdown.org/eugene-alt-right-trolls-behind-boston-antifa-exposed/.

Commonly Used Anti-Fascist Symbols

Antifa Dual Flag, originally a German anti-fascist symbol from the 1920s and 1930s, is also been seen with one flag as a different color, usually red, or for a specific community like the LGBT Rainbow or Trans Pride flags

The Three Arrows, originally a German anti-fascist symbol from the 1920s and 1930s, often also incorporated into other designs or logos

The Circled Ansuz, sometimes used by anti-fascist Norse Pagans and sympathetic non-Pagan groups and sites.

Making Community Work

Building community has its own unique challenges that go above and beyond being a part of an already existing community. Even so, if there are no active communities in your area that are meeting your needs, then the results of good community building make the work worthwhile. The work is long and at times will be difficult. What will always ease the burdens is sharing the load as much as possible, keeping decision-making transparent and holding people accountable in all things.

The next exercise will help for developing education, study groups, and materials for your community. This is based on similar exercises used by educators at all levels to help teach critical thinking and how to analyze written sources before using them in study groups. It is also useful for reading between the lines of other sources of information, including blogs, news outlets, and other works.

exercise
ENGAGING WITH SOURCES

For this exercise, you will need to go to your local library. Go to the history section and pick out two books on the same subject.

Once you have selected the books, there is some important information you will need to take down. Look up both authors of the books you have checked out. Take note of their education, qualifications, and prior work.

Open both books to the page with the publication information near the front cover. Write down the name of the publisher and the year it was published.

Next, open the books to their tables of contents. Compare how they organize the information on the subject and what is emphasized.

Now that you have taken down all this information, read both books. While you are reading them, pay attention to how each author discusses the subject. Write down any significant differences and arguments made. This is especially important to focus on in cases where both authors are discussing the same information, events, and evidence.

After reading and taking notes, check out a primary source that both authors mention or cite. Read it, and compare what it says in the source to what the authors say about it. Take note of the differences and similarities in what they say.

Analyzing how the authors approach the same subject is just as important as the events they describe. When reading other works, use a critical eye—pay attention to claims the author makes, and compare them to the claims made by others. True understanding of any material comes from analyzing the arguments of many different, credible perspectives.

AFTERWORD

Writing this book has been an incredible journey. I've gone to a lot of places I didn't expect when I started out. I hope what this inspires will continue to surprise me in the best way possible. I have no doubt what you do with the Way of Fire and Ice will be even more incredible than you could imagine.

This practice will always challenge you. Mistakes will happen. What matters is that you keep going, find the most effective solutions for the problems ahead, and use a compass made from worthy ideas to find the course forward. Your best days will always be ahead of you.

Do not shy away from great challenges; meet them as chances to grow. Let your journey lift up humanity. I hope someday we will cross paths. May you always rise above whatever you face, dare mighty deeds, and break chains.

May the Powers always watch over you.

appendix I

FURTHER READING

The following are additional books, articles, and other useful resources, organized by subject. They can help you learn on your own and better understand this book. You can also follow the growing conversation online at www.onblackwings.com.

Anti-Fascism

Books

Bring the War Home: The White Power Movement and Paramilitary America by Kathleen Belew

Antifa: the Anti-Fascist Handbook by Mark Bray

Fascism Today: What It Is and How to End It by Shane Burley

The Rage: The Vicious Circle of Islamist and Far-Right Extremism by Julia Ebner

Gods of the Blood: The Pagan Revival and White Separatism by Mattias Gardell

Black Sun: Aryan Cults, Esoteric Nazism, and the Politics of Identity by Nicholas Goodrick-Clarke

Right-Wing Populism in Europe: Politics and Discourse, edited by Ruth Wodak, Majid Khosravinik, and Brigitte Mral

Alt-America: The Rise of the Radical Right in the Age of Trump by David Neiwart

The Anatomy of Fascism by Robert Paxton

Against the Fascist Creep by Alexander Reid Ross

Websites

Anti-Fascist News: https://antifascistnews.net/

A Thousand Flowers: https://athousandflowers.net/

It's Going Down: https://itsgoingdown.org/

Searchlight Magazine: http://www.searchlightmagazine.com/#

Southern Poverty Law Center: https://www.splcenter.org/

Community Organizing and Education

Pedagogy of the Oppressed by Paulo Freire

Anarchist Pedagogies, edited by Robert H. Haworth

Cyberchiefs: Autonomy and Authority in Online Tribes by Mathieu O'Neil

The Empowerment Manual: A Guide for Collaborative Groups by Starhawk

Folklore and Mythology

The Penguin Book of Norse Myths: Gods of the Vikings by Kevin Crossley-Holland

Gods and Myths of Northern Europe by H.R. Ellis Davidson

The Road to Hel: A Study of The Conception of the Dead in Old Norse Literature by H. R. Ellis Davidson

Norse Mythology by Neil Gaiman

The Norse Myths: A Guide to the Gods and Heroes by Carolyne Larrington

Trolls: An Unnatural History by John Lindow

Scandinavian Folk Belief and Legend, edited by Reimund Kvideland and Henning K. Sehmsdorf

Jackson Crawford's Old Norse Channel: https://www.youtube.com/channel/UCXCxNFxw6-iqMh4uliYvufg

Mathias Nordvig's Nordic Mythology Channel: https://www.youtube.com/channel/UCnmluPOXod57_6M45Z-etuw/

History

Early Medieval Europe: 300-1000 by Roger Collins

Caliban and the Witch: Women, the Body and Primitive Accumulation by Silvia Federici

The Vikings: A History by Robert Ferguson

Nordic Religions in the Viking Age by Thomas A. DuBois

The Occult Roots of Nazism: Secret Aryan Cults and Their Influence on Nazi Ideology by Nicholas Goodrick-Clarke

Debt: the First 5,000 Years by David Graeber

Women in the Viking Age by Judith Jesch

The Pursuit of History by John Tosh

A History of the Vikings by Gwyn Jones

The Vikings by Else Roesdahl

Heimskringla by Snorri Sturluson

The Early Germans by Malcolm Todd

The Vikings and the Victorians: Inventing the Old North in Nineteenth-Century Britain by Andrew Wawn

The Roman Empire and Its Germanic Peoples by Herwig Wolfram

Inclusivity

Feminism is for Everybody by bell hooks

Gender Outlaw by Kate Bornstein

The Islamic Threat: Myth or Reality? by John Esposito

The Wretched of the Earth by Frantz Fanon

Disidentification by Jose Esteban Muñoz

Transgender History by Susan Stryker

Race Matters by Cornell West

Philosophy

The Ecology of Freedom by Murray Bookchin

The Philosophy of Social Ecology by Murray Bookchin

Mutual Aid: A Factor in Evolution by Peter Kropotkin

Ask: Building Consent Culture by Kitty Stryker

Runes

Runes: A Handbook by Michael P. Barnes

The Sorcerer's Screed by Jochum Magnús Eggertsson

Norwegian Runes and Runic Inscriptions by Terje Spurkland

Seiðr

The Nine Worlds of Seid-Magic by Jenny Blain

The Viking Way: Magic and Mind in Late Iron Age Scandinavia;Religion and War in the Later Iron Age of Scandinavia by Neil Price

Old Norse Religion in Long-Term Perspectives by Anders Andren, Kristina Jennbert and Catharina Raudvere

Sagas

Beowulf

Njal's Saga

Poetic Edda

Prose Edda

Saga of Grettir the Strong

Sagas of the Icelanders

Saga of the Jomsvikings

Icelandic Saga Database: http://sagadb.org

appendix II

THE ORIGINS OF THE PAGAN REVIVAL

The revival of Norse Paganism and Paganism is understood to be a long, complex process. There are many stories of glorified founders, larger-than-life figures, and teachers who led the way. They are not, however, all there is to the story of how Paganism in general and the Norse ways in particular returned after nearly a thousand years of suppression. A key part of this story is also how the neo-Volkisch movement began, became influential, and started losing their power in Paganism. There is a lot to this history, and much is poorly understood thanks, in part, to the limited nature of existing sources. What is presented here is an attempt at making sense of this process, starting with the roots of the modern revival in the eighteenth century.

Age of Spiritualism

For four hundred years after Scandinavia's conversion to Christianity by hook and crook, a new order settled over the European continent called Christendom. This social system was ruled by kings claiming divine right to rule and supported by allies in the church. Everyone who lived in this society saw themselves first and foremost as Christians before anything else. The crosses and crowns of feudal Christendom were supported by the vast majority of the population toiling under the yoke of serfdom. There were times when they rose up in rebellion, but many of these attempts were dealt with using the same harsh cruelty first inflicted on the pre-Christian peoples of the continent.

It took centuries for the solid, unified rule of the feudal system to crumble, beginning with the Reformation, which tore Christendom asunder between Protestant and Catholic. Ambitious kings, now armed with gunpowder and cannons, used the opportunity to crush unruly lords and reduce religious authorities from partners in power to subordinates. Merchants and bankers, who once had little power, became increasingly influential thanks to many monarchs' need for stable tax revenues to pay for everything. The last remnants of the old feudal order were swept away by the fires of the French Revolution and a quarter century of war unleashed by the ambitions of Napoleon Bonaparte. As Europe industrialized, invaded the Americas and Africa, and found its footing, cracks in the spiritual status quo opened. Created by centuries of turmoil, these breaches became wide enough for a breath of fresh air to slip in.

The first breeze was a movement known as Spiritualism, the direct precursor to modern Paganism. Spiritualism emerged in 1848 in the United States and was heavily influenced by Romanticism, a cultural and artistic movement that developed in reaction to the destruction of Napoleonic warfare. Its spread signaled the demise of Christianity as a central point of identity and the detrimental effects of the Industrial Revolution. In this way, Spiritualism was very much a product of its time. Members of this movement rejected what they saw as the detachment created by modern rationality while also embracing scientific processes to prove the existence of spirit.[203]

Spiritualists were and are most famous for their work in contacting the dead. Ouija boards, séances, and the practice of mediumship as we know it today were all developed, appropriated, and popularized by the Spiritualists. Others sought evidence of faeries, the hidden folk, and other beings attested to in folklore. Swept up in the fascination with all things seen as exotic to European colonial powers, some explored the spiritual practices of cultures around the world and those of pre-Christian Europe. A few started occult groups dedicated to the study of lost or hidden knowledge. This interest in folklore and mysticism was heavily influenced by the assumptions and norms of Vic-

203. Cathy Gutierrez, "Spiritualism," *Cambridge Handbook of Western Mysticism and Esotericism*, Cambridge University Press (New York: 2016), 240–242.

torian society, playing out as the tendency of Victorian Spiritualists to impose nineteenth-century ideas about race, nationalism, gender, and sexuality onto the past, mythology, and folk customs. As much as this work brought many sources for inspiration into the public consciousness, the material they produced was nevertheless distorted and removed from its original context via their deep-seated prejudices.[204]

The influence of Spiritualism waned from its origins in the 1850s to the 1930s. The times of greatest interest were in the aftermath of especially bloody conflicts such as the American Civil War and the First World War. People in these periods sought ways to contact relatives they'd lost in conflict, come to terms with so much destruction, and process the agony of industrialized warfare. These wartime surges were not solely responsible for Spiritualism's growth; interest endured well into the 1930s. Two of the more famous adherents of Spiritualism were Mary Todd Lincoln, First Lady to US President Abraham Lincoln, and Sir Arthur Conan Doyle, the author of many popular works of fiction, including the adventures of Sherlock Holmes, who also wrote extensive works promoting Spiritualism.[205]

Spiritualist occult societies and folkloric groups were the most direct predecessors of the modern revival. Some of the most historically significant groups for modern Pagans were the German Volkisch movement, the Hermetic Order of the Golden Dawn, and the Theosophy Society. These groups combined the ideas of the Spiritualist movement with fragments of folklore and remnants of

204. Gutierrez, 237–240.

205. Jean H. Baker, "Mary Todd Lincoln: Civil War First Lady," *White House Studies*, (Vol. 2, No. 1) 2002, 79; Angela Fowler, "Arthur Conan Doyle's British Spiritualist Commonwealth: 'the great unifying force,'" *English Literature in Transition (1880–1920)*, (59: 4) 2016, 458–460; Jennifer Hazelgrove, "Spiritualism After the Great War," *Twentieth Century British History*, (Vol. 10, No. 4) 1999, 404–407; David K. Nartonis, "The Rise of 19th-century American Spiritualism, 1854–1873." *Journal for the Scientific Study of Religion* 49, no. 2 (2010): 364–366.

older mystical traditions preserved by oral tradition or groups like the Rosicrucians and the Freemasons with their own developments. Their ideas provided inspiration for many who built modern Paganism in the twentieth century.[206]

The Volkisch movement is a particularly complicated example because there are some who claim they are a direct precursor to modern Norse Paganism. The core of their ideas was a mystical take on German nationalism, asserting what made a person German was blood and soil, which defined them on a deeply spiritual level. According to many Volkisch thinkers, true Germans lived in a direct spiritual relationship with a god very similar to that of Christianity. This deity was, according to them, the center of a powerful sun cult that was a direct manifestation of the Germanic peoples' desires, culture, and beliefs and was the true source of inspiration for Christianity. They argued only someone of true German heritage could study their lore or engage in their practices, a position that was used to justify excluding Jews and anyone else deemed insufficiently German from society. They used fabricated claims of "ancient wisdom," such as the writings of Guido List as proof while also arguing the Eddas were evidence of this solar cult. In reality, these ideas really set them apart from anything that could be described as Pagan. Such fervent nationalism also set them apart from the more ecumenical Spiritualist movement.[207]

All these groups are part of what could be described as proto-Pagans, movements who predated the Pagan movement with practices that helped inspire modern Paganism, even though many of their ideas were a far cry from the modern revival. These practices included using older source material such as occult grimoires and folklore as sources for inspiration, developing their own forms of practice and ritual, establishing systems of organization, and producing written material to perpetuate their ideas. These offshoots of Spiritualism saw themselves as pursuers of hidden and secret knowledge, a key difference from present-day Pagans, who generally see modern practices as a

---

206. Michael Gomes, "H. P. Blavatsky and Theosophy," *Cambridge Handbook of Western Mysticism and Esotericism*, Cambridge University Press (New York: 2016), 248–253, 257–259; Asprem Egil, "The Golden Dawn and the O.T.O.," *Cambridge Handbook of Western Mysticism and Esotericism*, Cambridge University Press (New York: 2016), 272–274; George L. Mosse, *The Crisis of German Ideology: Intellectual Origins of the Third Reich*, Grosset and Dunlap (New York: 1964), 41–44.

207. Mosse 40–45, 70–76, 129–133.

kind of religion or spirituality. This is especially the case for Norse Pagans and other similar practices, greater emphasis is put on the use of surviving ancient sources as inspiration for modern practice.

Fascism and Spirituality

As novel and experimental as their ideas were, these occult societies were not removed from the times they lived in. Political movements rooted in appeals to romanticized versions of the past, nationalism, tradition, and pseudo-scientific racism made some inroads into proto-Pagan groups. The best example of this was a Volkisch group known as the Armanenscheft, founded by Austrian mystic Guido List. List, whose practice was also known as Armanism, claimed to be channeling secret knowledge of a long-lost group of sun-worshiping priest-kings who, according to him, ruled over the ancient Germanic tribes. He also believed the Germanics were the purest of the so-called Aryan race, making them the greatest of all groups in the world.[208]

An offshoot of List's Armanen, the Thule Gelleschaft (also known as the Thule Society) were early supporters of the Nazi Party in Bavaria. They backed Hitler's organization prior to and during the 1923 Beer Hall Putsch, an attempt by Hitler and the early Nazis to overthrow the German government by force. They eventually fell out with the Nazis, partly due to the Nazi Party's attempts to appeal to church-going members of the German public, and were banished from any power or influence in the Nazi regime. One prominent Volkisch runologist and student of List, Friedrich Burnhard Marby of the Edda Society, was denounced as an anti-Nazi and imprisoned at the Welzheim concentration camp in 1936; he was released in 1945 when Allied armies liberated the camps. By the mid-1930s, the Volkisch were relegated to fringe status by a regime many of them had once helped propel to power.[209]

The main exception was SS-Brigadenführer Karl Maria Wiligut, Heinrich Himmler's personal occultist. Wiligut created his own Volkisch-derived practice known as Irminism, which claimed the ancient Germanics were monotheists

---

208. Mosse, 73–75.

209. Mosse, 228–233; Nicholas Goodrick-Clarke, *The Occult Roots of Nazism: Secret Aryan Cults and Their Influence on Nazi Ideology*, Tauris Parke Paperbacks (London: 2004), 160–161, 202–204.

who worshiped a god named Krist, who was appropriated by Christianity. The source of Wiligut's ideas was his "ancestral clairvoyance," and he claimed to have been initiated into these mysteries in 1890 by his grandfather's spirit and to have come from a prehistoric line of Germanic priests. Needless to say, there is no evidence to substantiate any of his claims. While Wiligut and other mystically-inclined Nazis like Heinrich Himmler continued to hold positions of influence, they largely stayed private in their practices while official regime religious policy focused on co-opting Christianity into a tool for expanding Nazi power.[210]

There is no better expression of how insignificant such groups were in Nazi Germany than the denunciations of occult practice in general by Hitler and the Nazi Party's open embrace of contemporary Christianity. As Hitler himself said on the subject in *Mein Kampf*:

> It is typical of such persons that they rant about ancient Teutonic heroes of the dim and distant ages, stone axes, battle spears and shields, whereas in reality they themselves are the woefullest poltroons imaginable. For those very same people who brandish Teutonic tin swords that have been fashioned carefully according to ancient models and wear padded bear-skins, with the horns of oxen mounted over their bearded faces, proclaim that all contemporary conflicts must be decided by the weapons of the mind alone. And thus they skedaddle when the first communist cudgel appears. Posterity will have little occasion to write a new epic on these heroic gladiators. I have seen too much of that kind of people not to feel a profound contempt for their miserable play-acting.[211]

This clear disdain is further reinforced by this portion of a 1938 public speech he gave in Nuremberg:

---

210. Goodrick-Clarke, 184–186.

211. Adolf Hitler, *Mein Kampf*, translated by James Murphy, 300.

> We will not allow mystically-minded occult folk with a passion for exploring the secrets of the world beyond to steal into our Movement. Such folk are not National Socialists, but something else—in any case, something which has nothing to do with us. [...] But since we set as the central point of this perception and of this profession of belief the maintenance and hence the security for the future of a being formed by god, we thus serve the maintenance of a divine work and fulfill a divine will.[212]

Between such sentiments and the marginalization of supportive Armanen practitioners by the Nazis, any sympathy on the part of the Volkisch movement for the regime was largely one-way and not reciprocated. Scholars like Nicholas Goodrich-Clarke have argued the influence of these groups on the Nazi Party (outside of Nazi usage of symbols popular with the Thule Society and the Armanen) was minimal.[213] Historian Peter Staudenmeier argues that any occult and Pagan influences on the Nazis are mostly sensationalism and attempts by former Nazis to create scapegoats. His argument against people taking these stories at face value is very direct:

"Attributing the horrors of Nazi Germany to obscure occult sources is all too often a convenient way of absolving ourselves from the hard work of understanding the past."[214]

This part of the history of Paganism is important to wrestle with for two reasons. The first is due to the common tropes in popular culture of Nazi occultism, mysticism, and association with otherworldly forces. Understanding the real history of the Nazi party's disdain for such practices is important for properly grappling with the true causes of Hitler's rise and march to genocide, and what it means for the modern day. The second is many in the neo-Volkisch

---

212. Speech in Nuremberg on September 6, 1938. *The Speeches of Adolf Hitler, April 1922-August 1939*, Volume 1, Edited by Norman Hepburn Baynes. University of Michigan Press, 396.

213. Mosse, 305–309.

214. Peter Staudenmaier, "The Nazis as Occult Masters? It's a Good Story but Not History, *Aeon* June 09, 2017. https://aeon.co/ideas/the-nazis-as-occult-masters-its-a-good-story-but-not-history.

movement point to this misunderstanding of history as justification for their beliefs while ignoring the open endorsements of Christianity by Hitler and Nazi disdain for the original Volkisch movement. As much as some of the neo-Volkisch work to forge connections with Hitler's Thousand Year Reich, their efforts would have been dismissed by the Nazis themselves. It also ignores how much of the modern white nationalist movement, whom they've allied with, has very similar opinions of the neo-Volkisch to the original Nazis.

Modern Revival

Spiritualism and occult practice generally receded into the background during the 1940s and 1950s. The once-vibrant Spiritualist movement was already in decline before the Great Depression hit, retreating to the fringe after the stock market crashed. Even so, the first significant modern Pagan groups—Aleister Crowley's Thelema and Gerald Gardner's Wicca—were organized during the 1920s and 1930s as Spiritualism's popularity was beginning to wane. This work wouldn't truly come into its own until the late 1950s and 1960s, when modern Paganism really took root.

There is little doubt the 1960s were critical in propelling Paganism from being a set of small, dedicated groups to the highly diverse religious movement it is today, thanks in part to challenges to the existing status quo rising from the counter-culture movement. For most people, "counter-culture" refers to hippies, Woodstock, and LSD. In fact, these were the only tip of the very large iceberg that was counter-culture, which had its birth in earlier forms of social criticism like the Beatniks and the Mods who challenged the conformity, regimentation, and general lack of personal satisfaction of modern life of their era. Three major strains of the counter-culture that had the greatest impact on the modern revival were the new wave of fantasy fiction, the "back to the land" movement, and exploration of Buddhist, Hindu, and occult spirituality.

Fantasy fiction is an under-appreciated element of counter-culture, even though it really exploded into popular consciousness during the 1960s. The vanguard of this element was, surprisingly enough, JRR Tolkien's *The Lord of the Rings* series, first published in 1954. As much as *The Lord of the Rings* is seen today as the archetypal fantasy novel, at the time of publication it was very subversive compared to the pulp fantasy literature of the time such as the Conan series, which was populated with all-conquering supermen and helpless damsels in distress. As BBC Culture points out, *The Lord of the Rings*'s main appeal for the counter-culture was due to its use of clearly pre-Christian folklore for ideas, the fashioning of the relatively ordinary hobbits and even women into heroes instead of being part of the background, the villains as part of a militaristic industrial wasteland, and victory achieved by breaking power instead of conquest. All these themes and ideas struck a chord with the rising counterculture. *The Lord of the Rings*'s place on the bestseller list was propelled primarily by the counter-culture movement.[215]

Incredibly influential in shaping the rest of the fantasy genre, Tolkien's books also saw impact outside of the literary world. Two examples from popular music of the time were bands like Black Sabbath and Led Zeppelin. Another was the founding of the Society for Creative Anachronism in 1966 in Berkeley, California, by a group of fantasy literature fans. From its humble beginnings as a themed outdoor party hosted by future *Asatru* author Diana Paxson, this organization was key in the rise of the broader medieval reenactment and recreation movement. The exploration of non-Christian or pre-Christian ideas in fantasy literature and the rise of re-enactment groups played a key role in raising awareness of these ideas in broader society.[216]

These groups were also influenced by the back-to-the-land movement, which was more or less spontaneously started by young people who were disenchanted with modern life, wishing instead to seek connection to nature. They set up communes, learned traditional crafts, and pursued primitive skills. Their escape from modern life was very similar to the desires and motives of the growing fantasy literature culture with considerable overlap.[217]

It's easy to see how the revolt against the shortcomings of modern life present in fantasy literature, medieval reenactment, and back-to-the-land was

---

215. Jane Ciabattari, "Culture—Hobbits and Hippies: Tolkien and the Counterculture" BBC News, November 20, 2014. http://www.bbc.com/culture/story/20141120-the-hobbits-and-the-hippies.

216. "What Is the SCA?" http://socsen.sca.org/what-is-the-sca/; "The Middle Ages as They Were, or As They Should Have Been?" NU HIST 2805: The Gunpowder Empires, https://faculty.nipissingu.ca/muhlberger/SCAREC2.HTM.; Michael J. Tresca, *The Evolution of Fantasy Role-Playing Games*, McFarland (Jefferson, NC: 2010), 182.

217. Ogden Publications, "The "Back to the Land" Movement" *UTNE Reader*, September 2016. https://www.utne.com/environment/back-to-the-land-movement-ze0z1609zfis.

influencing and shaping modern Paganism. These groups overlapped with other elements of the counterculture of spiritual explorers, as they all came out of the same general mindset. Desires for a simpler life, deeper truths, and meaning beyond simply having a nice house with a white picket fence, 2.5 kids, and the newest car in the garage propelled people to question their life decisions and society at large.

The most direct tie between these currents and Paganism was exploration of alternative spirituality. In 1972, sociologist Edward Tiryakian observed a clear connection between participants in the 1960s counterculture, campus politics, and the New Left with interest in the occult. He argued this was part of a broader surge of societal interest in the occult, pointing to films like *Rosemary's Baby*. Another example of this surge in interest can be seen in both the wild popularity of bands like Black Sabbath and the rise of heavy metal, an entire genre of rock and roll whose main sources of inspiration in this period were traditional occultism and social critique. All these factors helped to create an environment where individuals and small, grassroots groups around the world started exploring Norse mythology.[218]

The first known organized group that combined all these elements into Norse-inspired Paganism formed in Iceland. On the first day of summer in 1972, four men met at Hotel Borg in Reykjavík to discuss reviving traditional Icelandic spirituality. They were Sveinbjörn Beinteinsson, a farmer and poet; Jörmundur Ingi Hansen, a prominent participant in the Reykjavík hippie movement; Dagur Þorleifsson, an active member of the Reykjavík theosophy lodge; and Þorsteinn Guðjónsson, the leader of the esoteric group Félag Nýalssinna. They founded Asatruarfelagid, named Sveinbjörn Beinteinsson as the first Chairman or Alherjarsgodi, and they called their practice Asatru. They received recognition as a religion later in that year by the Icelandic government, making them the first government-recognized Norse Pagan group in the world.[219]

---

218. George A. T. Case, "Devil Music: A History of the Occult in Rock & Roll." *Medium*. January 06, 2016. https://medium.com/cuepoint/devil-music-a-history-of-the-occult-in-rock-roll-3e671a821ba5; Edward A. Tiryakian, "Toward the Sociology of Esoteric Culture" *American Journal of Sociology* 78, no. 3 (1972): 491–493.

219. Sveinbjörn Beinteinsson and Berglind Gunnarsdóttir. *Allsherjargoðinn*. Hörpuútgáfan, 1992, 132.

Shortly after, similar groups came together in Norway, Sweden, and Denmark. In Norway, the first known organized group was the Blindern Åsatlaglag, a campus-based group that formed in the 1980s. In 1996, a newer group founded on similar ideas, Asatrufelleskapet Bifrost, was recognized by the Norwegian government. Asastrufelleskapet Bifrost was founded as a strongly inclusive organization in structure and practice. Maintaining this position was assisted by outside actions undertaken by the Norwegian Antifa movement throughout the '90s, which thoroughly destroyed Norwegian fascism by 2001.[220]

Sweden followed suit in 1994 with the recognition of Sveriges Asatrosamfund, now known as Samfundet Forn Sed Sverige, which has continued to grow ever since. In 2000 Eldaring, a group based in Germany, was recognized by the German government. These groups were inspired by similar trends, ideas, and tendencies, tapping into the growing interest in pre-Christian spirituality, a return to nature, and disenchantment with the modern world.[221]

Unfortunately, it was in this period when the first neo-Volkisch groups emerged. These groups hijacked the broader tendencies in the counterculture so they could build a new vehicle for advancing fascist ideas. These organizations, along with Nazi appropriation of some symbols during the 1930s, led to many white power groups stealing Norse symbols and establishing influence within the community. In 1973, a group of individuals in England founded the Committee for the Restoration of the Odinic Rite, which became the Odinic Rite in 1979. The Odinic Rite embraced many of the same ideas advanced by the original Volkisch movement, including the claim of an inherent link between race and culture. They blended this ideology with existing opinions from the neofascist English National Front.[222]

---

220. "Rasekrig I Åsgard." Humanist. March 14, 2016. https://humanist.no/2016/03/rasekrig-i-asgard/; Bray, 60–61.

221. "About Samfundet Forn Sed Sweden | Samfundet Forn Sed Sverige." https://www.samfundetfornsed.se/samfundet/about-samfundet-forn-sed-sweden-25549657; Sven Speer, "Interview Mit Eldaring, Einer Heidnischen Gemeinschaft." Forum Offene Religionspolitik. July 26, 2017. https://offene-religionspolitik.de/interview-mit-eldaring-dem-verein-fuer-germanisches-heidentum/.

222. "FAQ." The Odinic Rite. http://www.odinic-rite.org/main/faq/.

The same process unfolded in a United States wracked by the turmoil of the 1960s. In 1973, Stephen McNallen advertised his own version of such a group, the Viking Brotherhood, in the notorious journal *Soldier of Fortune,* whose main readership included large segments of the white power movement and mercenaries who fought for dictators across the planet. Shortly after, he started his first major organization, known as the Asatru Free Assembly, which lasted until 1985. Towards the end of this period, he wrote an essay titled "Metagenetics" where he combined pseudoscience with the same ideas of the Odinic Rite, arguing that Asatru was a whites-only religion. Years later he founded the Asatru Folk Assembly in 1994 with metagenetics as its core doctrine, and called his organization's ideology Folkish Asatru.[223]

"Metagenetics" clearly argued that culture was a product of genetics, not people, and it was only possible for "the peoples of the North" to practice Asatru. In practice, it has been frequently observed that one's quality of being "of the North" is determined by skin color; no organization that practices metagenetics has ever actually defined what it means to be part of "the peoples of the North." That this idea didn't exist for the actual pre-Christian Norse peoples casts even more doubt on the claims that metagentics is about anything other than a justification for bigoted spirituality. And this form of bigoted spirituality is even in direct conflict with the words of the actual founders of Asatru, including Sveinbjörn Beinteinsson, who said, "Anyone can pray to the gods in whatever manner he likes."[224]

The conflict of Norse Pagan worship first manifested in the United States shortly after the end of the Asatru Free Assembly in 1985 with the founding of a new organization. Known as the Troth, or the Ring of the Troth, it was founded in 1987 by Stephen Flowers and James Chisholm, who pushed for

223. "Asatru's Racist Missionary: Stephen McNallen, Defend Europe, and the Weaponization of Folkish Heathery," GODS & RADICALS. September 14, 2017. https://godsandradicals.org/2017/09/14/asatrus-racist-missionary-stephen-mcnallen-defend-europe-and-the-weaponization-of-folkish-heathery/; "Stephen McNallen and Racialist Asatru Part 1: Metagenetics and the South Africa Connection." Circle Ansuz. September 10, 2013. https://circleansuz.wordpress.com/2013/08/19/stephen-mcnallen-part-one/.

224. Bil Linzie, "Sveinbjörn Beinteinsson." http://www.angelfire.com/nm/seiðrman/beinweb.html.

more inclusive Norse Paganism compared to McNallen's followers. They called their practice Universalist Asatru. Flowers would have a falling out with other Troth members and later changed his position on inclusion with the 2002 publication of the essay "Integral Culture" in the fascist periodical *Tyr.* In it, he advocated for the same argument as Stephen McNallen's metagenetics in more academic language. Since then, the Troth has been largely active in the United States and Canada, with some members in other parts of the world.[225]

McNallen put his words into action in 1998 when he plunged headfirst into controvery surrounding the Kennewick Man. The dispute began over what were then recently uncovered ancient remains, between the Washington State government and the Umatilla Native American tribe who, citing federal law, claimed the body was an ancestor whom they had the right to rebury. McNallen inserted the AFA in the controversy, claiming the body was an ancient European, hiring known Holocaust denier Michael Clinton, who had ties to white nationalist groups, as his lawyer. White nationalists, who were campaigning to turn the Pacific Northwest into a whites-only enclave, saw Kennewick Man as a critical battle. They believed if the body was proven to be European, it gave them a "claim" to the entire region. McNallen's motion was laughed out of court, and later investigations determined the body was, in fact, of Native American ancestry. However, even in defeat, this cemented his alliance with American white nationalists.[226]

Though what the neo-Volkisch groups preached was in direct conflict with the practices of the first Scandinavian organizations, they managed to endure and become a major factor in Norse Paganism. Such toleration was due to a phenomenon referred to in chapter eight as the unwritten pact of silence. This pact formed the general tendency that developed in North America to excuse

---

225. Diana Paxson, *Essential Asatru: Walking the Path of Norse Paganism*, Citadel Press (New York: 2006), 52; Stephen Edred Flowers, "The Idea of Integral Culture: A model for a Revolt Against the Modern World," *Tyr: Myth-Culture-Tradition Volume I*, (2002).

226. "Stephen McNallen and Racialist Asatru Part 2: The Roots of Racialized Religion," Circle Ansuz. September 10, 2013, https://circleansuz.wordpress.com/2013/08/26/stephen-mcnallen-part-two/; Lindzi WesselFeb, "After 20 Years of Legal Battles, Kennewick Man Is Laid to Rest." *Science,* December 08, 2017. http://www.sciencemag.org/news/2017/02/after-20-years-legal-battles-kennewick-man-laid-rest.

the obvious bigotry and quiet support for the neo-Nazi ideologies of groups like the Odinic Rite and the Asatru Folk Assembly.

The pact of silence manifested through peer pressure, castigating people who pointed out the problems with the AFA and Odinic Rite as "frith-breakers" and disturbers of the peace, social ostracism, and even the whitewashing of neo-Volkisch ideas and actions by more tolerant Norse Pagans. One example of such whitewashing is from Diana Paxson, a prominent advocate for inclusive Asatru, Troth member, and clergywoman, who wrote the following in 2006 on the Asatru Folk Assembly in her book *Essential Asatru*:

> As these goals should make clear, the AFA defines itself as a revival of the native spirituality of western Europe, a religion that belongs to the people of indigenous European stock in the same way that traditionalist tribal religions belong specifically to Native Americans. It states that it opposes racial hatred and honors other indigenous religions. McNallen received national publicity in the mid-90s when he claimed Kennewick man (a 9,000 year old body found in Washington state) as a European tribal ancestor.[227]

Since the publication of *Essential Asatru,* Paxson's position (along with many others) has changed. Paxson herself has since spoken out against the neo-Volkisch and personally took to the streets of Berkeley, California on two occasions recently to oppose fascist rallies. In her writings and actions, Paxson has left her earlier words on the neo-Volkisch firmly in the past.[228]

The circumstances that created the pact of silence in the United States are somewhat understandable. One major factor was how small and relatively insular their communities were in this period. Many were afraid to upset others or be identified as trouble-makers. The underground, small-scale nature of the American community is what made the peer pressure at the heart of the pact so incredibly effective.

---

227. Paxson, 176.

228. Sigal Samuel, "What to do when racists try to hijack your religion," *The Atlantic,* November 02, 2017. https://www.theatlantic.com/international/archive/2017/11/asatru-heathenry-racism/543864/.

Another factor was a new moral panic during the 1980s known as the Satanic Panic, a wave of persecution aimed at practitioners of the occult, alternative spirituality, heavy metal music, and even Dungeons & Dragons. Accusers claimed there were secret cults of Satanists with members in all levels of society who were kidnapping children for sacrifice, sexual assault, and other horrendous crimes. The panic became so widespread in the popular consciousness that Oprah Winfrey hosted a discussion of the subject on her show. Many innocent people went to prison based on false accusations in this modern-day witch hunt.[229]

Even though these circumstances partially explain how the pact of silence happened, they do not excuse it. Many people were driven out of the Norse Pagan community, particularly in the United States, due to threats and intimidation by the neo-Volkisch. Others swore off associating with a practice they loved due to neo-Volkisch activities. The failure to decisively confront the neo-Volkish (who have always been a minority in the community) in these early years set the stage for one of the central conflicts in Norse Paganism just as it entered its greatest period of growth.

Digital Revolution

If the counterculture was the soil in which Norse Paganism sprouted, then the internet was the fertilizer that accelerated its growth. Before the internet, Paganism in all its forms spread very slowly, depending on word of mouth and personal connections. Contacting groups required knowing where and who to ask. The common availability of the internet made it possible for Pagans of all stripes to reach out, organize, share information, and exchange ideas with people all over the world, while websites provided often cash-strapped groups free do-it-yourself media outlets.

There were two big waves in how the Digital Revolution shaped Norse Paganism that coincide with Web 1.0 and Web 2.0. During the Web 1.0 period,

229. Aja Romano, "The History of Satanic Panic in the US—and Why It's Not Over Yet." *Vox*, October 30, 2016, https://www.vox.com/2016/10/30/13413864/satanic-panic-ritual-abuse-history-explained; Kurt Andersen, "How Oprah Winfrey Helped Create Our Irrational, Pseudoscientific American Fantasyland," *Slate* magazine, January 10, 2018, https://slate.com/health-and-science/2018/01/oprah-winfrey-helped-create-our-irrational-pseudoscientific-american-fantasyland.html.

beginning with the birth of the internet in 1991, email lists and free websites were the backbone of community organizing. Web 2.0 began with the rise of social media sites like MySpace, and things really took off when Facebook opened to the public in 2006, leading to a new explosion of interest, outreach, and organizing. Social media's ubiquity globalized the Pagan community, making national and international communication incredibly easy while at the same time bolstering local groups.

It was during this period the first documented groups emerged in Latin America. The first was the Hermandad Óðinnista del Sagrado Fuego of Mexico in 2004. In 2010, they would be joined by the Irminsul Fellowship of Costa Rica, who became the Asociación Ásatrú Yggdrasil in 2015. Across Brazil, new local groups emerged and developed into many different vibrant communities. At the time of this writing, Latin America has one of the fastest-growing Norse Pagan communities in the world by all accounts.[230]

Just as Norse Paganism was reaching new places, new ideas developed. Before the Digital Revolution, the dominant form of Norse Paganism (excluding the neo-Volkisch) were Asatru and Theodism. Vanatru, which focused on the Vanic deities over the Aesir while following similar forms, was the one main divergence that slowly emerged during the Web 1.0 period. The rise of social media over the course of the mid-to-late 2000s was paralleled by the development of Reconstructionist Heathenry. This also saw the rise of Lokean practice as an organized movement. This was started by people who honored the God of Mischief that now had the means to build community and develop their ideas without fear of harassment or persecution.

All this growth, change, and rapid development led to newer and younger Norse Pagans challenging the pact of silence. Just as Reconstructionist and Lokean practice developed thanks to the emergence of new networks outside of existing organizations, the same was true for breaking the pact. People were able to freely exchange ideas, compare notes, and air grievances on the state of the community. In these spaces, the most common objection was to the abuses and silent toleration of the neo-Volkisch in officially inclusive, Universalist

---

230. Hermandad Odinista del Sagrado Fuego. http://www.angelfire.com/folk/sagradofuego/principal.htm; Heathenry & Liberdade, https://asatrueliberdade.com/; Esteban Sevilla, "Inicio" AsoYggdrasil. March 28, 2018, http://asoyggdrasilcr.com/.

groups. Social pressure, which long maintained that silence, lost its potency thanks to Norse Pagans now having the means to find or build new networks. In some ways, the rise of these dissenting movements parallels similar dynamics seen in the Occupy movement and the Arab Spring.

This simmering discontent erupted in September of 2013, when a group of Norse Pagan anarchists and anti-fascists known as Circle Ansuz published a highly detailed exposé on Stephen McNallen, the AFA, their ideology, and other connected organizations. Their work can be found online at circleansuz .wordpress.com. Much of what Circle Ansuz pointed out was already known to some extent. The Circle's work was powerful because they were the first documented case of a Norse Pagan group connecting the dots and showing the truth neo-Volkisch propaganda had hidden. The conversation changed rapidly—people who were once forced to keep quiet or were driven out of the community through intimidation tactics could finally raise their voices.

Following these revelations, a number of grassroots groups emerged, including organizations like Heathens United Against Racism,[231] the Svinfylking, Heathens Against Hate, Heathens for Racial and Cultural Diversity, Heathens for Social Justice, and many other groups. In other cases, individuals lobbied administrators of the larger Norse Pagan discussion groups to change moderation policies and implement bans on neo-Volkisch material. Tactics varied from raising awareness to educating people on neo-Volkisch ideas, social justice advocacy, agitation, and, in some cases, direct action and anti-fascism.

The older organizations responded differently to these developments. Asatrufelleskapet Bifrost of Norway, Asatruarfelagid of Iceland, Forn Sed Sverige of Sweden, and Eldaring of Germany made strong inclusivity statements, openly banning the neo-Volkisch from their organizations, while most groups in Latin America had already taken such steps early on. The only major holdout among the established organizations at the time was the Troth. Though some Troth members advocated for taking similar steps, their organization's leadership consistently refused to make such changes.

Then, on January 31, 2016, the chief officer of the Troth, Steer Steven T. Abell, openly denounced anti-racist work and HUAR's founders in a public blog post on Patheos, one of the largest general Pagan blog channels in the

231. Which was co-founded and led for its first five years by the author of this book.

English-speaking world, that also included McNallen and the AFA. The result was immediate and widespread condemnation by many other Pagans, culminating in the cancellation of Abell's Patheos blog. Many other sites, individuals, and groups joined the growing chorus of outrage. The tide was decisively turning.[232]

The wave of fascist denoucement continued and gained momentum throughout the year. On September 5, the blog Huginn's Heathen Hof released a joint statement by a global coalition of Pagans organizations denouncing the AFA, known as Declaration 127. The Declaration (found at: http://declaration127.com) declared the AFA and its members were no longer welcome at any of the signatories' events or spaces. Since its release, a total of 180 Norse Pagan organizations from twenty different countries around the world have added themselves to the Declaration, making it clear that the AFA is no longer seen as part of the broader community. The pact of silence was dead.[233]

Today the Norse Pagan community continues to grow. A 2016 demographic survey by Huginn's Heathen Hof shows this spiritual movement consists overwhelmingly of younger people and solitary practitioners. What were formerly problems in the community now face challenges, such as the women of the Havamal Witches' movement (they confront entrenched sexism rather than accommodate it) that began in the summer of 2017. The Havamal Witches have only begun their work, and there's no question there are many challenges ahead for them. They are also one of many different groups in Norse Paganism confronting bigotry of all kinds, including racism, queerphobia, transphobia, and anti-immigrant attitudes. Though challengers are growing stronger, these problems are still a source of struggle.[234]

---

232. Steven T. Abell, "Letters From Midgard: Yes, Enough." Faith on the Couch, January 31, 2016. http://www.patheos.com/blogs/agora/2016/01/guest-post-yes-enough/; Jason Mankey, "There Are Some People I Don't Want Under the Umbrella." Faith on the Couch, February 01, 2016. http://www.patheos.com/blogs/panmankey/2016/01/there-are-some-people-i-dont-want-under-the-umbrella/.

233. Declaration 127. September 5, 2016. http://declaration127.com/.

234. "World Wide Heathenry." Huginn's Heathen Hof, http://www.heathenhof.com/world-wide-heathenry/; "#HavamalWitches: We Are the Witches the Havamal Warns You About" *Spiral Nature* magazine, August 7, 2017, http://www.spiralnature.com/spirituality/witches-the-havamal-warns-about/.

The neo-Volkisch now face open opposition, with bans on sharing their material becoming more common in the broader community. Stephen McNallen has solidified his alliance with the alt-right by founding a new organization, the Wotan Network, openly calling for putting race over religion. He is also reaching out to atheist and Christian alt-right groups, despite their obvious disdain for him. And non-Pagan groups, such as the Nordic Resistance Movement and the Soldiers of Odin, are using the same neo-Volkisch trappings to advance open bigotry.[235]

Yet these groups face increasingly fierce opposition. In April of 2016, Heathens United Against Racism and Anti-Fascist News conducted an operation that hamstrung the anti-immigrant Soldiers of Odin's organizing in the United States. A month later, on May 1, Norse Pagans from more than two hundred locations around the world lit beacons in solidarity with inclusive community and opposing fascism. In 2017 Norse Pagans joined counterprotests to alt-right demonstrations in Berkeley, California, facing down attempts by fascists to march through the streets. Direct action against fascism is becoming more accepted in Paganism than ever before.[236]

What it means to be a Norse Pagan continues to change, as practitioners wrestle with applying its ideals in our lives. Even with its obstacles, Norse

---

235. Press Release, August 22, 2018, "Nordic Resistance Movement (NRM)," Counter Extremism Project, https://www.counterextremism.com/threat/nordic-resistance-movement-nrm; Ben Makuch, "Soldiers of Odin: Inside the Extremist Vigilante Group that Claims to be Preserving Canadian Values." *VICE News*, February 01, 2017, https://news.vice.com/en_us/article/434z4n/soldiers-of-odin-inside-the-extremist-vigilante-group-that-claims-to-be-preserving-canadian-values; Carl Bonebright, "The Wotan Network Part 2—How to Exploit a God" *The Adventurous GIT*, June 30, 2017. https://adventurousgit.blogspot.com/2017/06/the-wotan-network-part-2-how-to-exploit.html.

236. Antifascistfront, "Soldiers of Odin Plan Meet-Up in Lodi Lake, CA on April 30th," Anti-Fascist News, April 21, 2016, https://antifascistnews.net/2016/04/21/soldiers-of-odin-plan-meet-up-in-lodi-lake-ca-on-april-30th/; "Light the Beacons 2016," Heathens United Against Racism, May 2, 2016, www.facebook.com/events/135921890127980/permalink/206787726374729/; "Heathens United Against Racism," April 16, 2017, https://www.facebook.com/HeathensUnited/photos/a.254508398012164/1125471097582552/?type=3&theater; "Heathens United Against Racism," August 27, 2017, https://www.facebook.com/HeathensUnited/posts/1242829335846727.

Paganism continues to grow, develop, and mature as a diverse, global spiritual practice. The new generation is learning from the past, rising to meet these and other problems head-on. They are enthusiastically building a stronger community than ever before. And the challenges created by the past are facing stiff resistance in the present—many are building a better future for all.

The lessons of Norse Paganism's history show many challenges had to be overcome for this movement to reach the place it is now. There have been many setbacks, mistakes, and obstacles along the way. Even though great strides have been made in recent years, there still is much work to be done. It would be wrong to say victory is around the corner, but there is little doubt Norse Paganism has passed the end of the beginning and the beginning of the end is in sight.

BIBLIOGRAPHY

"Neo-Volkisch." Southern Poverty Law Center. Accessed March 23, 2018. https://www.splcenter.org/fighting-hate/extremist-files/ideology/neo-volkisch.

"Northern-Tradition Paganism & Heathenry." Northern Tradition Paganism. Accessed November 06, 2017. http://www.northernpaganism.org/general/northern-tradition-paganism-heathenry.html.

"World Wide Heathenry." Huginn's Heathen Hof. Accessed July 10, 2018. http://www.heathenhof.com/world-wide-heathenry/.

"#HavamalWitches: We Are the Witches the Havamal Warns You About." *Spiral Nature Magazine*. August 7, 2017. Accessed July 10, 2018. http://www.spiralnature.com/spirituality/witches-the-havamal-warns-about/.

"10 Tips on Becoming a More Effective Teacher." Inclusion Lab. Accessed August 04, 2018. http://blog.brookespublishing.com/10-tips-on-becoming-a-more-effective-teacher/.

"1179 (Svensk Etymologisk Ordbok)." Project Runeberg. Accessed August 22, 2018. http://runeberg.org/svetym/1267.html.

"30 Days of Deity Devotion: Loki Day Three." Lokean Welcoming Committee. June 27, 2015. Accessed August 28, 2018. http://lokeanwelcomingcommittee.tumblr.com/post/122544282338/30-days-of-deity-devotion-loki-day-three.

"About Samfundet Forn Sed Sweden | Samfundet Forn Sed Sverige." Accessed July 09, 2018. https://www.samfundetfornsed.se/samfundet/about-samfundet-forn-sed-sweden-25549657.

"Asatru: Norse Heathenism." ASATRU (Norse Heathenism). Accessed November 06, 2017. http://www.religioustolerance.org/asatru.htm.

"Celebrating the Solstice: Midsummer in the Nordics." A Little Something About Easter in the Nordics. Accessed August 26, 2018. https://www.nordicvisitor.com/blog/celebrating-the-solstice-midsummer-in-the-nordics/.

"David Lane." Southern Poverty Law Center. Accessed November 06, 2017. https://www.splcenter.org/fighting-hate/extremist-files/individual/david-lane.

"Don't Confuse Jargon with Rigor." Education Next. January 23, 2015. Accessed August 04, 2018. https://www.educationnext.org/dont-confuse-jargon-rigor/.

"Eugene, OR Alt-Right Trolls Behind 'Boston Antifa' Exposed." It's Going Down. March 30, 2017. Accessed August 15, 2018. https://itsgoingdown.org/eugene-alt-right-trolls-behind-boston-antifa-exposed/.

"FAQ." The Odinic Rite. Accessed July 09, 2018. http://www.odinic-rite.org/main/faq/.

"Former Skinhead on the Threat of White Supremacist Violence in the U.S." WBUR. August 30, 2017. Accessed August 17, 2018. http://www.wbur.org/hereandnow/2017/08/30/life-after-hate-white-supremacy.

"Former Skinhead T.J. Leyden Tells His Story." Southern Poverty Law Center. Accessed August 17, 2018. https://www.splcenter.org/fighting-hate/intelligence-report/1998/former-skinhead-tj-leyden-tells-his-story.

"Frozen Factors: Nordic Influences on the Festive Season - BBC News." BBC. December 20, 2014. Accessed August 26, 2018. https://www.bbc.co.uk/news/uk-scotland-highlands-islands-30411490.

"Gymnosperma (Pine)." Afzender. Accessed November 13, 2017. http://www.vcbio.science.ru.nl/en/virtuallessons/gymnosperma/.

"Heathenry & Liberdade." Heathenry & Liberdade. Accessed July 09, 2018. https://asatrueliberdade.com/.

"Heathens United Against Racism." April 16, 2017. Accessed August 30, 2018. https://www.facebook.com/HeathensUnited/photos/a.254508398012164/1125471097582552/?type=3&theater.; "Heathens United Against Racism." August 27, 2017. https://www.facebook.com/HeathensUnited/posts/1242829335846727.

"History | Icelandic Coat of Arms." Prime Minister's Office. Accessed November 12, 2017. https://eng.forsaetisraduneyti.is/state-symbols/icelandic-coat-of-arms/history/#Guardian_spirits.

"How Do Molecules Interact?" OpenLearn. August 08, 2006. Accessed August 22, 2018. http://www.open.edu/openlearn/science-maths-technology/science/chemistry/how-do-molecules-interact.

"How Do Pine Trees Reproduce?" Sciencing. Accessed November 12, 2017. https://sciencing.com/do-pine-trees-reproduce-5173107.html.

"How Long is Apprenticeship Training Typically?" Learn.org -. Accessed August 12, 2018. https://learn.org/articles/How_Long_is_Apprenticeship_Training_Typically.html.

"How to Train an Apprentice - Business Voice." CBI. Accessed August 12, 2018. http://www.cbi.org.uk/businessvoice/latest/how-to-train-an-apprentice/.

"How Trees Survive and Thrive After a Fire." National Forest Foundation. Accessed November 12, 2017. https://www.nationalforests.org/our-forests/your-national-forests-magazine/how-trees-survive-and-thrive-after-a-fire.

"KS3 Bitesize Science - Cells to Systems : Revision, Page 5." BBC. Accessed August 22, 2018. http://www.bbc.co.uk/bitesize/ks3/science/organisms_behaviour_health/cells_systems/revision/5/.

"May Day 2018: Ancient Origins, Strange Customs and Modern Interpretations." *The Week UK*. Accessed August 26, 2018. http://www.theweek.co.uk/58343/may-day-2018-ancient-origins-strange-customs-and-modern-interpretations.

"Neurotheology: This Is Your Brain On Religion." NPR. NPR, December 15, 2010. https://www.npr.org/2010/12/15/132078267/neurotheology-where-religion-and-science-collide.

"Othala Rune." Anti-Defamation League. Accessed August 31, 2018. https://www.adl.org/education/references/hate-symbols/othala-rune.

"Rasekrig I Åsgard." Humanist. March 14, 2016. Accessed July 09, 2018. https://humanist.no/2016/03/rasekrig-i-asgard/; Bray 60–61.

"Religions - Paganism: Autumn Equinox." BBC. June 07, 2006. Accessed August 26, 2018. http://www.bbc.co.uk/religion/religions/paganism/holydays/autumnequinox.shtml.

"Religions - Paganism: Heathenry." BBC. October 30, 2003. Accessed November 06, 2017. http://www.bbc.co.uk/religion/religions/paganism/subdivisions/heathenry_1.shtml.

"Scandinavian Mountains over 2000 metres - James Baxter." Scandinavian Mountains - Flora and Fauna. Accessed November 12, 2017. http://www.scandinavianmountains.com/flora-fauna/trees-shrubs/index.htm.

"Soldiers of Odin Plan Meet-Up in Lodi Lake, CA on April 30th." Anti-Fascist News. April 21, 2016. Accessed August 30, 2018. https://antifascistnews.net/2016/04/21/soldiers-of-odin-plan-meet-up-in-lodi-lake-ca-on-april-30th/."

"Sonnenrad." Anti-Defamation League. Accessed August 31, 2018. https://www.adl.org/education/references/hate-symbols/sonnenrad.

"Starting and Managing a Study Group." Western Sydney University. February 2017. Accessed August 12, 2018. https://www.westernsydney.edu.au/__data/assets/pdf_file/0005/1082795/Starting_and_managing_a_study_group.pdf.

"Stephen McNallen and Racialist Asatru Part 1: Metagenetics and the South Africa Connection." Circle Ansuz. September 10, 2013. Accessed July 09, 2018. https://circleansuz.wordpress.com/2013/08/19/stephen-mcnallen-part-one/.

"Stephen McNallen and Racialist Asatru Part 2: The Roots of Racialized Religion." Circle Ansuz. September 10, 2013. Accessed August 24, 2018. https://circleansuz.wordpress.com/2013/08/26/stephen-mcnallen-part-two/.

"Stephen McNallen and Racialist Asatru Part 3: In His Own Words." Circle Ansuz. September 10, 2013. Accessed November 06, 2017. https://circleansuz.wordpress.com/2013/09/02/stephen-mcnallen-part-3/.

"Supplementary Learning and Teaching Materials." Unesco IIEP Learning Portal. https://learningportal.iiep.unesco.org/en/issue-briefs/improve-learning/curriculum-and-materials/supplementary-learning-and-teaching.

"The Middle Ages as They Were, or as They Should Have Been?" NU HIST 2805: The Gunpowder Empires. https://faculty.nipissingu.ca/muhlberger/SCAREC2.HTM.;

"The Seasonal Cycle of Atmospheric Heating and Temperature." American Meteorological Society. Accessed November 30, 2015. http://journals.ametsoc.org/doi/abs/10.1175/JCLI-D-12-00713.1

"The VAK Learning System." Southwestern Community College. Accessed August 04, 2018. https://www.southwesterncc.edu/sites/default/files/VAK_Learning_Styles.pdf.

"Theodish Belief: Oft-Askings (Frequently Asked Questions)." The Ealdríce Théodish Fellowship. May 04, 2017. Accessed November 06, 2017. https://ealdrice.org/theodish-belief-oft-askings-frequently-asked-questions/.

"Today Is the Shortest Day of the Year. Just Thought You'd Like to Know." The Local. December 21, 2016. https://www.thelocal.se/20161221/sweden-shortest-day-of-the-year-winter-solstice.

"Wayfinders: Wayfinding." PBS. Accessed November 13, 2017. http://www.pbs.org/wayfinders/wayfinding2.html.

"What is Rökkatru?" Northern Tradition Paganism. Accessed November 06, 2017. http://www.northernpaganism.org/rokkatru/what-is-rokkatru.html.

"What Is the SCA?" Welcome! Accessed July 09, 2018. http://socsen.sca.org/what-is-the-sca/.

"Wisdom." Dictionary.com. Accessed March 29, 2018. http://www.dictionary.com/browse/wisdom?s=t.

"Wolfsangel." Anti-Defamation League. Accessed August 31, 2018. https://www.adl.org/education/references/hate-symbols/wolfsangel.

"Light the Beacons 2016." Heathens United Against Racism. May 2, 2016. https://www.facebook.com/events/135921890127980/permalink/206787726374729/.

Abell, Steven T. "Letters From Midgard: Yes, Enough." *Faith on the Couch*. January 31, 2016. http://www.patheos.com/blogs/agora/2016/01/guest-post-yes-enough/.

Andersen, Kurt. "How Oprah Winfrey Helped Create Our Irrational, Pseudoscientific American Fantasyland." *Slate Magazine*. January 10, 2018. https://slate.com/health-and-science/2018/01/oprah-winfrey-helped-create-our-irrational-pseudoscientific-american-fantasyland.html.

Aragones, Enriqueta and Santiago Sanchez-Pages. "A theory of participatory democracy based on the real case of Porto Alegre," *European Economic Review*, September 21 2008. http://www.iae.csic.es/investigatorsMaterial/a12231123057archivoPdf88451.pdf.

Asprem, Egil, "The Golden Dawn and the O.T.O." *Cambridge Handbook of Western Mysticism and Esotericism*, Cambridge University Press (New York: 2016)

Bagge, Sverre, "The Structure of the Political Factions in the Internal Struggles of the Scandinavian Countries During the High Middle Ages," *Scandinavian Journal of History*, 24:3-4, 1999.

Baker, Jean H. "Mary Todd Lincoln: Civil War First Lady," *White House Studies*, Vol. 2, No. 1, 2002.

Barnes, Michael P. *Runes: A Handbook*. Suffolk, UK: Boydell Press, 2012.

BBC. "Master the Classroom: The Power of Teacher Credibility." http://www.bbcactive.com/BBCActiveIdeasandResources/ThePowerofTeacherCredibility.aspx.

Beinteinsson, Sveinbjörn and Berglind Gunnarsdóttir. *Allsherjargoðinn*. Hörpuútgáfan, 1992.

Bellows, Henry Adams. *The Poetic Edda: The Mythological Poems*. Mineola, NY: Dover Publications, 2004.

Beowulf. Translated by Seamus Heaney. New York: W.W. Norton and Company, 2000.

Blain, Jenny. *Nine Worlds of Seid-Magic: Ecstasy and Neo-Shamanism in North European Paganism*. London: Routledge, 2002.

Bonebright, Carl. "The Wotan Network" Part 2 - How to Exploit a god." *The Adventurous GIT*. June 30, 2017. Accessed August 30, 2018. https://adventurousgit.blogspot.com/2017/06/the-wotan-network-part-2-how-to-exploit.html.

Boyd, Brian. *On the Origin of Stories: Evolution, Cognition and Fiction*. Cambridge, MA: Harvard University Press, 2009.

Bray, Mark. *Antifa: The Anti-Fascist Handbook*. New York: Melville House, 2017.

Brunning, Sue. "A 'DIVINATION STAFF' FROM VIKING-AGE NORWAY: AT THE BRITISH MUSEUM," *Acta Archaeologica*, Vol. 87, Issue 1 (December 2016).

Burley, Shane, *Fascism Today: What It Is and How to End It*. Chico, CA: AK Press, 2017.

Burley, Shane, and Ryan Smith. "Asatru's Racist Missionary: Stephen McNallen, Defend Europe, and the Weaponization of Folkish Heathery." *GODS & RADICALS*. September 14, 2017. Accessed July 09, 2018. https://godsandradicals.org/2017/09/14/asatrus-racist-missionary-stephen-mcnallen-defend-europe-and-the-weaponization-of-folkish-heathery/.

Burrows, Hannah. "Rhyme and reason: lawspeaker-poets in medieval Iceland." *Scandinavian Studies*, 81, no. 2 (2009).

Byock, Jesse L. "Governmental order in early medieval Iceland". *Viator: Medieval and Renaissance Studies* 17, 1986.

Case, George A T. "Devil Music: A History of the Occult in Rock & Roll." *Medium*. January 06, 2016. https://medium.com/cuepoint/devil-music-a-history-of-the-occult-in-rock-roll-3e671a821ba5.

Chase, Eric. "The Brief Origins of May Day." Industrial Workers of the World. 1993. https://www.iww.org/history/library/misc/origins_of_mayday.

Ciabattari, Jane. "Culture - Hobbits and Hippies: Tolkien and the Counterculture." BBC News. November 20, 2014. Accessed July 09, 2018. http://www.bbc.com/culture/story/20141120-the-hobbits-and-the-hippies.

Collins, Roger. *Early Medieval Europe 300-1000*. London: MacMillan, 1991.

Cooke, Ember. "What is Vanatru? Who are the Vanir?" *EmberVoices: Listening for the Vanir*. October 28, 2015. Accessed November 06, 2017. https://embervoices.wordpress.com/2013/10/02/what-is-vanatru-who-are-the-vanir/.

Crossley-Holland, Kevin. *The Penguin Book of Norse Myths: Gods of the Vikings*. London: Penguin, 1993.

Davidson, HR Ellis. *The Road to Hel: A Study of the Conception of the Dead in Old Norse Literature*. Westport, CT: Greenwood Press, 1968.

———. *Gods and Myths of Northern Europe*. Harmondsworth, UK: Penguin, 1986.

———. *Myths and Symbols in Pagan Europe: Early Scandinavian and Celtic Religions*. Syracuse, NY: Syracuse Univ. Press, 2006.

Declaration 127. September 5, 2016. http://declaration127.com/.

Downham, Clare. "Viking Ethnicities: A Historiographic Overview." *History Compass* 10, no. 1, 2012.

Eoghan. "Declaration of Purpose." Asatru Folk Assembly. http://runestone.org/oldsite/index.php?option=com_content&view=article&id=69&Itemid=475.

Ferguson, Robert. *The Vikings: A History*. New York: Penguin Books, 2009.

Fernstål, Lotta. "Spoken words: equality and dynamics within a group of women skalds in the third century AD," *World Archaeology*, 39: 2, Skovgårde, DK, 2007.

Flowers, Stephen Edred. "The Idea of Integral Culture: A Model for a Revolt Against the Modern World," *Tyr: Myth-Culture-Tradition* Volume I, 2002.

Fowler, Angela. "Arthur Conan Doyle's British Spiritualist Commonwealth: 'the great unifying force,'" *English Literature in Transition* (1880-1920), volume 59, no. 4, 2016.

Gallo, Carmine. "TED Talks Are Wildly Addictive For Three Powerful Scientific Reasons." *Forbes*. March 05, 2014. https://www.forbes.com/sites/carminegallo/2014/02/25/ted-talks-are-wildly-addictive-for-three-powerful-scientific-reasons/#22912e426b6a.

Gomes, Michael. "H.P. Blavatsky and Theosophy." *Cambridge Handbook of Western Mysticism and Esotericism*. New York: Cambridge University Press, 2016.

Goodrick-Clarke, Nicholas. *The Occult Roots of Nazism: Secret Aryan Cults and Their Influence on Nazi Ideology*. London: Tauris Parke Paperbacks, 2004.

Gutierrez, Cathy. "Spiritualism," *Cambridge Handbook of Western Mysticism and Esotericism*. New York: Cambridge University Press, 2016.

Hazelgrove, Jennifer. "Spiritualism After the Great War," *Twentieth Century British History*, Vol. 10, No. 4, 1999.

Hedenstierna-Jonson, Charlotte; Anna Kjellstrom, Torun Zachrisson, Maja Krzewinska, Veronica Sobrado, Neil Price, Torsten Gunther, Mattias Jakobsson, Anders Gotherstrom and Jan Storå. "A female Viking warrior confirmed by genomics," *American Journal of Physical Anthropology*, 2017;164: 853-860, https://onlinelibrary.wiley.com/doi/epdf/10.1002/ajpa.23308.

Hedges, Kristi. "Five Communication Traits That Turn People Off." *Forbes*. June 25, 2014. Accessed August 04, 2018. https://www.forbes.com/sites/work-in-progress/2014/06/25/five-communication-traits-that-turn-people-off/#2f14ce7f4b28.

Heide, Eldar, "Hǫrgr in Norwegian names of mountains and other natural features," *Namn og nemne* 31, 2014.

Hermandad Odinista Del Sagrado Fuego. http://www.angelfire.com/folk/sagradofuego/principal.htm.

Hill, Charlotte. "Most Humans Have an Attention Span of about 10 Minutes, after That They Will Revert to Daydreaming." *Psych2Go*. September 09, 2014. https://psych2go.net/most-humans-have-an-attention-span-of-about-10-minutes-after-that-they-will-revert-to-daydreaming/.

Hitler, Adolf. *Mein Kampf*, translated by James Murphy, 1936 [n.l.].

Hucbald. *The Life of St. Lebuin*, translated by M. J. A. Moltzer, 1909, [n.l.].

Jesch, Judith. "History - Viking Women." BBC. March 29, 2011. http://www.bbc.co.uk/history/ancient/vikings/women_01.shtml.

Jones, Gwynn. *A History of the Vikings*. Oxford, UK: Oxford University Press, 1984.

Konung Skuggsja. Translated by Laurence M. Larson. New York: The American-Scandinavian Foundation, 1917.

Kvideland, Reimund, and Henning K. Sehmsdorf. *Scandinavian Folk Belief and Legend*, Minneapolis, MN: University of Minnesota Press, 1988.

Laskowski, Amy. "The History of All Hallows' Eve." *Boston Hospitality Review RSS*. October 31, 2013. http://www.bu.edu/today/2013/how-did-halloween-get-started/.

Lindow, John. *Trolls: An Unnatural History*. London: Reaktion Books, 2014.

Linzie, Bil. "Sveinbjörn Beinteinsson." http://www.angelfire.com/nm/seiðrman/beinweb.html.

Makuch, Ben. "Soldiers of Odin: Inside the Extremist Vigilante Group That Claims to Be Preserving Canadian Values." *VICE News*. February 01, 2017. https://news.vice.com/en_us/article/434z4n/soldiers-of-odin-inside-the-extremist-vigilante-group-that-claims-to-be-preserving-canadian-values.

Mankey, Jason. "There Are Some People I Don't Want Under the Umbrella." *Faith on the Couch*. February 01, 2016. Accessed July 10, 2018. http://www.patheos.com/blogs/panmankey/2016/01/there-are-some-people-i-dont-want-under-the-umbrella/.

Marsh, Sarah. "Effective Teaching: 10 Tips on What Works and What Doesn't." *The Guardian*. October 31, 2014. https://www.theguardian.com/teacher-network/teacher-blog/2014/oct/31/effective-teaching-10-tips.

Maybee, Julie E. "Hegel's Dialectics." *Stanford Encyclopedia of Philosophy*. June 03, 2016. https://plato.stanford.edu/entries/hegel-dialectics/.

McLaren, Brian D. "Charlottesville: 'Alt-Right' Has Created Alt-Christianity." *Time*. August 25, 2017. http://time.com/4915161/charlottesville-alt-right-alt-christianity/.

Miller, Stevie. "Urglaawe: One of History's Best-Kept Secrets." *Huginn's Heathen Hof*. September 16, 2016. http://www.heathenhof.com/urglaawe-one-of-historys-best-kept-secrets/.

Mosse, George L. *The Crisis of German Ideology: Intellectual Origins of the Third Reich*. New York: Grosset and Dunlap, 1964.

Nartonis, David K. "The Rise of 19th-century American Spiritualism, 1854—1873." *Journal for the Scientific Study of Religion* 49, no. 2, 2010.

"The 'Back to the Land' Movement - Environment - UTNE Reader." *Utne*. September 2016. https://www.utne.com/environment/back-to-the-land-movement-ze0z1609zfis.

Page, R.I. *An Introduction to English Runes*. Woodbridge, UK: Boydell Press, 1999.

Paxson, Diana. *Essential Asatru: Walking the Path of Norse Paganism*. New York: Citadel Press, 2007.

Paxton, Robert. *The Anatomy of Fascism*. New York: Vintage Books, 2004.

Press Release, August 22, 2018. "Nordic Resistance Movement (NRM)." Counter Extremism Project. https://www.counterextremism.com/threat/nordic-resistance-movement-nrm.

Price, Neil. *The Viking Way: Religion and War in Late Iron-Age Scandinavia*. Uppsala, Sweden: Department of Archeology and Ancient History, 2002.

Roesdahl, Else. *The Vikings*. New York: Penguin Books, 1987.

Romano, Aja. "The History of Satanic Panic in the US - and Why It's Not over Yet." *Vox*. October 30, 2016. https://www.vox.com/2016/10/30/13413864/satanic-panic-ritual-abuse-history-explained.

Ross, Alexander Reid. *Against the Fascist Creep*. Chico, CA: AK Press, 2017.

Ross, Margaret Clunies. *Prolonged Echoes: Old Norse Myths in Medieval Northern Society*. Odense, DK: Odense University Press, 1994.

Runic and Heroic Poems of the Old Teutonic Peoples, edited by Bruce Dickens. Cambridge, UK: Cambridge University Press, 1915.

Saga of the Jomsvikings, translated by N. F. Blake. London: T. Nelson, 1962.

Schnurbein, Stefanie V. "Shamanism in the Old Norse Tradition: A Theory between Ideological Camps," *History of Religions*, Vol. 43, No. 2, November 2003.

Self, Kathleen M. "The Valkyrie's Gender: Old Norse Shield-Maidens and Valkyries as a Third Gender" *Feminist Formations* (26:1) Spring 2014.

Sevilla, Esteban. "Inicio." *AsoYggdrasil*. March 28, 2018. http://asoyggdrasilcr.com/.

Sigmunsdottir, Alda. *The Little Book of the Hidden People*. Reykjavík, IC: Little Books Publishing, 2015.

Skogsberg, Markus Räv. "What is Forn Sed?" *Huginn's Heathen Hof.* July 07, 2016. http://www.heathenhof.com/what-is-forn-sed/.

Sommern, Bettina Sejbjerg. "The Norse Concept of Luck," *Scandinavian Studies*, Vol. 79 No. 3, Fall 2007.

Sørenson, Preben Meulengracht. *Saga and Society: An Introduction to Old Norse Literature,* translated by John Tucker. Odense, DK: Odense University Press, 1993.

Speer, Sven. "Interview Mit Eldaring, Einer Heidnischen Gemeinschaft." *Forum Offene Religionspolitik*. July 26, 2017. https://offene-religionspolitik.de/interview-mit-eldaring-dem-verein-fuer-germanisches-heidentum/.

Spurkland, Terje. *Norwegian Runes and Runic Inscriptions*, translated by Betsy van der Hoek. Woodbridge, UK: Boydell Press, 2005.

Starhawk. *The Empowerment Manual: A Guide for Collaborative Groups*. Gabriola Island, CA: New Society Publishers, 2011.

Staudenmaier, Peter. "The Nazis as Occult Masters? It's a Good Story but Not History." *Aeon*, June 09, 2017. https://aeon.co/ideas/the-nazis-as-occult-masters-its-a-good-story-but-not-history.

Sturluson, Snorri. *Egils Saga*, translated by Bernard Scudder, and Svanhildur Óskarsdóttir. New York: Penguin Books, 2004.

Sturluson, Snorri. *Heimskringla*, translated by Samuel Laing. London, [n.p.], 1844.

Tacitus. *Germania*, translated by Thomas Gordon. Harmondsworth, UK: Penguin, 1957.

Tan, Edwardson. "Jung's Shadow: Two Troubling Essays by Jung." October 27, 2013. http://www.cgjungpage.org/learn/articles/analytical-psychology/47-jungs-shadow-two-troubling-essays-by-jung.

Team Building. "Forming - Storming - Norming - Performing." https://www.teambuilding.co.uk/theory/Forming-Storming-Norming-Performing/html.

The Saga of Erik the Red translated by J. Sephton, 1880, Icelandic Saga Database http://sagadb.org/eiriks_saga_rauda.en.

The Secret Teacher. "Secret Teacher: Jargon Is Ruining Our Children's Education." *The Guardian*. August 09, 2014. Accessed August 04, 2018. https://www.theguardian.com/teacher-network/teacher-blog/2014/aug/09/secret-teacher-jargon-education-pupils/.

The Speeches of Adolf Hitler, April 1922-August 1939, Volume 1. Edited by Norman Hepburn Baynes. London: Oxford University Press, 1942.

Tiryakian, Edward A. "Toward the Sociology of Esoteric Culture." *American Journal of Sociology* 78, no. 3, 1972.

Todd, Malcolm. *Everyday Life of the Barbarians: Goths, Franks and Vandals*. London: BT Batsford, 1972.

———. *The Early Germans*. Oxford, UK: Blackwell Publishing, 2004.

Tresca, Michael J. *The Evolution of Fantasy Role-Playing Games*. Jefferson, NC: McFarland, 2010.

Walton, Alice G. "7 Ways Meditation Can Actually Change The Brain." Forbes. January 17, 2018. https://www.forbes.com/sites/alicegwalton/2015/02/09/7-ways-meditation-can-actually-change-the-brain/#4b37c4791465.

Wawn, Andrew. *The Vikings and the Victorians: Inventing the Old North in 19th Century Britain*. Cambridge, UK: D.S. Brewer, 2002.

WesselFeb, Lindzi. "After 20 Years of Legal Battles, Kennewick Man Is Laid to Rest." Science | AAAS. December 08, 2017. http://www.sciencemag.org/news/2017/02/after-20-years-legal-battles-kennewick-man-laid-rest.

Wolfram, Herwig. *The Roman Empire and Its Germanic Peoples*. Berkeley, CA: University of California Press, 2005.

Wyrddesigns. "Wyrd Designs - The Holy Tides - Ostara, Sigrblot & Summer Nights." *Faith on the Couch*. March 18, 2011. . http://www.patheos.com/blogs/pantheon/2011/03/wyrd-designs-the-holy-tides-ostara-sigrblot-summer-nights/.

Xander. "The Reconstructionist Method." *Huginn's Heathen Hof*. October 27, 2016. http://www.heathenhof.com/the-reconstructionist-method/.

INDEX

Core Values

Creation

Deities

Group Ritual

History

Holidays

To Write to the Author

If you wish to contact the author or would like more information about this book, please write to the author in care of Llewellyn Worldwide Ltd. and we will forward your request. Both the author and the publisher appreciate hearing from you and learning of your enjoyment of this book and how it has helped you. Llewellyn Worldwide Ltd. cannot guarantee that every letter written to the author can be answered, but all will be forwarded. Please write to:

Ryan Smith
℅ Llewellyn Worldwide
2143 Wooddale Drive
Woodbury, MN 55125-2989

Please enclose a self-addressed stamped envelope for reply, or $1.00 to cover costs. If outside the U.S.A., enclose an international postal reply coupon.

Many of Llewellyn's authors have websites with additional information and resources. For more information, please visit our website at http://www.llewellyn.com